HOW TO PLAN, ESTABLISH, AND MAINTAIN

ROCK GARDENS

By George Schenk

A Sunset Book

Photographs by Don Normark

LANE BOOK COMPANY · MENLO PARK, CALIFORNIA

Author's Preface

I BUILT MY FIRST ROCK GARDEN when I was eighteen. It was such a geological mish-mash that I even had pieces of coal worked into it. But it grew wild plants—and that encouraged me.

Ever since, during my travels in America and abroad, I've collected small wild plants and grown them in my garden near Seattle. For years I kept on collecting without much thought as to why. (Collecting, I decided, was the sort of delightful dementia that requires no reason.) Then I began to develop a special interest in rock plants—some new and some well known—that seemed useful for landscaping. My work as a landscape designer and author has grown from my own experience in working with plants and plantsmen.

The photographs in this book are no random collection. They are the work of Don Normark, one of the most talented garden photographers in America —and, in my opinion, *the* most patient. He and I traveled thousands of miles together, seeking out and photographing the plants and techniques we felt would capture the true spirit and the "feel" of rock gardening.

I don't expect all garden enthusiasts to agree completely with my views; in fact, if a bit of controversy comes out of this book, I will welcome it. My greatest hope (and belief) is that this book will serve not only the experienced plantsman but also the neophyte who is being introduced to the fascinating world of rock gardening for the first time.   GEORGE SCHENK

Eighth Printing October 1969

Contents

The Origins of Rock Gardening

We do more gardening, more imaginatively, with natural stone and with rock plants than ever before. And yet classical rock gardening, as Reginald Farrer described it in *The English Rock Garden,* has almost disappeared from the American garden scene. It is not likely to come back strongly. Farrer's rock garden is a jewel-box of tiny, delicate plants which are enormously costly in hand-and-knee labor. Today's quickened tempo of living and high labor costs have made easier gardening a practical fashion and have largely outmoded Farrer's rock garden as a popular garden form.

Our new work in America with stones and rock plants can't be fitted within the old definition of rock gardening, and yet it descends from classical rock gardening. This book proposes to call it American rock gardening.

American rock gardening tends to become an ever larger and more diffuse subject, whose boundaries are no longer easy to define. The garden influence of Japan, the design influence of abstract art, and the extensive use of ground covers have all entered into American rock gardening, and have become fused with it. There is no longer complete distinction between a rock garden and a stone design; a rock plant, a ground cover, and a plant for pattern making.

This book offers a new definition of rock gardening for our time and our country, a definition set down in the broadest terms: American rock gardening is the decorative garden use of natural stone in any manner other than strictly utilitarian (as in unplanted paving or retaining walls); American rock gardening is also the cultivation of rock plants in any garden setting, with or without rocks. This definition holds a key to an understanding of the new significance of natural stone and of rock plants in the present day garden, and relates newly employed stones and plants to their old places in Farrer's rock garden.

The rock garden as Farrer knew it is not dead in the United States. We have a lively coterie of several hundred jewel-box gardeners. These American plantsmen and plantswomen, and their colleagues around the world, are the classicists of rock gardening, the curators of its science, its lore, and its plants. Most significantly of all, they act as agents for the introduction of plants from the world of botany, with its dried herbarium specimens and its Latin-heavy tomes, into the layman's world of practical gardening. An enthusiasm for plants is the nucleus of rock gardening, and it is also the nucleus of this book.

Classic rock gardeners seldom confine their interest to plants which originate in rocky places. Their rock gardens include small wild plants from any natural setting—wooded, grassy, marshy and sandy, as well as rocky. Their enthusiasm for plants has led to the merger of the rock garden with the woodland garden, the container garden, the cactus garden, and the bog garden. Just so have we merged these gardens as topics in this book.

Rock gardening began by following nature, and until yielding to the recent influences which tend to pull it away from its beginnings, rock garden design has remained true to the world of wild stones and the plants which cling to them.

This book begins by visiting this world of stone and plants so that we can better understand the garden art that has evolved from it.

At top of page is *Arabis breweri,* emblematic of the big-flowering, small growing plants of high rocky places.

Natural Rock Gardens

Garden stone compositions which seem clumsy and unnatural are often the result of the designer's having never studied stone design in nature. Much bad rock garden planting is similarly the result of having never taken the opportunity to study plants and stones in natural association. To the right are three photographs of natural stone work and natural rock plantings to serve as a guide and inspiration to your own work. They are presented without captions to preserve the silence and dignity, too deep for language, which is always a part of natural stonescapes. (For the botanically minded reader, the daisy-like flowers in the top photograph are *Erigeron glaucus;* in the other two photographs is *Dudleya farinosa.*)

Not all natural rock gardens serve as desirable examples of composition—according to human standards. Our pictures were selected, with an eye for order, out of the frequently chaotic ways that nature arranges stones. The human senses call for order in composition, and nature is not always an orderly gardener.

Men's senses have guided them into two distinct schools of stone composition, the British and the Japanese. The British have gone to the mountains and taken the strata of stone for their chief inspiration. The Japanese use stone more loosely scattered, following the way that stones lie in the maple-canopied stream beds of their islands.

The American artist with natural stone sometimes follows either the British or the Japanese school, but much recent American work blends elements of both schools.

The great themes

Natural rock gardens are not pretty places. There's too much greatness in them. Immortality is here in the stone itself, and the passage of time is etched in its surface. The struggle of living things to live is molded in the muscled clench of tree trunks, in the clasping of cliff plants. The death of wood is written in whiteness and lichen. All the great themes are stated here for us to see and to use as examples when we bring stones and plants together in our gardens. With the incorporation of any of these themes, another theme, beauty, will come of its own accord.

Don't turn away from the possibility of capturing the great themes in your garden on the basis that nature performs them in landscapes of vast size. Garden art is a matter of relative proportion. The Japanese, in the garden arts of bonsai and bonkei, have analyzed these great themes—time, green-burgeoning life, white death, and immortality—and captured them in bowls and trays, with stones and plants the size of fists and fingers.

Above: Granite hills and modern highway combine to make a rock garden of grand scale. *Below:* Outcroppings and meadow grasses show good landscape proportion of stones to plants.

The relationship of stones and plants

The stone-like plant represents nature's harmonious approach to the combination of plants and stones. There is another equally beautiful relationship of plants and stones—the relationship of dissimilar textures. The heft, solidity, immortality of stone, sets off the grace, fragility and measurable life of plants. Especially is this opposition of natures and textures pronounced in the most graceful leaves of all—the arching leaves of waterside grasses against stream-bed stones and the lacework of fern fronds in the crevices of cliffs.

Leonardo da Vinci was aware of the artistic effectiveness of this opposition of living things and stone when he painted plants and women with petal-soft skin against stonescapes as austere and as mysterious as the moon.

Another lesson about rock gardening can be garnered from da Vinci's painting: The element of man must enter the picture in order to complete it and to make it sympathetic to our senses. This lesson is present in the photograph at left. The highway tames this natural rock garden and makes it traversable in the same manner that a path invites us to stroll through a man-made rock garden. By the device of a path, this colossal rock garden of worn sandstone boulders thrusting from 600-foot hills becomes restful to our emotions, while at the same time it remains visually stimulating. There are some other reasons for the balance of stimulus and composure which we feel in this landscape. The outcroppings are well separated, the area between mantled with oaks and meadows. Neither stone nor greenery dominates. The areas that they occupy offer a balance of interest to our eyes. The heroic quality of the stone is balanced by the quality of repose inherent in forest and meadow.

How can we translate this balance of forms and qualities into practical use when we group stones and plants? The illustrations suggest these conclusions:

Don't use too many rocks. A dominance of stone will make the rock garden seem stark. Rocks should probably not cover more than two-fifths the area of the rock garden. (On retaining walls, where nearly a solid surface is covered by stone, a balance of two parts stone to three parts foliage can be achieved with wall plants.)

But the rocks should not be lost among the plants. To hold the garden together visually, rock should probably not cover less than one-tenth the total rock garden area.

The rocks should be of different sizes. Notice in the photographs that the boulders are of different sizes, some dominant, some subordinate. A variance of size makes the stone composition rhythmic instead of static. The rocks should be unequal distances apart. Unequal spacing gives the stonework further rhythm and vitality.

The successful rock garden never employs stone as ballast—as deadweight. Stones are included and arranged to signify the greater life of our universe.

The British Background

The history of classical rock gardening is largely a British story. Francis Bacon envisioned rock gardening in Elizabethan times, when he wrote that he would like to see a little garden of irregular hillocks planted with wild strawberries and the other herbage of copse and hedgerow. But nothing much of the sort materialized until the nineteenth century. Then mounded rockeries, much as Bacon envisioned, began to appear in cottage gardens. (They are still popular.) At the same time, massive rock work, simulating natural outcropping, began to become fashionable at manor houses.

By the twentieth century, there was much call for specialists in rock placement. Edward K. Balls was retained by Lionel Rothschild of Exbury to lay out rock work totaling some thousands of tons. (For the Rancho Santa Ana Botanic Garden in Claremont, California, this same Mr. Balls has designed some of the finest naturalistic stone composition in North America.)

In the early twentieth century, at about the time Mr. Balls was guiding five-ton rocks into place for Lionel Rothschild, equally heroic efforts were going on in the mountains of the world, from Tibet to Colorado, to find all the alpine plants worth growing and bring them down to the botanic gardens of Europe. (Quite a few of these discoveries have turned out not to be worth growing, after all, but they are still cherished by collectors.)

The great era of plant discovery both contributed to and resulted from the great popular interest in rock gardening which occurred at the same time. Specialty nurseries sprang up under the rain of new plant species. The catalogue of Henri Correvon of Geneva offered 7,000 different rock garden plants for sale.

The work of Reginald Farrer belongs in the foreground of this gardening era. Farrer was involved with alpine plants as an explorer, a collector, a painter, and a writer. His book *The English Rock Garden* is the classic on the subject. It is an ottoman of a book—couched in opulent Victorian English, studded with wit and pleasantly exasperating opinion over which rock gardeners are still arguing. *The English Rock Garden* is reprinted from time to time and can be ordered for you by most book dealers.

With this book as its credo, rock gardening came on strongly in the United States in the 1920's and stayed strong even into the depressed 30's. At the same time there was a pronounced English accent in the architectural detail of American homes. The rock garden, itself a transplant from the British Isles, became the fashionable garden for the fashionable house. But the subject had been overdone—had generated a fatal over-excitement. By degrees a great many people grew tired of rock gardening. Then the war came and suspended the spirit of rock gardening, and of almost all leisure-time pursuits. For this and for other reasons, the English-born rock garden began to seem a period piece.

But out of the war came a strange revival of rock gardening. Americans in Japan had seen plants and stones used in ways which were fresh and new to them (although as old to Japan as Buddha) and they were deeply impressed.

An Inheritance from Japan

American gardeners have a keen eye on Japanese garden art these days. There is much direct imitation—which will probably go under as a consequence of changing fashion. But there is also much adaptation which is far more likely to stay afloat in the main stream of America's garden heritage for some generations to come. On pages 9 and 10 are photographs of authentic Japanese garden art (of which stone work is an inseparable part) and of ideas adapted from this art by American homeowners. The text in this chapter touches on the religion and the philosophy underlying Japanese gardening, and discusses Japan's role in the future of America's gardens.

The thought behind it

Earlier in this chapter we named the scattered stones of streambeds as a natural source of Japanese stone arrangement. But the Japanese work has meaning beyond simple imitation of nature. It is not merely the world that the Japanese garden artist means to encompass—it is the world plus man's thoughts about his world. He looks for a personality in each stone he selects for his garden. Stones are to be used to suggest things beyond themselves. Stones of varied and curious form are placed to serve as touchstones to the imagination. Their form, size, number and placement are all charged with symbolic meanings. An upright stone may symbolize a mountain, a guardian deity, masculine force. Prostrate stones may suggest bridges, repose, or feminine submissiveness. The origins of these symbols lie back in undated pantheism; their refinement spans centuries of the meditations of Zen monks. At the monastaries of these scholarly, subtle and ascetic friars of Buddha first appeared much of the Japanese garden art we know today.

Perhaps the most famous of these gardens still in existence is the Ryoanji rock garden in Kyoto. This centuries-old garden exerts a vital influence over present day landscape gardening in the United States. In 1963 the Brooklyn Botanic garden opened an exact replica of Ryoanji constructed with stones imported from Kyoto. There are several replicas in private gardens in the United States, and there are innumerable gardens which have inherited the spirit of Ryoanji.

Ryoanji is timeless—almost time proof. It consists of 15 stones in 5 groups which arise like islands in an infinite-seeming sea of sand raked into wave patterns. Around it, stone paving and a wall form the boundary of the universe. These are all the physical properties of Ryoanji. Its larger properties are not to be seen— they are to be envisioned.

On a pilgrimage to Ryoanji one walks barefoot through the monastery halls and sits facing the garden alongside Zen monks and nuns, shaven-headed men and women. There is at first a sense of calm in response to the simplicity of the physical garden. Then there is a vision of a world of islands and sea seen from great height. There follows a largeness of thought, an expansion of imagination which grows from this vision of the world made small.

The essence of Japanese garden art is irreducibly expressed at Ryoanji.

Find the essence

A formal study of Japanese garden art could be expanded to fill a lifetime of research and a library full of books. But it is hardly necessary to assume the lotus position and think in terms of Zen mystique in order to understand and incorporate the essence of Japanese garden art in our own gardens. The essence of Japanese garden art can be found in several tangible features:

Simplicity and spareness. Evergreen foliage is used heavily for year around effect. Flowers are used sparingly.

A balance of space and mass. Shrubs are spaced openly so that space itself becomes as important an element as mass. Some trees and shrubs are pruned to control the space they occupy. There is an old saying: "The purpose of Japanese gardeners is to keep things from growing."

A balance of proportion. The proportions of all things—stones, leaves, flowers, trees and shrubs— are related so that the garden, no matter how small, becomes a harmonious landscape where nothing is outsized.

Great themes. For all their petiteness, Japanese gardens inspire noble thoughts. These thoughts result from the presence of great themes which we discussed earlier in this chapter.

The Japanese garden contains more of the world of air, water, stone, time in progress, and life in heroic struggle than we are likely to see elsewhere contained in so small a space—except, perhaps, on a microscope slide.

Adaptation or limitation?

In the United States today we know the Japanese garden as transplanted regional art, but we have not come to its real position in the changing tide of America's garden art. It is in assimilated form that a regional art stays alive and current in a new environment.

All regional garden art, such as the Spanish, the British, and the French, which has come into this country intact, has soon passed from fashion and has become submerged in America's cultural ferment. Then once more it comes to the surface, but in fragments. We retain only fragments of the original body of the work: the Spanish patio, the British lawn, the French ironwork. The great influx of Japanese culture in our country today can't escape this cyclic change in the near future.

The American homeowner can with great profit absorb the essence of Japanese gardening and accept its basic elements of stone, water and foliage in quiet arrangement. But for the protection of his property investment, he should be chary of installing a formal Japanese rock garden, complete with stone

These are authentic Japanese designs

Top left: Naturalistic falls in an O-cho style garden lead to a quiet stream course. Design: Juki Iida.

Top right: Stream in photograph at left flows into this pond from which symbolic stones arise to watch and to guard.

Bottom left: The Japanese garden is a dell—a secluded place protected by woodland foliage.

Bottom right: Large and small stones are effectively contrasted in these steps designed by Juki Iida.

This work is by Japanese-inspired Americans

Top left: Focal point of this composition is the upright stone which might symbolize many things—a mountain, a sculpture, man in abstract, or a monk in his robes.

Top right: Trough of pebbles catches runoff from roof without rain gutter. Shady side garden includes sword ferns *(Polystichum munitum),* vine maple *(Acer circinatum).*

Bottom left: Dry stream bed modified into driveway. Flat stones are placed within stream bed; raked gravel forms smooth surface for car tires. Design: George Schenk.

Bottom right: Stones alone are used to suggest fall and flow of water. River rocks, gravel channel rain water away from house. Design: Eckbo, Dean and Williams.

Above. Mound gardens planted with kinnikinnick (*Arctostaphylos uva-ursi*) and strawberry trees (*Arbutus unedo*) seclude this house from the street. The paths are crushed granite.

lantern. He should wait and ruminate a good long time—three years perhaps—before deciding how far to style his garden after the Japanese tradition. He may in that time witness a significant change in the popular appeal of the trappings of the Japanese garden.

Japanese mound gardens

A common feature in Japanese rock gardens is the miniature hill, mounded (we might say modelled) with great refinement and plasticity of line. Sometimes the mounds *(koyama)* are meant to resemble peaks and foothills and are planted with dwarf conifers such as *Pinus densiflora* 'Umbraculifera'. Other mounds of sand are designed purely for abstract sculptured effect.

Both these Japanese conceptions of soil mounding are in vogue in western America. However, their best use here is practical rather than stylistic. Mounded soil is being used instead of fences or hedges to separate house and garden living areas from the street with its traffic sights and sounds.

The planting of koyama with ground covers (an American innovation) brings this Japanese garden form quite close to the hummock gardens of the British Isles.

Below. Koyama separates walk from driveway. Alpine firs (*Abies lasiocarpa*) will grow into a narrow screen. Ground cover is Irish moss (*Arenaria verna caespitosa*).

Elements of the Rock Garden

We have seen in Ryoanji a rock garden without plants; we shall see many rock gardens without rocks. It may seem that we are playing with definitions here, but only the widest possible definition can embrace the reality of the American rock garden.

Although we can dispense with rock, with pools or streams, and even with plants, most of us feel that the ideal rock garden will have all these elements. Let us then consider for a moment the basic components.

The Stone Itself

What is stone? In one definition stone is the stuff the earth is made of—the substance to which we anchor our houses, our lives, and our thoughts. "Solid as a rock," people say, and "Down to bedrock" when they mean to plunge to the core of a matter. Stone is our symbol of surety, the foundation of our world.

Why have stone in the garden? Because it is our symbol of security and permanence, stone brings a feeling of settlement into the garden. The fact that most of us find the patina of age—the oxidation, the sun glaze, the moss and the lichens—to be the most attractive feature of stone, indicates further our preoccupation with time itself. Perhaps these readings of time's passage give us a sense of transcending time.

Quarried stone

Quarried stone, with raw broken surfaces, seldom gives us much feeling of timelessness. Neither does it hold for us the strange and half-realized feeling of calm that we know from natural stone. Instead of these nearly wordless feelings, quarried stone conveys a sense merely of the contemporary and mechanized hands of men.

Quarried stone should not be used in the naturalistic garden with the hope of ornamental effect. Except in garden architecture, its absence is more attractive than its presence. Whenever possible its use should be restricted to walls, walks, bridges and other structures.

Stone is more permanent than any other paving, retaining or bridging material suitable for the garden. While there are probably certain metals more enduring than stone, let's hope that an age never comes for stepping stones made of them.

Artificial stone

When we think of artificial stone, we remember strange, ersatz situations—imperiled Pauline of the silent films hanging by her thumbs from a not-quite-believable stone cliff, or sad lions in zoo grottoes, pacing on stuccoed outcroppings of nonstone. The mere thought of artificial stone brings on feelings of disappointment and distaste—to rock gardeners especially. We use natural stone in the garden as a monument to the natural world. Artificial stone cancels the esthetic premise of stone in the garden—because we can almost always see at a glance that it doesn't belong to the natural world.

In the days of silent movies, Hollywood studios employed old-world specialists in the making of artificial stone. Inadvertently their skill came to have a

"Fibrorok" is easy to work with, has appearance of natural granite. (See description on facing page.) Plant at lower right is umbrella plant (*Cyperus alternifolius*).

substantial effect on American rock gardening. After the movies passed the cliff-hanging era, these stone makers began to make artificial stones for retaining purposes in hillside gardens in Southern California. Some of their specialty is still in place—concrete work stuccoed over the hillside soil and troweled sensitively into imitations of the ridges, hollows and striations of natural stone. The work fools the eye at a little distance. A vogue developed for this skill which has never completely subsided, but most of the actual skill of artificial stone making died with the old artisans.

Today there are a very few men left in the United States who keep the old art alive with all its meticulous trowel work. Aside from the accomplishments of these experts, jobs of artificial stone retaining that we've seen about the United States usually range in quality from disappointing to embarrassing to grotesque. Most jobs of bank retaining accomplished with stucco-stone could better have been accomplished by some other means. An honest concrete wall is preferable to a dishonest face of non-stone.

Lately, an entirely different type of artificial stone has come into being. The best of the new artificial stones are so cunningly made that the closest inspection, even hand magnification, can't tell them from the real thing. Their weight is only about one-twentieth the weight of real stone the same size.

We recommend this new artificial stone for enclosed patio gardens or for indoor gardens where the unique effect of natural stone is wanted, but where it would be impractical to carry in real stone because of the weight.

Among the most successful artificial stones of this new type is "Fibrorok" which can be seen on display in the Arboretum Foundation—*Sunset Magazine* Demonstration Home Gardens in the Los Angeles State and County Arboretum at Arcadia, California. A fibrorok is a thin, hollow cast of a natural stone. The cast is formed of fiber glass and plastic impregnated with finely crushed granite. The example shown on page 12 is 6 feet across, weighs 47 pounds, and faithfully reproduces the smallest creases and knobs of naturally eroded stone. The color and texture can't be told from natural granite.

The product has limitations. Its thinness makes it subject to chipping. Two small chips appeared in the shell of one of the sample fibroroks at Arcadia after it had been on display in the open air and weather for three years. We have no record of the length of life of this product, or of the effect of hard frost on it.

Fibrorok is produced by Fibro Design Company and distributed by Ray Sanders and Company, Pasadena, California.

Several nurseries about the United States have developed their own formulas for making creditable plastic casts of natural stones.

Stones for fun

Have you ever picked up an odd stone and carried it home because it piqued your imagination by its resemblance to something in the animate world? If you're a stone saver, it seems safe to say that you have a strong sense of sculpture.

Restraint is required on the part of the finder and user of such animal forms of stone (or driftwood) not to doctor them up with added eyes or whatnot. The danger is the shattering of their fragile, imaginative quality and substitution of the obvious and commonplace.

Above and below. Landscape Architect Garrett Eckbo is a stone saver. He uses his finds as sculpture in beds of plants about his garden. We would call this use of stone delightful, whimsical, and personal. Above: Egg-like stones are nested in Chilean strawberry beside aggregate-textured concrete stepping stones. Below: Animal-like pieces of sandstone peer from forest of agapanthus leaves. These natural sculptures are quite as stimulating to the imagination as a sculpture by Arp.

Stones and Water

Since rock gardening began in Japan a thousand years ago, rock gardeners have been fascinated by the movements, changes, and reflections of water and have been eager to embody them in the rock garden.

For the past century, imitative alpine rills have been considered highly desirable to the pictorial completion of rock works in both British and American gardens. Currently, small alpine gardens built around artificial falls and cascades are popular in several western American cities. But the Japanese work is concerned more with the moods of water than with its pictorial presentation.

A body of water need not be large in order to instill a mood. A hollowed stone full of rain water can contain the reflective peace of a woodland pond.

Photographically this page takes you down a stream where you can see the movement of water among stones, the shatter of sunlight on its shallows and the glide of shadows in its deeps, the way water molds stone into primordial sculpture, and the yielding way in which waterside sedges grow and prepare for the water's sudden rise and power.

What Are Rock Plants... and What Are Their Needs?

The first definition of a rock plant is the natural one established by the plants themselves: *A rock plant is a plant found in association with rocks.*

The second definition of a rock plant is that established by the rock gardener. His definition is far more embracing: *A rock plant is any plant which, rightly or wrongly, he wants to grow in his rock garden.*

Rock gardeners as a rule are far more interested in plants than in rocks. They gather and grow small wild plants from every climate and setting—woods, meadows, sand dunes, and bogs as well as rocky places.

We are concerned here with both right and wrong plant selections for the rock garden; in other chapters we will describe rock garden plants which originate in non-rocky places. But first let's examine the two definitions in more detail.

Nature's definition of a rock plant

Flowering plants are found chinked in the rocks of all the world's mountains and deserts, except those that are devoid of warmth and moisture. There is a simple procession of events by which some of the world's most brilliant and fragile flowers are able to spring from stone. Like all simple things, these same events are also as complex and mystic as the universe in which they take part.

Sun, frost, wind and rain hammer at the stone, pitting its surface.

Lichens and mosses—primitive flowerless plants —fix themselves to the stone's surface and slowly dissolve it with the acids of their growth and decay.

A crevice forms in the stone.

A soil formed of stone dust and plant dust blows into the crevice, where it catches and holds the rain.

A seed blows into this soil.

It sprouts, flowers, fruits, and discharges its seed.

It lives out its time, dies, and becomes itself a fleck of soil waiting to receive new seed.

Typical vanguards of the flowering plants are sedums, saxifrages, and sempervivums. They have so conformed themselves to the exacting situation of living on stone that they hardly seem different from the stone itself. In general form these plants have become low, rounded masses, resistant to wind and snow. Their leaves have developed into thickened lobes in order to store the uncertain supply of moisture. Their predominant leaf color is stone-gray. It is only with their flowers, which they hold up bright

The popular "alpine garden" consists of falls among natural stones, a pool, alpine conifers, dwarf conifers, and ground covers. (Falls are supplied by a recirculating pump.) This example is well turned out. Too many "alpine" grottos are shoddily put together, with glaring exposures of concrete; too often they are placed in the wrong gardens. They look best with a deep foliage backing—a woodland setting. Urban and structural gardens call more for a fountain than a grotto.

A hollowed stone serves as a reflection pool. The owner and designer is Les Le Blanc.

Saxifrages and sempervivums are beautiful the year around. To left of stone is *Saxifraga hostii*. Below is *Sempervivum arachnoideum* 'Stansfieldii' (the larger), *S. a.* 'Minus' (the smaller). To right of stone is *Saxifraga cotyledon*.

Three typical rock plants pried out of the rocks to show whole structure. Left: *Geranium sessiliflorum* 'Nigrum'. Center: *Armeria juniperifolia*, which grows as a weather-resistant dome. Right: *Aquilegia scopulorum* of the Colorado Rockies.

and brave as flags, that they announce they are plants.

Bright and sizable flowers are common among rock plants. Their colors, of molten purity and intensity are found in great flows on mountain tops and deserts during the short, swift season of growth and fruition. There is a biological purpose for these big, bright flowers. We are not the only ones who find them eye-stopping. They attract bees and other insects, which come to gather nectar, and in the process unknowingly carry the pollen vital to the plants' reproduction on their bumbling feet.

An English translation of the genus names *Sedum, Saxifraga,* and *Sempervivum* tells much about the nature of all rock plants. *Sedum* means to sit, a succinct description of the plants' huddled, adhesive habit of growth. *Saxifraga* means to break stones, a name that dramatizes the ability of the plants to wedge themselves into the narrowest cracks in the stone. *Sempervivum* means to live forever.

Because of their endurance and their "at home" appearance among rocks, sedums, saxifrages, and sempervivums might be called the three S's of rock gardening. But it is also possible to plant a richly beautiful rock garden without using one of the hundreds of plants found under these three names. The three S's form but a fraction of the beauty and variety of the plants in our world which have become naturally associated with rocks.

Virtually any plant you might think of has relatives which have been modified to a life on stone, or rather in stone. Most of these plants show only a fraction of their structure; the greatest portion of their bulk is submerged. Their tap roots often lead several feet down into the crevices of the stone, and the thread-like extensions of their tap roots may lead still farther, following microscopic cracks in seemingly solid stone. In their search for moisture these thread-like roots stretch to the thinness of a single cell.

Natural rock plants, reduced in their surface portions to wind-resistant mounds only a few inches in height, are found abundantly among plant groups commonly considered to be forest dwellers. Columbines, primulas, bleeding hearts, and anemones all are found growing on sun-heated stone. Meadow plants such as daisies, daffodils, gentians, and iris all have representatives there, as have such a random selection of plants as willow trees, orchids, rhododendrons, ferns, and bamboos. The world's natural rock plants total several hundred thousand species. No one rock gardener, however severely he is bitten by the collecting bug, will ever grow them all.

The rock gardener's definition of a rock plant

Because most plants look attractive against stone, only the gardener's taste will limit what he will put in his rock garden. However, most rock gardeners agree that certain types of plants and flowers are unsuitable for rock gardens. They exclude such plants as roses, camellias, and tulips, all of which have a highly bred appearance and are usually associated with formal gardening. Because rock gardening in its purest form is the cultivation of wild plants, many rock gardeners reject double flowers such as the double daffodils and *Rhododendron indicum* 'Balsaminaeflorum' *(R. rosaeflorum)*. They consider such plants out of place in the naturalistic setting of the rock garden.

How big is a rock garden plant?

There is a classic limitation of the size of rock garden plants to one foot in height. This rule makes sense for rock gardens under 15 by 15 feet in dimension, and for retaining walls under four feet in height. The size limit of rock garden plants is relative to the size of the rock garden and the size of the rocks in it. Oak trees may be in good scale if you are gardening on natural outcropping, and a draba the size of a pincushion may be the largest plant allowable in a container garden.

The basic garden needs of rock plants

There are no comprehensive rules for growing rock plants. They come from climates which are poles apart and where growing conditions are as opposite as sun and shade, bog and desert. However, the basic rock plant comes from uplands, where draining is good. The general rules of rock gardening have been built around the requirements of these plants. They ask for:

A fertile, loamy soil with sufficient sand to prevent caking. Old notions about the need to starve rock plants to keep them healthy have been disproved by practically all present day growers. But apply fertilizer with restraint or some of the high alpines will grow lax and out of character.

A steady abundance of water during the season when they are in growth. Plants of mountains, woods and meadows have an insatiable thirst during their growing season, especially during the heat of summer. Taper off the summer watering of prairie plants, desert plants, and species crocuses which will naturally die down and go dormant during the summer. During the winter most rock plants prefer receiving just enough water to keep the soil from drying out, but most will withstand the soaking rains winter brings to many localities.

A fast draining soil. An upland soil which is basically sand is most favorable. If your soil is heavy and slow draining you can grow rock plants on a raised scree.

Sufficient light and fresh air. Avoid planting rock plants—even shade-craving rock plants—in dank, dark places. Stagnant air which sometimes hangs between closely standing buildings is detrimental to rock plants. It builds up ground surface moisture and encourages mildew and rotting off. Rock plants which grow naturally in meadows do best in full sun or light shade. High alpine plants appreciate part shade in lowland gardens. The ideal light for alpine rock plants is a moving pattern of sun and shade provided by a lath structure. Other sun-shade providers for alpine rock plants are the east side of a house, which is sunny in the morning, shady in the afternoon; the dappled shade of open branched trees; a bank which runs from north to south. Rock plants from prairies and deserts grow best in full, hot sun.

What rock plants *do not* require:

It may come as a surprise to rock garden beginners, but rock gardens do not require lime or rocks.

Lime. The value of lime in the rock garden is an hereditary notion, the pros and cons of which cover stacks of paper. The author's collection of 1500 species of rock plants, including many which are in nature confined to limestone soil, is growing in acid, sandy loam suitable for rhododendrons. Perhaps the plants which keep to limestone soil in nature grow there not because they demand lime, but because the plant species with which they are in competition for growing space can't tolerate lime. There may be a few rock plants that require lime but these, if they exist, are so rare that most rock gardeners will never obtain one. If you are pro-lime, go ahead and use it if you wish. The psychological effect is sure to be good.

Rocks. Nothing adds so great a feeling of timelessness and strength to a rock garden as rock, and rock plants never seem so appropriate as when they are growing among rocks. We can take the association of plants and rocks as a rock garden ideal. *But it is by no means a necessity.* Virtually all rock plants, if they accept cultivation at all, grow equally well with or without the presence of rocks. If the end in view is to grow and enjoy these plants for their individual qualities rather than for landscape effect, they can be grown almost anywhere in open, correctly prepared soil—at the edge of the perennial border or in beds by themselves.

Sedum album clutches stone like an octopus. This succulent plant grows among mosses in a crevice on the face of a cliff. Wind blew the seed which gave it birth into the crevice; decayed particles of the mosses helped to lodge and sustain it. In this manner, flowering plants spring from stone.

Rock gardeners at work

The hands of a rock gardener. *(Top left.)* Dirt-stained and callused, the human hand seems too obtuse a tool to care for plants this fragile. Sometimes it is; work gets down to jeweler's dimensions, and weeding must be done with forceps. Among stepping stones (upper right to lower left): *Soldanella alpina, Trillium rivale, Primula clarkei, Woodsia obtusa.*

Unwrapping. *(Bottom left.)* Nothing elicits a broader smile from the rock gardener than a mail order shipment of plants received in prime condition. There is an ever-present challenge of newness—new plant names and habitats, new foliages and flowers, new growing conditions to be provided.

Weeding. *(Top right.)* The tiny plants in collector's rock gardens are in chronic need of hand-weeding. Some find the work relaxing; others groan and drag themselves toward it, but get it done nevertheless; others give up rock gardening because of it. There are no successful rock gardeners who are not willing weeders—or clever delegators of work.

Sharing. *(Bottom right.)* For many rock gardeners, the greatest gardening fun is in giving spare plants away. The collector at left, having laden a visiting hobbyist with rock plants from the greenhouse propagating bench, seems to be pronouncing some arcane blessing over them.

The American Rock Garden

We have already seen an instance of how American rock gardeners have taken a Japanese landscape element (the koyama, or earth mound), added a native element (the ground cover), and put it to practical use (screening an entry). This boldness in combining elements and in adapting them to practical as well as aesthetic ends is characteristic of the best American rock gardening.

Except for a few favored areas, North America affords a climate which is hostile to the cultivation of the classic alpine rock garden plants. The ingenious gardener faces the challenge of his climate in a number of ways: he modifies the climate (not so impossible as it seems); he grows plants which are native to his climate; or he takes from the vast number of general garden plants in his area certain ones which, by virtue of their low stature and high quality, will be likely rock garden subjects.

The American gardener *can* be a rock gardener no matter where he lives.

A Look across America

A rock garden tour of America in May would be a feast of color. May brings the crest of rock garden color all over the continent. In Seattle on thousands of retaining walls, in New England and in Victoria, British Columbia, on natural outcropping, there is a blaze of yellow alyssum, rosy phlox, purple aubrieta, white iberis.

May is the prime time to see the flowering stone wall at Rancho Santa Ana Botanical Garden in Claremont, California, and its desert wash flowering with incienso, evening primroses and many other drought resistant native plants.

The Ohme Gardens in Wenatchee, Washington, usually reach their peak from mid-April to mid-May. And this is the high season for the rock garden at the Strybing Arboretum in Golden Gate Park in San Francisco.

While rock gardens are found all over America, many states have only a few; a few states have thousands. Why should this be so? Are there some localities in the United States more suitable for rock gardening than other localities? The answer depends on your approach to rock gardening. If you're a classical rock gardener, there is a decided and narrow locality limitation to rock gardening. If you're a rock gardener whose primary interest is in combining plants and stones for landscape effect, any climate in North America is a perfectly acceptable climate for a rock garden. For garden success you have only to stick to plants which are compatible with your climate. You'll find compatibility in the plants native to your area and in plants from regions around the world which have climates similar to your own. These plants will usually prove to be the hardiest and the most harmoniously beautiful plants for your garden. The case for a garden of native plants and analogous non-native plants will come up again in several chapters in this book. It is important enough to re-emphasize.

The classical rock gardener makes a different case out of rock gardening. He delights in achieving the near impossible—the cultivation of high alpine plants in lowland gardens. Only a few locations in the United States will permit him success.

We hear classical rock gardeners speak of good rock garden climates and bad rock garden climates, of good rock plants and bad rock plants—the good climates being the ones in which the high alpine plants can be coaxed into growing, and the good plants being the most fastidious of these alpines made famous by Farrer and other writers.

If the cultivation of alpine plants were the only dimension of rock gardening, the cool coastal shelf of the Pacific, from Alaska to northern California, would have a distinct rock gardening advantage over the rest of the continent. The famous European and Asiatic high alpines grow passably well here. In most localities they will not grow at all. The only garden location in North America where mountain plants might be expected to grow better would be a garden in the mountains. (There is proof of this in a mile-high garden near Denver.)

Western Washington and Oregon are considered by many people as the rock gardening capital of the country. Here are many rock gardens, here is much talent and enthusiasm for rock gardening.

There are reasons other than climate for the development of rock gardening in the Northwest. The influence of Victoria, British Columbia, is one. Victoria, a world center of rock gardening, is just a few hours from Seattle by ferry. Then there is the fact that Seattle and Portland are hilly cities, where rock plants have been used to line dry stone retaining walls, which sometimes extend for a mile, interrupted by steps and streets. Down the length of these walls you often see a uniform planting of bergenia and other stalwart rock plants. (Bergenia is one of those plants which get neighbors together. It grows and divides with such consummate ease that there is soon plenty for the entire neighborhood. You wonder which gardener originally owned the bergenia, and how many years it took to line a street with it in neighborly fashion, one gardener giving his thinned-out excess of the plant to the gardeners next door.)

There are secondary centers of rock gardening interest about the United States. New York and the New England states, with their magnificent granite outcroppings, their rock-inhabiting phloxes and ferns, have given rise to a regionally inspired group of rock gardeners.

While Western Washington and Oregon comprise one of the few favored areas in the United States where plants assembled from a wide range of elevations and climates will acclimatize almost equally well, the area perhaps most favorable to plant acclimatization in our country surrounds San Francisco Bay. The Bay Area seems to be several climates in one. If you're a Bay Area gardener, you can grow subtropicals, temperate zone forest plants, alpines, and desert plants. Of course they require different degrees of sun and shade. In shady Bay Area gardens, rhododendrons from the Himalayan monsoon forests grow with greater success than anywhere else in the United States. Combine them with forest plants —trilliums, ferns, oxalis and others to create a woodland planting of rich variety.

The sunny, well-watered garden in the Bay Area will suit the entire range of rock garden conifers and a surprising number of the "good" alpine plants of America, Europe, and Asia. Many of the wonderfully strange plants of Australia, New Zealand, and Tasmania will grow and flower for Bay Area gardeners as they do in their native islands—and then they'll give you a plant's final vote of confidence: they'll set seeds or berries.

In gardens at Berkeley, where the Bay's fog cover consistently breaks and admits the sun, succulents from South Africa and cacti from North and South America are completely at home. For example, *Opuntia floccosa,* a woolly-white cactus from the Peruvian Andes which is the despair of rock gardeners in the British Isles, is so settled here that it spreads by means of self-detached pads.

But neither the Bay Area—nor any area—possesses the ideal climate for the culture of rock plants. By specializing in those plants most suited to your climate, you'll have the key to successful rock gardening wherever you live.

Try plants native to your own area

Wild plants make the most appropriate subjects for the rock garden. There are many small plant species native to every section of the United States.

Following, you'll find the names of some of these plants listed section by section across our nation.

California and the Southwest: *Arctostaphylos* (dwarf species), cacti and succulents, *Ceanothus* (dwarf), ferns, *Heuchera, Penstemon, Phlox,* and *Zauschneria.*

The Northwest: *Cornus canadensis,* ferns, iris, *Lewisia, Linnaea, Mahonia, Oxalis oregana, Penstemon, Sedum, Trillium, Vancouveria.*

Alaska: *Andromeda polifolia, Chrysanthemum arcticum, Cypripedium, Dodecatheon, Erigeron, Geranium erianthum, Iris setosa, Loiseleuria procumbens, Rubus arcticus, Silene acaulis.*

The Great Plains and the Rocky Mountains: *Aquilegia, Dryas octopetala, Eriogonum, Leucocrinum, Mertensia, Opuntia* and other native cacti hardy to sub-zero temperatures, *Penstemon, Phlox, Sedum, Viola.*

The Northeast: *Cypripedium, Erythronium, Houstonia, Iris cristata, Leiophyllum, Phlox divaricata, Phlox subulata, Silene, Trillium.*

The South: *Chrysogonum, Chrysopsis,* many ferns, *Galax, Pachysandra procumbens, Phlox, Ruellia, Shortia, Silene, Trillium.*

Wherever you live in the United States, the mountains, woodlands, prairie, deserts, or seaside will yield plants of unequalled beauty for you to try in a rock setting. Before you dig, check to make sure that digging plants is permissible by law in the area. If you dig on private land, be sure you have permission from the owner. Generally, the best procedure is to buy native plants from a nursery that specializes in them.

A Rockery Is Not Quite a Rock Garden

Webster may not recognize the difference, but the term "rockery" as it is widely understood among American gardeners has come to mean something quite different from a rock garden. While there are few rock gardens in America (as Farrer defines the rock garden), America is a land of rockeries, and has been so since its early days. The ratio of rockeries to rock gardens in America is probably a thousand to one.

The core of the difference is simply this: rock gardens are places where rock plants are grown exclusively; rockeries are stoneworks planted with almost anything. There are some other differences which are usual but not consistent. Rockeries are usually dry stone retaining walls built for utilitarian purposes rather than as homes for plants. Rockery planting is usually an afterthought to conceal the massiveness of the stonework. Other rockeries—heaps of earth studded with stones and garnished with nasturtiums and such—are neither utilitarian nor unpremeditated. They are perfectly serious attempts undertaken for no other reason than to arrange plants and stones together. (In England such attempts are called "dog's grave rockeries".)

Rockery plantings are as unpredictable as the gardeners who plant them. True rock plants may be mixed together in a surrealistic way with annuals, tulips, roses, peach trees, border perennials — anything. But there is often a saving grace about these rockery mixtures. They may lack everything we consider essential in the way of taste, composition, plant ecology and color sequence—and still be beautiful. The flowers account for part of this. Well grown, well tended flowers are always beautiful no matter what the setting. But there is something more: there is a personality about a rockery which is a reflection of the gardener's own personality. This expression of personality gives the rockery significance as a folk art. Rockeries with their bright, jarring masses of colors and textures have the same cheerful naivete as the paintings of American "primitive" artists of an earlier day.

Rock gardening is a more studied art than rockery gardening. Rock gardens usually exist for themselves. Their stones may hold up banks of soil, but their design and construction are done with as much thought for beauty as for utility. They are planted entirely with natural rock plants or with other wild plants of suitable proportion. The arrangement of these plants is naturalistic and ecologically sound. Roses, annuals, and other "improved plants" will not be found here, having been relegated to their own garden territory.

It is not the place of this book to dictate that rock gardens are more satisfactory than rockeries. A good rockery, by way of its gaiety and personality, makes up for whatever it lacks in the way of sophistication. America without the springtime banner of rockeries would be a bit less enjoyable than it is.

Garden tulips and border iris, interlopers in a rock garden, spring among genuine rock plants, conifers. Yet the total effect of this rockery beside an old mansion is charming.

Antique rockery and antique house live on timelessly in Jacksonville, Oregon. One of those anachronistic gold rush towns, Jacksonville seems to have slept, unchanged, a hundred years in the sun, lulled by the monotone of katydids.

Terraced rockeries running continuously across these city lots give the houses a measure of unity.

In Seattle, one of the brightest May-time garden pictures is the rockery of the Harold Rasmussens.

Working with Nature

The American rock gardener's problems do not all arise from a hostile climate, although this is likely to be the strongest limiting factor in choosing plant material. Soil and water, sun and shade, are limiting, or at any rate challenging factors that the gardener has to deal with.

The farmer deals with stony sites either by avoiding them or by using them for pasture; he handles the desert by irrigating it; he cuts down the forest to bring sun to the soil; and he drains wet, boggy places. The rock gardener doesn't fight nature; he works with it, adapting his plant lists and his design techniques to the site and to the climate.

Gardening on a Naturally Stony Site

The most logical situations for rock gardens are where the raw material lies—rock terrains, rough with outcroppings and a-scatter with fragments of stone. Except to provide footing for houses and for people, hardly any change need be made in the lay of these stones.

There is a careless perfection about the way stones are placed by the combined forces which cause their upheaval, fissuring, sliding, aging and mellowing. With money, thought and muscle we can imitate natural stone placement, but we may hardly equal it. (We, after all, are subjects of the same force of upheaval, fissuring, sliding, aging and mellowing.)

If your garden site is a stone field, consider it a challenge to your ingenuity and by all means make bold use of stone in your garden plans. In rural areas the closer the relationship you can give your garden to the countryside, the more pleasing it is apt to be. Instead of the usual garden of conventional trees, shrubs and flowers, think about basing your garden on rocks and ground covers.

Unforgettable garden effects have been achieved on the basalt cliffs of the Ohme Gardens of Wenatchee, Washington; in the desert stone fields of the

House and garden are built on a hill of sandstone, where elbows of stone break through thin coat of soil. In the top photograph, broad concrete steps between sandstone outcroppings are surfaced with crushed aggregate from same ochre sandstone. In the lower photograph, dooryard is dominated by a Gibraltar of a boulder and southern sword ferns.

southwestern United States; and in the Pedregal district outside Mexico City, where lava outcroppings are allowed to form the basic garden element, and where, for their sculptural quality, they are sometimes built into the houses.

In these rockiest of rock gardens the natural lay of the stone along with its own community of mosses, ferns, and succulents is altered as little as possible. The most harmonious of these gardens depend largely on rock plants, native and exotic, for color and pattern. Tame plants (such as vegetables and annuals) are kept to man-dominated areas defined by terraces, walls, walks or raised beds.

The Desert Rock Garden

Stone is abundant in many desert regions. For that reason, and for the quality of the stone, the desert garden is very often a rock garden. There is a special warmth and vibrancy about the colors of desert stones which makes them irresistible to gardeners. But these colors owe so much to their desert context of piercing sun and crystal sky that the desert is perhaps the one place where we should use desert stones in a garden. Desert colors in general don't transplant well to other settings. We must go to the desert to really see rose and ochre sandstones blending in their environment, and the fierce reds and gold of cactus flowers balanced by an equally primary sun. In coastal gardens against the backdrop of a soft, maritime sky, these same stones and flowers may seem strident and out of place.

The world's biggest sun stands welded in the desert sky, and a gardener must be able to retreat from it. Life in the desert is still dependent on a walled oasis of one sort or another. The oasis of the latter-day American desert is an air conditioned house, and sometimes it is the house together with a walled garden.

The walled garden

Within its walls the desert garden may become a garden room as individual to the gardener as the rest of his home. Sometimes it is as extraterritorial in its motif as Italy or Japan.

Outside its wall the desert garden should reflect its surroundings, incorporating native stones, shrubs, and cacti. The desert gardener who is a plantsman will probably want to augment natives with plants brought from deserts as far away as Brazil and Egypt. Almost all desert plants have enough in common in their appearance to be good landscape companions.

But the native desert taken just as it is, with nothing added and nothing removed, is a complete landscape of subtle harmony. The complete desert landscape is worthy of preservation wherever possible in the suburbs of desert cities, and sections of the virgin desert are worthy of inclusion as parks within the cities themselves.

As elementary as these facts might seem to the science and to the conscience of conservation, in the practice of land clearance they are being hugely disregarded. Many thousands of acres of residential land surrounding some of our mushrooming cities in the desert are being subjected to the scorched earth policy —to the eradication of native plants and the table-topping of land contours.

Following this, there are sometimes attempts to patch up the land and make it reflect the leafy greenness of coastal gardens. Visually and climatically these attempts are at odds with the land. A surprisingly large number of gardeners who have chosen to live and garden in the desert *fight* the desert instead of coming to terms with it in the selection of the landscape theme and the plant material for their gardens. The gardener who fights the desert by imposing lawns, shade trees, and other non-desert material on it is lucky to gain a draw. His lawn often suffers despite frequent attention. His shade trees are inclined to be sparsely leafed and unshady.

The first settlers of a region often tend to be hostile toward the land as it is. They want to "break" it, beat back its plants, level its soil, and attest that men are in control. They import plants and garden style from older, more admired regions. But then, when the land is thoroughly cowed and its native cover is dwindling toward extinction, an interest develops in the land as it was. After a certain time in residence people come to have a patron's admiration for the unique plants, stone and fauna of their land. Preservation and restoration become the cry of this eleventh-hour conscience.

As a society we have repeatedly taken this back-tracking route before arriving at the simple truth we rejected in the beginning: Plants and materials native to a region are the best possible plants and materials for gardens in that region. But with the final arrival of a regional garden conscience, American gardeners, region by region, become more aware and appreciative of native materials.

The plants of our deserts

The larger, more spectacular plants of the American desert, such as fan palm, saguaro, agave, Joshua tree, ocotillo, and cholla are well known, justly popular, and available at nurseries.

In addition to these, the American desert offers a host of other plants just as extraordinary (as their English names suggest) but probably not yet available commercially. They include such shrubs, perennials and bulbous plants as live-forever *(Dudleya saxosa),* a gray rosetted, red-stemmed, yellow-flowered succulent; the hollyhock-like desert mallow *(Sphaeralcea ambigua),* with grenadine red flowers;

A **wall** of slate blue, river-smoothed stones sets a theme of strength and simplicity at the street side of this suburban desert garden. Wall's matrix of blue-tinted grout is deeply recessed and not visible. Raked gravel covers soil. Composition evolves in spirit from Ryoanji rock garden in Kyoto, Japan.

the desert lily *(Hesperocallis undulata)*; blue dicks *(Brodiaea pulchella pauciflora)*; the vermilion desert mariposa *(Calochortus kennedyi)*; the cottony flowered winter fat *(Eurotia lanata)*; hop-sage *(Grayia spinosa)*, with reddish flower bracts; the crepe-white prickly poppy *(Argemone corymbosa)*; evening primroses *(Oenothera)*, with opulent, satin-white and satin-yellow blossoms; feathery-seeded Apache plume *(Fallugia paradoxa)*; quinine bush or cliff-rose *(Cowania mexicana stansburiana)*, with cream white wild rose flowers; *Prunus fremontii,* the desert apricot, with angular branches and cherry-like blossoms; *Calliandra eriophylla,* the fairy-duster, whose flowers are rosy tufts of inch-long stamens; blue sage *(Salvia dorrii)*, twiggy-branched, puffy-flowered *Salazaria mexicana,* the bladder sage; beard tongues *(Penstemon)* of scarlet, carmine, rose, white and lavender; daisies of many forms and colors—white, cream, butter color and orange-yellow, and notable among them, the incienso *(Encelia farinosa)*, a small rounded bush covered with sunflowers from March to May.

Potentially, each of these plants ranks among the most cultivable and curiously beautiful subjects for the desert garden. You can see and judge the garden performance of many of these plants at certain botanical gardens. But for the present, you probably will have to collect them if you want to grow them.

Most desert plants have deep-driving roots which make them impossible to move after they are more than a year old. Seedlings can be collected and re-established by watering and shading them until they have begun to grow again. But seed gathering is the easiest and most productive means of acquiring a collection of desert plants. Before sowing, file a notch in the flint-hard casing of desert seeds of the pea family. Soak other varieties in water for several days

to leach out germination-inhibiting salts present in the seed and casings of many desert plants. (The plants have learned to hold back the sprouting of their seeds until they're sure that there is plenty of moisture in the ground.)

Sow seeds in sandy, fast draining soil and keep them moist. As soon as the seedlings appear, let them receive sunshine and fresh air. This will reduce losses from damping off, to which desert seedlings are especially prone. Use a fungicide if necessary.

Small ferns with firm grayish fronds grow among stones in the desert canyons, and sometimes in flat areas. Such species as cloak fern *(Cheilanthes parryi)*, bead fern *(Cheilanthes covillei),* and the desert goldenback fern *(Pityrogramma triangularis maxoni),* are readily transplanted. Grouped with stones they make interesting container plants. They can also be grown on the shady side of a stone in the cactus garden.

Most elusive of all plants of the western deserts are the "belly plants," inch-high bulb flowers and jewel-bright annuals which pop up, flower, and die back within days after the spring rains. Wildflower enthusiasts say that you must lie flat to get close enough to appreciate them. Look for them after the February rains recharge the desert with life.

Plants from the Mediterranean and Near East

We can only make a hopeful guess about the American potential of most of the plants from Europe's dry coasts and Near Asia's dusty, boulder-strewn mountains. But representative plants from both these regions are flourishing in our desert where shade temperatures exceed 120°. Among them are olive trees; Aleppo pine *(Pinus halepensis);* prostrate rosemary *(Rosmarinus officinalis* 'Lockwood deForest') even now much used as a ground cover in desert gardens; *Matricaria (Chrysanthemum) tchihatchewii; Helianthemum; Santolina;* and *Achillea.*

These encouraging successes suggest that the untried majority of rock plants from the Mediterranean and Near East will also acclimatize to the American desert. These include: *Acantholimon, Anthemis, Artemisia, Carlina, Dianthus, Dictamnus, Digitalis* (the perennial species), *Dracocephalum, Eryngium, Euphorbia, Frankenia, Genista, Globularia, Gypsophila, Hypericum, Hyssopus, Iberis, Lavandula, Morisia, Ononis, Onosma, Origanum, Ruta, Salvia, Scilla, Satureja, Sedum, Senecio, Stachys, Tanacetum, Teucrium, Thymus,* and *Tulipa. Tulipa,* the wild tulips which come from such dry lands as Turkey, Persia, and Greece, seem especially promising.

Certain Mediterranean and Near Eastern plants are legendary among British and American rock gardeners for their rarity, beauty and difficulty of cultivation. The first rock gardeners to try such plants as oncocyclus iris in the American desert may find them as much at home as cholla.

The cactus garden

However much they search, devotees of cactus and succulents can always find one more new plant. Perhaps a thousand different plant species are available from dealers in cacti and succulents in western America. The hundreds of different cacti of western America, Mexico and the Andes are equalled by a bulk of unbelievable cactiform euphorbias, puffy-leaved senecios, and "living stones" from Africa.

Few gardeners will claim that cacti and succulents are vegetatively beautiful (although their flowers may be), but few will deny interest in their bizarre forms.

Throughout the world, plants have discovered the same wonderfully ingenious means of existing in places of little rainfall. In the main, their discoveries have been these: turn gray or white to repel excessive sunshine; reduce leaves to spines to prevent evaporation and to discourage foraging animals; thicken the trunk and stems to store water, and harden the skin to seal in water.

You need plenty of sun the year around and mild winters to grow the widest range of these plants. They like drainage just as much as the alpine plants. They look appropriate among stones, to which they often bear a structural resemblance, and they crave heat. These conditions exist most perfectly in our Southwestern deserts.

Such native cacti of our Great Plains as *Opuntia polycantha* and *Coryphantha vivipara* have fully adapted themselves to −50° winters. Great Plains cacti and some of the species from the higher elevations in the Southwest, Mexico and South America can be grown outside the year around in scree gardens in most areas of North America—even in the cold damp winters of Seattle and New York.

Working with cactus is very prickly business. Use blacksmith's or baby bottle forceps for grasping them and a sharp knife to disjoint the pads for propagation. For weeding under clumps, a filed-down scuffle hoe works well. Most gloves offer little protection against cactus spines.

Upper right: Reminders of the surrounding desert were brought inside the wall. Pots contain pencil plants *(Retanilla ephedra)*. Landscape architect: James Hayes.

Lower right: Spectacular *Nolina parryi* of the Mojave Desert makes a 5-foot burst of rapier-like leaves which shimmer with deflected sunlight. A colony of *Opuntia erinacea ursina* spreads about its base. The flowers of nolina are cream-yellow, clustered and yucca-like on a massive stem.

Gardening in an oak canyon. Home and garden of Architectural Designer John W. Pitman are fitted in a wooded canyon near Santa Barbara, California. Native live oaks canopy the entire area. Brick surfaces the garden living areas. All around the garden the woods are left alone to grow their own way. *Acanthus mollis* flanks the house. *Ajuga reptans* 'Purpurea' flows up to it (at right), makes a minor seconding of its dark, lacquered leaf tone.

Woodland Gardening

The majority of America's keenest rock gardeners happen to live and garden beneath shade trees. This circumstance has given American rock gardening close merger with woodland gardening. The woodland gardener who is a plantsman employs all the techniques of rock gardening and all its enthusiasm for rarity and variety in plants. It is beside the point that his shady rock garden often contains no rocks.

However, if there are rocks in the woodland garden so much the better. Many shade plants are genuine rock plants native to mossy cliffs. Even if they are not rock plants by birth, virtually all woodland plants gain interest by the textural contrast of rock.

The gardener in shade has more use for wild plants —and more need for knowing about them—than the gardener in sunshine. His garden, if it is fully shaded, will not support a grass lawn, nor most man-made garden flowers. In denying him the use of ordinary garden plants, his garden offers him the stimulus of original and exploratory use of little-known plants. There is no scarcity of plants to try. The range of plant material suitable for shade gardens is encyclopedic.

The shade garden is more leaf than flower; more subdued for its greenness than the flower garden. But it is never monotonous. Forest foliages are infinitely varied in hue, in texture, in shape; and in size they vary dramatically from the elephant ears of gunnera to the lacework of bleeding hearts.

The flowers of forest plants, while generally fleeting, have matchless grace of carriage and colors of melting softness.

Not all woodland floral effects are demure. In the open woodland such plants as narcissus, the hybrid heucheras, and *Primula burmanica* can be massed to form lakes of color.

The basis of the woodland garden is shade, with its accompanying coolness of air and ground. Trees are the usual shade source, but artificial shade is as good or better for woodland plants. You can control its intensity and keep the competition of tree roots away from forest footlings.

The north side of a building is an excellent shade provider for a small woodland garden. Some gardeners have adapted the nursery lathhouse to the home garden. Basically a grid of laths and beams, the lathhouse offers as many architectural possibilities as an open fence. The shade manufactured by a lathhouse is especially valuable in climates too severe for most shade trees. One lathhouse gardener in the heat of California's lower San Joaquin Valley grows and flowers alpine rhododendrons. Other lathhouse gardeners have perfect success with ferns and alpine heaths in the 100°-plus summers of Medford, Oregon, and Spokane, Washington.

On a hot summer day a lath structure is as pleasant to people as it is to plants. With chair and book you can make it a garden room.

In an established woodland...go easy

If the woods are old, the trees virgin or mature second growth, and the community of life settled beneath them, it is wiser to interfere as little as possible. The trees, the undergrowth, the snails and slugs, the burrowing and nibbling animals are a complete, balanced society which will work relentlessly to shade out, starve out, or eat up any foreign plant that you place among them.

Complete landscapes

Enjoy the woods for what they are. Old woodlands are complete landscapes. A house built among the sculptured cypresses of the Monterey coast, beneath the moss-deep Douglas firs of the Olympic Peninsula, within the dogwood groves of the Catskills, or among the oaks and pines of numberless places in America, is a house in a fully landscaped natural garden.

No non-native plant really improves a complete natural landscape. The gardener need do no more than restore the native plants to the soil areas about his house disturbed by construction.

But most woodland gardeners don't take this purist view. They clear the natural undergrowth back some distance from the house. They set traps, scatter snail-and-slug bait. They add non-native plants. From their viewpoint, added plants are added interest. And while the woods work relentlessly to destroy these plants and erase the gardener's efforts, the gardener who is watchful and persistent eventually wins out.

The woodland gardener may have to work rather

hard in the beginning; however, woodland gardens become progressively easier to maintain as they grow older. There comes a day when the forest undergrowth which the gardener has willed into being achieves its own community balance. At last the gardener has something as lovely in its own way as the original woods.

Gardening under young second-growth trees

Forests of young second-growth trees are usually unsettled communities. Either the trees are spindlings standing so closely together that no plants can grow beneath them, or they are so sparse that the undergrowth is a jungle of native shrubbery mixed with brambles, nettles, and thistles. In the latter case you may have to clear all the undergrowth, sacrificing the native plants in order to get rid of the weeds. In the case of spindling trees you can either clear them back, leaving an open area for house and garden surrounded irregularly by a living fence of trees, or you can leave small groups of trees standing 10 to 50 or more feet apart over your entire property.

Leaving groups of trees is more attractive and safer for the health of the trees than having them stand alone, gaunt and pole-like. If you want to turn a spindling stand of trees into serviceable shade umbrellas that you can walk beneath, garden beneath and rest beneath, you'll probably have to cut down some trees and remove many lower limbs from those that remain within the grove. Don't remove limbs from trees along the edge of your woodland or you will lose more in the way of a woodland's insular mood than you gain in light.

If you intend to garden beneath your trees, enough tree thinning must be done to bring life-giving light to the woodland floor. The test for light sufficiency in a woodland is this: Are there native forest plants growing vigorously beneath the trees? Unless light conditions are correct for the growth of native plants,

Lath shelter *provides partial shade for plants, people, and nearby coldframe. Owner-designer: Arthur Menzies.*

there is little chance of establishing non-native plants. Walk to the edge of your woodland to find out the conditions of light under which plants grow naturally beneath your trees. Then match these conditions.

Tree-thinning and bulldozing

The work is necessary desecration, and the less done the better. We know one home-owner-to-be who wisely strung a length of rope from tree to tree to form a corral; he then told the bulldozer operator and the construction crews to confine their machinery and their activities within it.

Any thinning-out of an old grove of trees should be done sparingly. The remaining trees may receive a fuller force of wind than they have roots to withstand.

It is advisable not to let bulldozers clear the soil at the base of trees that are to be saved. The treads of the machine are capable of compressing the soil, barking the roots and causing the death of the tree over a period of years. If possible, keep the bulldozer outside the circle of soil under the extremities of the tree's branches. Often referred to as the "drip line," this outer extremity usually indicates the perimeter of the root system.

Selective bulldozing — saving certain trees and areas of undergrowth—takes a little more time and thought than scalping the entire property. It may cost a little more, and you will have to come to terms with the contractor and then direct the bulldozer operator in order to get the job done right. Selective bulldozing is well worth the small extra cost involved.

Mulching the soil

After tree thinning and ground clearing, it is beneficial to mulch the soil 3 to 6 inches deep with leaf mold, peat moss, or rotted sawdust. This fresh medium, free of competitive roots, will give new plants an equal chance with the trees already there. Replenish this mulch annually. If your woods are deciduous let the fallen leaves remain to protect the woodland plants against frost over winter, and to then decay and enrich the soil. *Exception:* Oregon maple (*Acer macrophyllum*) has platter-sized leaves which can smother non-native plants on which they fall.

Planting your own woods

Even if you start with a bare lot you can create woodland conditions in as short a time as 4 years using trees no more than 6 feet high.

Trees with open, spreading branches and refined root systems are the best companions for woodland plants; they cast about the right amount of shade, and they don't take all the moisture and food out of the soil. Most of the trees which fit these qualifications are deciduous trees such as birches and oaks.

Some trees are definitely hostile to almost any underplanting, and it takes a skillful gardener to grow much of anything under them. They include: *Liriodendron, Populus, Robinia, Salix, Ulmus, Arbutus menziesii, Eucalyptus, Cedrus, Chamaecyparis, Thuja.*

Pines can also be considered an excellent choice for a woodland garden. A planting of pines provides shade quickly and makes an open, pleasant, needle-carpeted woodland. Many woodland plants will grow beneath pines if you water them frequently to compensate for the relatively dry soil conditions.

Space trees 10 to 20 feet apart depending on how patient you are about receiving effective shade. Six-foot birches, maples, pin oaks, or dogwoods spaced 10 to 15 feet apart should provide half shade (enough for many woodland plants) within 4 years, full shade within 8 years. Cut some lower limbs from the trees each year until they reach the desired height and openness.

Following is a list of some of the best trees and plants for woodland gardening:

Deciduous Trees: *Acer circinatum, Acer ginnala, Acer palmatum, Betula* in variety, *Cornus* in variety, *Juglans, Magnolia, Malus, Oxydendrum, Parrotia, Prunus cerasifera* 'Atropurpurea' (*P. pissardii*), *Prunus subhirtella autumnalis, Quercus, Sorbus, Stewartia, Styrax.*

Broadleaf Evergreen Trees: *Castanopsis, Cornus capitata, Lithocarpus, Magnolia, Quercus.*

Coniferous Evergreen Trees: *Cryptomeria, Picea engelmanii, Picea sitchensis,* pines in variety, *Pseudotsuga menziesii (P. taxifolia), Sequoia, Tsuga.* (Woodland gardens beneath coniferous trees require extra water and control over density of shade.)

Best of the woodland plants: Ferns: *Adiantum, Asplenium, Athyrium, Blechnum, Camptosorus, Cystopteris, Dicksonia, Osmunda, Phyllitis scolopendrium, Polypodium, Polystichum, Pteridium, Woodsia, Woodwardia;* Flowering plants: *Acanthus, Achlys, Actaea, Ajuga, Alchemilla, Anemone, Aquilegia, Asarum, Asperula, Astilbe, Boykinia, Campanula, Claytonia, Clintonia, Coptis, Cornus canadensis, Corydalis, Cotula, Cyclamen, Dentaria, Dicentra, Digitalis, Disporum, Dodecatheon, Epigaea, Epimedium, Erythronium, Fragaria, Francoa, Fritillaria, Galanthus, Galax, Gaultheria, Geranium, Gunnera, Hedera, Helleborus, Helxine, Heuchera, Hosta, Iris douglasiana, Jeffersonia, Leucojum, Leucothoe, Linnaea, Maianthemum, Mazus pumilio, Mertensia, Mitchella, Mitella, Narcissus, Omphalodes, Ophiopogon, Oxalis, Paeonia, Penstemon, Petasites, Plumbago, Podophyllum, Polemonium, Polygala, Polygonatum, Primula, Pulmonaria, Pyrola, Ranunculus, Rhododendron, Rubus, Ruellia, Sanguinaria, Saxifraga, Scilla, Scutellaria, Shortia, Smilacina, Tanakaea, Tellima, Thalictrum, Tiarella, Tolmiea, Trientalis, Trillium, Uvularia, Vancouveria, Viola, Xerophyllum.*

Foliage Patterns...

Leaves are the warp and woof of the woodland garden. Over the deep, soft humus spreads a texture of greens, varying with the colonies of different plants, blending where the different colonies meet.

Above: Along the course of a slow woodland stream, tea-colored with the tannin of redwood needles, grow skunk cabbages *(Lysichitum americanum)*, broad-leafed rosette at upper right; lady ferns *(Athyrium filix-femina)* at left; and colt's foot *(Petasites palmatus)* at bottom. Entire landscape —stream, trees, stones and plants—is a man-made garden.

Upper right: A 3-foot buttercup, *Ranunculus cortusaefolius,* at lower left, sets the scale for the vast umbrellas of *Gunnera manicata* (center) and Australian tree fern (top).

Lower right: Rhododendron foliage spreads fanlike beneath a roof of Douglas firs. Beneath the rhododendrons grows a carpet of *Cornus canadensis,* with white-bracted flower clusters to be followed by scarlet "bunch berries."

Below: A rotting log makes a grandstand seat for a colony of false lily-of-the-valley *(Maianthemum dilatatum)*.

In a small artificial bog grow white Japanese skunk cabbages (*Lysichiton camtschatcense*) in center. At lower left is *Montia parvifolia flagellaris*. Above skunk cabbages on drier soil held by weathered wood is *Andromeda polifolia* 'Minima'. Near top of photograph, where the soil is moist but not boggy, is *Anemone nemorosa* 'Robinsoniana'.

The Bog Garden

Boggy ground is no liability to a plant collector. Some of the world's most fascinating and most specialized plants grow only in sopping soil. Other bog plants are conditioned to life on a mattress of pure sphagnum moss. If you haven't a natural bog, both these types of plants will adapt to small artificial bogs.

One sort of man-made bog garden is simply a filled-in concrete basin. Choose a semi-shady place for an artificial bog garden. Bogs in full sun suit many plants but require watering every day or so in hot weather.

Dig out an area of ground to a depth of two feet. Slope the sides of the excavation 45°. Line it with chicken wire and shovel on concrete. Trowel the concrete up the sides of the excavation until it is six inches from the level of the ground surface. The below

ground level of the concrete reduces the danger of winter freezing and cracking. The six inches of free soil allow the roots of the bog plants slight but required aeration.

After the concrete has cured for a couple of days, fill the basin with rich loam if soil-requiring bog plants are to be grown, or with pure peat moss (topped with living sphagnum if you can get it) for the plants which grow naturally in peat bogs. Water the filled-in basin until the soil becomes quaggy.

Wet soil plants include the rampant mat makers *Mazus* and *Montia parviflora;* the scarlet staffs of *Lobelia cardinalis;* the candelabroid *Primula japonica;* marsh marigold (*Caltha palustris*); *Athyrium filix-femina,* the stately lady fern; the great, tropical fronds of *Osmunda regalis,* the royal fern; and the skunk cabbages, *Lysichiton americanum* and *Symplocarpus foetidus,* whose hooded arum flowers come out at catkin time in spring, followed quickly by vast leafage.

Smaller plants more suited to small, concrete bogs are the bog orchids *Epipactis* and *Habenaria;* thyme-leaved *Houstonia caerulea* and *H. serpyllifolia; Parnassia,* the white-starred grass of parnassus; the shooting stars, *Dodecatheon meadia* and *D. jeffreyi; Gentiana calycosa* of western American mountains; and *Primula rosea* of the Himalayas.

The sphagnum lovers include the insectivorous plants *Dionaea, Sarracenia, Darlingtonia,* and *Drosera;* bog orchids such as *Habenaria; Eriophorum,* the cotton sedges; *Empetrum,* the crowberry; bog-laurel, *Kalmia polifolia,* and its smaller form, *K. polifolia microphylla;* and *Ledum,* the Labrador tea.

Unfortunately, birds delight in pecking and pulling at the sphagnum bog. To discourage them, cover the entire surface around the plants with marble-sized gravel.

Almost all bog plants will grow in bowls, tubs, and other containers in areas where frosts are not deep. They are more subject to frost damage in containers than in the deeper soil of the bog. Fill the containers with rich soil or sphagnum, according to the requirements of the plants. The containers should have drainage holes to prevent the toxic accumulation of salts from evaporated water. Containers of two-quart capacity are large enough to grow a few insectivorous plants; skunk cabbages and other bog giants should have at least 5 gallons of soil to make full growth.

Many bog plants will adapt to upland soil conditions, with no more water than you give to polyanthus primroses. Bog plants tend to grow more compactly and more slowly under upland conditions than when free in their native bogs. Bog plants readily adaptable to drier-than-bog-soil include *Vaccinium macrocarpon* (cranberry), *Andromeda polifolia, Houstonia, Chamaedaphne, Caltha palustris, Mazus, Ledum, Kalmia* and *Empetrum.*

The Collecting Bug

Although the rock gardener may build his first rock garden to handle a specific landscape problem, he is likely to go on to collecting. Charmed by the beauty (or oddity) of his first rock plants, he will acquire newer, rare plants. Since some of these require more care and coddling than his earlier acquisitions, he will remodel his rock garden to accommodate them; or he will build and plant a scree garden when he can attempt the high alpine plants, the successful flowering of which will move him up to the big leagues of rock gardening.

He may even dispense with rocks altogether and take to growing his collection in pots under lath or in an alpine house. He is almost certain to join with other dedicated rock gardeners in societies which exchange information and plant material.

What is the collecting bug ?

Rock plant collecting is a delightful impracticality indulged in presently by a few thousand gardeners in the British Isles, a few hundred in the United States, and a few hundred more in other parts of the world.

The collector cares nothing for the time he devotes to his collection. There is something different to see every day, and there is always something to putter with. He invests a thousand hours or more each year and considers the time well and restfully spent. He builds lathwork and lanais to temper the light that strikes his plants, and constructs glass houses to create microclimates for them. He mixes and sifts soils: sandy soils for desert plants, peaty soils for woodland plants, gritty soil for alpines, sphagnum for bog plants.

For clues and for inspiration the collector pores over whatever he can find to read about a new plant— notes on its habitat made by the botanist in the field, notes on its garden performance made by other gardeners. But the successful grower of rare plants must rely mainly on his own plant sense built on personal experience (which often means learning the hard way what *not* to do). And the truly great grower of rare plants seems to rely on something more than what he has read or experienced. He has established that mystical rapport with his subject which we call a green thumb.

The collector's plant

Rarity and diminutiveness are prerequisites of a collector's rock plant. Showiness of flower is unnecessary. Beyond a certain point it is even repellent to the more sensitive collectors. Such grand old rock plants as

The spirit of the collector is evident in the hundred examples shown here. Giving free rein to his bounding delight in variety, the collector has more plants than he has ground space. Tables hold overflow from crowded walkways; they must be as heavy as baronial banquet tables to support the weight.

arabis, iberis, alyssum, and aubrieta, with their easygoing habits and splashy colors, usually make them shudder.

That's not to say collector's plants don't have beauty. What they lack is merely splashy brilliance. If you take time to examine them closely you'll discover flower forms and richness of color unequalled in the floral world. The reduction of leaf size and stem length that these plants have undergone in their adaptation to fierce climates has not been accompanied by

A typical collector's rock plant, *Primula bilekii* is rare, diminutive, and recalcitrant—and suddenly rewarding with a burst of big, brave flowers.

reduction in their flowers. In fact, the strength these plants save on leafage seems to be applied in the explosive production of big, bold flowers.

The trouble is that this color explosion, which is the summer event of the rock slides and alpine meadows where these plants are native, is not so consistent when the same plants are grown in lowland gardens.

Take *Primula bilekii,* for example. The photograph on page 31 shows a 2-inch primrose growing between raised stepping stones. There are some eighteen rosettes of toothed leaves and ten comparatively enormous flowers of intense aniline rose. This is the gardener's entire stock of the plant and these are the first flowers he has obtained after seven years of weeding, watering, and pampering. Obviously this kind of gardening has very little general appeal. Why not plant *Primula* 'Wanda' and have the entire walk laced with foliage and flowers every year—and have an excess to dig up and hand to admiring visitors?

The collector's persuasion

The answer lies in the difference in persuasion between the landscape gardener and the collector-gardener. As pure types these gardeners may not exist, for there's probably a bit of the collecting bug in everyone who assembles plants in a garden, and there is also the wish in every gardener to display his plants artistically. But the motives that tend to separate landscape gardeners and collector-gardeners are as different as logic and love. The gardener who is pre-eminently a collector is the romantic of the two, a person who looks for and finds the aura of romance that surrounds rare plants.

In *Primula bilekii* there is the romance of far places and of discovery. It has been found only once or twice, and then as a single plant, growing in crumbling limestone cliffs of the Hintere Onne in the Brenner Alps. It is a natural hybrid of two high alpines, *Primula minima* and *Primula hirsuta.*

The collector values the plant further for its rarity both in nature and in gardens. The exclusiveness of possessing *Primula bilekii* (possibly only half a dozen Americans do) appeals to the very human, very general desire for exclusive possessions. The successful growing and flowering of this plant (which has little willingness to do either) brings the gardener a feeling of competence for having done a difficult thing well.

Each of the wild plants portrayed in this book has its own story of remote mountains or meadows, of forests or dry lands, of discovery, and of entry into the gardening world. Although these plants are domesticated they have never lost their individuality as wild plants, nor their unsophisticated charm as wild flowers. Above all else these plant qualities provide the impetus for rock gardening.

Rhododendrons and woodland plants grow together in this banked rock garden. The "rocks" are actually pieces of mountain driftwood. A grove of alpine firs is in the background.

Rhododendrons for the Rock Garden

Rock gardening means rhododendron gardening (especially dwarf rhododendrons) to many Americans. Collecting, hybridizing, or just plain growing and enjoying these shrubs has come to a high degree of popular interest. The rest of the rock plants usually play a supporting—but not necessarily narrow—role in the garden of the rhododendron enthusiast.

The name *Rhododendron* covers a gigantic genus. Nearly 1,000 rhododendron species have been discovered around the northern hemisphere. The contributions from Japan, the United States, and Europe are small in number but horticulturally important. The vast majority of the world's rhododendron population grows in the Himalayan fastness of monsoon

Rhododendron hanceanum 'Nanum' is a slow grower.

Rhododendron williamsianum has heart-shaped leaves and clear pink flower bells. This clonal selection begins flowering generously when only a few years old.

forests and foggy crags. There, the forest species become trees as high as 80 feet with leaves 30 inches long, while the alpine species, in typical alpine fashion, reduce themselves to ankle-high shrublets with half-inch leaves.

The rhododendron belt across western China, Burma and Tibet coincides generally with the primula belt. Here is the hotbed of species proliferation for both these groups of plants.

Give rhododendrons primula conditions in the garden—a light, sandy, fast draining soil with plenty of humus dug into it. Rhododendrons are shallow rooters. Water them plentifully and keep a mulch of leaves or peat moss about the plants. Some growers prefer a living mulch of such trailing ericaceous subshrubs as *Gaultheria* and *Vaccinium*.

While relatively few primulas can be taken out of

Rhododendron lepidotum, bright yellow, grows inch a year.

the Asian mountains and made to live in the open in other continents, rhododendrons are far more accommodating. The botanic garden at Edinburgh, Scotland, grows about 500 species. Several collectors and nurserymen in Oregon, Washington, and British Columbia grow about 200 different species.

The West Coast down as far as California's Monterey Peninsula suits a greater number of rhododendron species than any other area on the continent. The giants from the Himalayan forests do best in shade on the southern end of this foggy, rainy, coastal strip. The high alpine dwarfs prefer more northerly gardens in full sun. Full sun stimulates flower production in rhododendrons and in almost all plants, while shade turns most plants to leaf production. The trick is to find how much sun plants will take without scorching.

A few alpine species are hardy enough to tolerate East Coast winters north into New England. It may seem paradoxical that rhododendrons which grow at elevations of two to three miles in the Himalayas are not oak-hardy in American gardens. But remember that the zone of Arctic cold falls much higher on the Himalayas than it does in our mountains; 10,000 feet in Yunnan may correspond to 2,000 feet in Virginia or Oregon.

A number of the best Japanese and American rhododendrons are equally adaptable to the West Coast, the Gulf Coast, and the East Coast north of Boston.

Certain rhododendrons will grow in the hot interior valleys of Washington, Oregon, and California if they are given shade, shelter, and the essential acid soil. Of course you'll be taking on unnecessary trouble and expense if you choose to grow rhododendrons in so inhospitable an environment. This may, however, be just the sort of challenge you like.

The plants that come under the name of *Rhododendron* are a diverse lot, including trees and shrublets and (in the Azalea series) both evergreen and deciduous plants. For a better understanding of the genus, botanists have divided rhododendrons into more than 40 "series"—groups of related species. The species within each series are similar in flower and leaf form, and often in their cultural requirements.

The Lapponicum series has given us the greatest number of rock garden shrubs. The more than 50 species in this series grow mainly in western China at elevations of 12,000 to 14,000 feet (even as high as 18,000 feet). The Lapponicum rhododendrons are twiggy, 1 to 4-foot shrubs with tiny leaves and small flowers in showy clusters. In the Himalayas, Lapponicum rhododendrons grow together by the millions, covering mile after mile of stony moorland. The plant explorer Kingdon Ward described the flowering colonies as "a chromatic, storm-tossed surf—rose, pink, purple, lavender, and amber—through which one may wade ankle-deep for days on end."

The Saluenense series has also provided favorite

rock garden rhododendrons. Like the Lapponicums, the Saluenense rhododendrons colonize the stony pastures 2 to 3 miles high in the rhododendron belt. The typical Saluenense rhododendron is a typical alpine plant—a dense, slow growing, domed growth with comically large flowers sitting directly on the leaves. On young plants the wide-open flowers, 1½ inches across, are as large as the body of the shrub. The flower colors of the Saluenense series are in the reddish purple zone.

In the garden, Lapponicum and Saluenense rhododendrons flower most heavily and keep their neatly compressed alpine habit best in full sun. But many gardeners take the safer way, planting these rhododendrons in half shade and settling for lanker growth and fewer flowers.

Turn to the chapter at the back of the book and read about some of the best rhododendrons in these and a number of other series. Shrub measurements at a given age are included in the biographies of many species. These measurements were taken from copiously watered plants growing in full sun (with noted exceptions). In shade these same shrubs would be larger and more loosely branched.

Scree Gardening

The most written-about, argued-about, and misunderstood way of growing rock plants is on a scree. The one area of agreement among scree gardeners is that a scree is nature's way of growing rock plants, and that —faithfully recreated in the garden—a scree will work tonic wonders on the garden health and the floriferousness of these same rock plants. The hitch in this is that many scree gardeners are not clear about the formation of a natural scree and how it works as a home for plants.

Natural screes are deep piles of detritus (flaked or fragmented stone) which lie at the base of cliffs or on ridges in the mountains.

Natural screes provide homes for the most rock-oriented of all rock plants. The typical scree plant has a deep-driving cord of root; a little tuft or cushion of leaves huddled, wind-shy, between the stones, and (during the brief mountain springtime) incredibly big, vividly colored flowers.

A scree plant's lean, stony diet and its cautious expenditure of growth each year often give it far longer life than plants which grow fatter and faster in soil. Climbers in the Alps have made annual pilgrimages to certain scree plants and, after measuring their growth over a period of years, have been able to make approximate estimates of the plants' ages. Some of these scree plants are over a century old. Every year when the melting snow uncovers them, and the air is abuzz with the insects which fertilize them, they still flower furiously.

Natural screes, then, are stony places—growing mediums of loose, fragmented stones which hold air, but quickly drain away excess moisture. Scree plants, having adapted themselves to life on this extremely porous growing medium, require it in our rock gardens. However, natural screes are not dry places.

The more successful scree plant communities occur on screes which are charged with fresh water from melting snows above them or from subterranean springs. During the growing season, scree plants require copious amounts of fresh water as much as they require the rapid draining of water. Here is where many garden screes fail. Because the well made garden scree disperses water as quickly as a sieve, it requires constant water replenishment. Alpine scree plants are such little living things that if their demands for water are not met during the heat of summer when they need water most, they may dry up and die in a single hot day. Even desert scree plants require a constant supply of moisture during their growing season.

Building a scree

While there are just about as many recipes for scree making as there are rock gardeners, the basic intent of the scree maker is to provide drainage for alpine plants or desert plants in gardens where drainage is poor. The scree provides other benefits. It is both a stage and a garden sanctuary for rare and small plants. The scree is an open (and often raised) area where these small plants can be seen, and can be protected from engulfment by the larger, stronger plants of which the rest of the garden is composed.

Before deciding to build a scree, first establish that your garden conditions actually call for one. If your garden is of basically sandy soil and is fast-draining at all times of the year, it is in effect an over-all scree. Your concern is not to add drainage, but to provide sufficient water during the summer. Screes are advantageous for rock gardening on clay or peat soils, or in loam soils of average drainage (average enough to grow daffodils, roses, cherries and the mass of garden plants).

Wait for a time of year when the soil is dry enough to crumble before beginning construction. In soils of average drainage the scree can be constructed so that its surface is level with that of the surrounding soil. But where drainage is definitely slow—in gardens where water will collect and stand in a hole at any time of the year—the scree must be built entirely above the level of the surrounding soil.

The scree contains these ingredients: crushed stone or gravel, sand, clay, and humus in a mixture. The scree mixture should be at least a foot deep, but need not be more than 2 feet. As an optional feature, stones, gravel, or broken flower pots can be placed at the bottom to a depth of three inches to assure maximum drainage. Cover the drainage with a thin sprink-

How to make a scree

Upper left: Scree will be placed against this group of stones. A bed 18 inches deep is being dug about the "face" (steep, exposed portions) of the stones to simulate a natural scree.

Upper center: Completed excavation is partly filled with a 3-inch layer of inexpensive ½-inch gravel and "builders'" sand in equal proportions.

Upper right: Mix gravel, sand, and soil by scooping them up together and letting them trickle from the side of the shovel.

Left: Blue-gray crushed stone, selected to match color of scree's stone grouping, is poured 1 inch deep over top. Stone of various colors is available from suppliers listed under "Rock" in yellow pages of phone book.

Below: By end of first summer, scree has become a settled community of plants. At lower left is cushion of *Draba rigida;* above its right edge is *Juniperus communis* 'Compressa'. Background grove is *Picea glauca* 'Conica'.

The 4 by 4-foot boulder in foreground was split along its seams with a hammer and wedge. Fragments were then pieced together with an inch or so of the scree mixture between. Result is both container and display table for a score of scree plants. Hummock scree rises behind the upthrusting conifer (*Chamaecyparis lawsoniana* 'Fletcheri'). Design: W. Bogard.

Dudleya and other dry-land plants give this scree-filled planter a desert motíf. Design: Percy Everett.

ling of coarse leaf mold to prevent the scree mixture from sifting down and clogging it.

For the main depth of the scree, mix 1 part crushed rock (½ inch minus or ¾ inch minus) or pea gravel, 1 part coarse sand, and 2 parts fertile garden loam. If you haven't the loam you can prepare it by sieving together equal parts of clay, humus (leaf mold, well rotted sawdust, compost, or peat moss), and sand. Exact proportions are unimportant. In scree making, the basic idea is to provide a growing medium that stays porous. Experienced rock gardeners are inclined to mix unmeasured amounts of these different ingredients until the mixture looks right and feels right. (It should crumble when you squeeze it.)

Stonier scree recipes than ours are advocated by many rock gardeners. But screes of 4 to 5 parts stone to 1 part loam become desert-dry much too easily.

The incorporation of air into the scree by the mixing of its solid ingredients has an importance equal to the incorporation of sand and stone. Tamp the mixture into place with your feet, but don't "hammer" it. Allow for settling by piling the scree mixture 25 per cent higher than the desired final grade.

The top inch of the scree should be crushed stone or pea gravel without the admixture of any soil. Where their leaves meet the soil, alpine plants appreciate especially fast drainage.

Watering a scree

The hose is the usual means of watering a scree, but there are other systems worth knowing about.

The water requirements of garden screes are sometimes met by burying water pipes with tiny holes drilled in them at intervals of 1 or 2 feet. The water is turned on in the spring and turned off in the fall. But roots or mineral salts are apt to clog the holes in time —even as short a time as a year.

In the public rock garden at Geneva, Switzerland, (one of the world's finest) there is a large scree which banks a terrace. A trough, lipped at intervals, runs along the edge of the terrace and trickles water down among hundreds of minute, high-alpine plants.

The mist spray system is the ideal way to water many scree plants. So far it has been little tried. Reports indicate that open, airy locations favored by many scree plants are not favorable to the accumulation of the life-giving mist. A breeze will whisk it away. But in sheltered spots such plants as *Cassiope, Phyllodoce, Gentiana,* and *Meconopsis* have given spectacular garden performances under mist culture.

Pipes, troughs, and mist sprays are for specialists. The weekend gardener can't be expected to invest in them. Foregoing some elaborate system of plumbing, the next best way to keep a scree moist is to construct it in a half shady place and to water it frequently with the hose (every day if possible) during dry summer weather.

The scree as a garden composition

The raised scree can take the simple form of a hummock, with or without surface stones larger than the scree topping. Hillside screes seem especially well-wedded to cliff-like outcroppings of large stones, as screes are disposed in nature.

If these outcropping stones set the scale for a cliff, the dwarfest conifers represent forests, the alpine cushion plants take on the dimension of shrubbery, and the inch-high mat plants equal the turf of the alpine meadow.

The sand scree

Coarse sand spread over the ground to a depth of 4 inches works well as a growing medium for many scree plants, providing the ground beneath is well drained. The roots of the plants grow into the soil beneath to receive nutrition. The neck of the plant stays well aerated in winter.

Light-colored sand is valuable for increasing the intensity of light in shady places. Cacti have been successfully grown in shade by this means.

Sand alone provides an interesting texture much appreciated in Japanese stone gardening.

The scree-in-a-planter

Scree-filled planters have interesting landscape uses. A long narrow container can form a low wall at the edge of a patio. In rural gardens, such raised beds can be retained appropriately with dry stone or railroad ties; in more tailored gardens, with mortared stone or aggregate faced concrete.

As in the open scree, the scree-in-a-planter can be made a complete composition or subordinated to the surrounding garden areas. If planter is all the garden for which there is room, this is still room enough for an entire "little world'" encompassing stones, trees, shrubs and perennials.

Representative plants for screes

Acantholimon venustum, Androsace lanuginosa, A. sarmentosa, A. sempervivoides, Armeria juniperifolia (A. caespitosa), Campanula aucheri, C. tommasiniana, C. waldsteiniana, Carmichaelia enysii, Cheilanthes siliquosa, C. tomentosa, Crassula sarcocaulis, Crocus, Cryptomeria japonica 'Vilmoriniana,' *Cytisus decumbens (C. humifusa), Daphne arbuscula, D. collina, D. retusa, Dianthus alpinus, D. microlepis, Edraianthus pumilio (Wahlenbergia pumilio), Edraianthus serpyllifolius (Wahlenbergia serpyllifolia), Elmera racemosa, Erigeron compositus, E. leiomerus, E. pinnatisectus, Genista villarsii, Geranium cinereum, Globularia incanescens, G. repens (G. nana), Hebe pimeleoides,*

Helichrysum selago, Hypericum coris, Iberis saxatilis, Juniperus communis 'Compressa,' *Leucogenes grandiceps, Lewisia cotyledon, L. rupicola, Morisia monantha (M. hypogaea), Myosotis alpestris (M. rupicola), Narcissus pseudo-narcissus* 'Nanus' *(N.* 'Nanus'), *N. cyclamineus, Oxalis enneaphylla, Penstemon menziesii, P. pinifolius, Phlox diffusa, Potentilla nitida, P. verna* 'Nana,' *Primula hirsuta,* P. *minima, Saxifraga* (choice high alpine saxifrages), *Silene acaulis, Synthyris lanuginosa, Talinum spinescens, Thalictrum kiusianum.*

There might be added to this list the greater portion of plant species grown in the name of rock gardening.

Rock Gardening in Pots, Coldframes, and Alpine Houses

Around the world many major collections of rock plants—those of botanic gardens, nurseries, and private collectors—are grown in pots which are kept under glass for the winter. The usual glass cover is the coldframe sash.

Rock gardening in pots and coldframes offers certain comforts to both the gardener and the plants. The gardener benefits from the compactness of his garden. He can grow a great variety of plants in a small area. Watering, spraying, and fertilizing can be done with a minimum of motion. The plants benefit from the partial climate control—especially the control of alternate winter rains and frosts which are damaging (and sometimes deadly) to many alpine plants.

Almost any garden coldframe that receives full sun or part sun can be prepared as a home for the general run of rock plants. You can grow the rock plants directly in the frame without pots by placing a foot of scree mixture in the bottom of the frame. (Mix the scree according to the formula in the preceding section.) Or you can grow the plants in pots sunk in 6 inches of sand or peat moss placed in the frame to act as a moisture and temperature regulator. (Some collectors prefer doing without this sand or peat base.)

Place coarse drainage material in the pots up to one-third the pot height. Then fill them with various growing media according to the needs of the plants. Scree plants require a scree mixture; woodland plants and ericaceous plants prefer a mixture of one part leaf mold, peat moss, compost, or well-rotted sawdust to one part scree mixture; bog plants enjoy rich peaty loam or living sphagnum moss, according to habitat.

The sashes should be removed from early spring until fall to prevent the etiolation (the stretching toward light) of the plants growing within the frame. The potted plants themselves can be removed from

Scree-filled pots house the *Lewisia* collection in the San Francisco garden of Arthur Menzies. Square pots at lower center and round pot at lower right contain *L. rediviva*. Just above right-hand square pot is *L. cantelowii,* exhibiting a few of its quiet little flowers. Three pots toward upper left hold the bold, strap-leafed rosettes of *L. cotyledon.*

the frame for the summer to be enjoyed on a patio railing or elsewhere.

Water potted rock plants frequently—they may need daily watering during the summer. Never let them become dry. The aestival (summer dormant) prairie and desert plants are excepted. It is their nature to die down to the ground by midsummer, after they have flowered and set their seed. After they've begun to die down, give them just enough water to keep the soil from becoming dust-dry. If they show signs of rejuvenation in the fall, resume the full watering schedule; otherwise wait until spring.

Fertilize the potted plants once a month during their growing season. A mild solution of organic fertilizer is the safest tonic for rock plants.

Division and repotting should be done as needed —every year or two.

Many collectors in the British Isles (and a few in North America) fill whole greenhouses full of potted rock plants. A greenhouse adapted to the culture of rock plants is known as an alpine house. Alpine houses must be sunny, well ventilated, and well aerated (electric fans are used). Usually they are unheated, but some collectors prefer keeping the temperature a degree or two above freezing during frosty winter weather. Daily and seasonally, plants are cared for essentially the same as plants in coldframes.

If an alpine house sounds intriguing to you, read Stuart Boothman's *The Alpine House and Its Plants.* The book is published in England, but it is available from book dealer Lynn Ranger, Lynn Shore Drive, Lynn, Massachusetts, and probably from other American dealers in hard-to-track-down garden books.

Trenches and Hummocks... Rock Gardens of Ingenuity

In a land of general flatness, British rock gardeners have invented ways of making garden elevations. They either dig trenches or they pile earth into hummocks. Often these two earth works are combined, in microcosmic imitation of mountains and mountain gorges. The results seldom come close to nature, but at best these trench-and-hummock gardens possess an unexpected charm—the charm of suspended disbelief that we feel in all miniature things.

To make a trench garden, a flat piece of land is dug out with a meandering network of broad, man-deep trenches. The trench walls are sloped gradually, moderately, or steeply, and banked with stone. As a rule, walls of gradual slope are more pleasing than steep ones.

The gardening advantages of the trench garden are these: a variety of exposures from full shade to full sun; elevation from ankle level to eye level for the better display of small plants; coolness and moisture retention in the shadier aspects of the trench, a valuable asset in areas where summers are hot and evaporation is rapid. (Desiccating sun and wind are among the worst garden enemies of delicate alpine plants.)

Hummock gardens are built of soil piled in irregular elongated mounds interconnected with paths. The mounds are never too even, too high, or too steep. Rocks are used with great restraint and linked to each other with careful artistry to avoid a "raisin cooky" effect. The gains to be made from hummock gardening are: elevation for easy viewing; some variation in sun and shade exposure; and, best of all, good drainage in locations where drainage is poor.

The hummock garden and the raised scree (discussed earlier in this chapter) are closely related rock garden techniques. In fact, the hummock becomes a scree with the incorporation of sand and crushed rock in its soil.

The Societies and the Nurseries

In England, Scotland, and the United States there are three rock gardening organizations which have much to offer you. These three societies welcome all who apply for membership. Each society has its own journal or bulletin which is sent to all members. These publications are mines of authoritative information about rock plants in the wild and in the garden.

The articles in the British *Journal* and the Scottish *Bulletin* are more technically and botanically advanced than those in the American *Journal*. (Remember that alpine rock gardening was founded in the British Isles.) But there is plenty of substance in the American *Journal,* presented more in the nature of a neighborly chat over the back fence than in the formal manner of a technical journal.

Equally valuable are the seed exchanges which these societies arrange for their members every winter. Seeds of rock garden plants are contributed by society members, who collect them in their gardens or from wild plants. Contributions come in from such scattered addresses as Colorado, the Falkland Islands, Japan, Chile, Soviet Russia, and New Zealand. These seed contributions are catalogued in lists of astonishing length. A selection of 1,500 to 3,000 different kinds of plants is available to all members at a few cents per seed packet. All this is as good as it sounds, and considering the necessarily limited offering of the rare plant nurseries in North America, it is about the only way to build up a plant collection of any size.

"The necessarily limited offering" of our rare plant nurseries has resulted from a limited demand. However, as a source for the staple rock plants, these nurseries are indispensable. The seed of many staple

Plant sale. Several of the regional units of the American Rock Garden Society conduct plant sales to fatten up their treasuries. Members bring surplus plants from their gardens; plants are then auctioned off. A plant sale is a lively happening which brings many a "sometime member" out of hibernation, offers opportunity to obtain new and rare plants.

rock plants is practically unobtainable. Dealing with these nurseries is also the easy way to obtain a considerable number of rare plants—often much easier than raising them yourself.

We've found a number of nurseries that deal in rock plants. Their names, addresses and terms of business are outlined in the following list. The addresses of the three rock garden societies are there, too. One way or another these sources offer you the making of a rock garden.

The Rock Garden Societies

For a year's membership in the American Rock Garden Society, mail a check for $5.00 to
Lawrence Hochheimer
Ridge Farms Road
Norwalk, Connecticut
Membership in the Scottish Rock Garden Club costs $3.00, payable by a check made out to
J. J. Boyd-Harvey
Boonslie, Dirleton
East Lothian, Scotland

For membership in the Alpine Garden Society send a check for $2.80 to
The Secretary of the Alpine Garden Society
10 Rochester Row
London, S.W. 1, England

Specialty nurseries

Alpenglow Gardens
13328 Trans-Canada Highway
North Surrey P.O.
New Westminster, B.C., Canada

All manner of rock plants, shrubs and trees for sale at the nursery and by mail order. Plant catalogue and seed list. (Americans should send an import permit along with their orders to Canadian nurseries. The permits are free and can be obtained by writing to the U.S. Department of Agriculture, Agricultural Research Service, Plant Quarantine Division, 209 River Street, Hoboken, New Jersey.)

American Perennial Gardens
P.O. Box 37
Garden City, Michigan
Perennials and rock plants of proven hardiness. Cash and carry, mail order. Catalogue, seed list.

Claude A. Barr
Prairie Gem Ranch
Smithwick, South Dakota
Great Plains plants, hardy cacti. Mail order catalogue, seed list.

E. C. Robbins
Ashford, McDowell Co.
North Carolina
Pioneer firm still operated by the founder. Forest plants of the Blue Ridge—many of them dug from the wild by the mountain people. Cash and carry, mail orders. Catalogue.

The Three Laurels
Marshall, North Carolina
List, mail orders. This is their complete, if somewhat cryptic address. (Both of the Carolina nurseries listed here offer some of America's best buys in plants.)

Mayfair Nurseries
R.D. No. 2
Nichols, New York
Rock garden conifers, heathers. Mail order catalogue.

MacPherson Gardens
2920 Starr Ave.
Oregon 16, Ohio
Mail order list. Sempervivum specialists—one of world's largest selections, with the right names attached to each kind.

Charles Thurman
Route 2, Box 259
Spokane, Washington
Rock plants, perennials for sale at the nursery and by mail order. Offers many useful plants native to the severe climate of the interior plateau country of the Northwest. Catalogue (50 cents) and seed list.

George Schenk
Box 487
Bothell, Washington

Perennials, ground covering shrubs and plants in wide variety selected for landscape value. Wholesale prices. Minimum quantities: 15 of a kind. Minimum order: $35. Price list: 10 cents.

The following are home nurseries, none of which issues a price list:

A. R. Heineman
540 Second Avenue
Milton, Washington
In this nursery near Tacoma are several dozen varieties of rock plants (including the best *Gentiana acaulis* in North America), many rhododendrons and shrubs. Mr. Heineman, an octogenarian, gives all the care to his plants that the Benedictine monks give to their liqueur. Mrs. Heineman may be America's last gardener in a poke bonnet.

Frank Newland
Rt. 2, Box 2914
Woodinville, Washington
Another unique operation by an old-time grower. With gentle courtesy Mr. Newland will show you rock plants and many perennials grown to a perfection that is not often found on the market.

Donald Stryker
Langlois, Oregon
Greenhouse and lathhouse chock-ablock with unheard of rarities, presided over by a man of wide knowledge and experience. He's sure to tell you about his plants, will probably give you one, and—if your interest is really keen—he may sell you some.

Ray Williams
108 Meidl Avenue
Watsonville, California
For forty years Mr. and Mrs. Williams have specialized in plants and shrubs so rare that you must be reassured by the locality labels that they did indeed originate somewhere in the world.

Rock Gardens for Landscape Effect

The near opposite of the collector's rock garden is the rock garden planted primarily for landscape effect. The variety of plants in this rock garden is purposely limited to produce an effect of strength and unity. The plants chosen for this rock garden possess hardiness, ease of culture, rich foliage values and, quite often, a bright gift of flowers. By and large, these plants are the best of rock plants.

The photographs on this page show a garden of such plants—a landscape garden of stones, coniferous trees, and mat-forming plants, mainly *Phlox subulata,* various sedums, and thyme. In flower, the garden becomes such rich color fare that a visitor's eyes very much welcome the change of pace provided by the perfectly kept lawns which separate the masses of flowers. This is the public rock garden of the Gordon and the Herman Ohmes of Wenatchee, Wash.

The Ohmes use tough, competitive, spreading alpine plants almost exclusively in their garden for large scale effect. The plantings are to a large degree self-maintaining—a necessary consideration in a four-acre rock garden. A valuable conclusion can be drawn here: the rock garden need not be a high maintenance garden. An area of ground planted with the strongest rock plants requires less maintenance than a lawn or a perennial border of the same size.

Some of the best looking and the strongest rock plants for landscape effect are found in these genera: *Achillea, Aethionema, Ajuga, Alyssum, Anthemis, Aubrieta, Cotoneaster, Dianthus, Dryas, Fragaria, Geranium, Genista, Gypsophila, Helianthemum, Iberis, Juniperus, Phlox, Saponaria, Sedum, Thymus.*

In the United States there are representative collections of these plants in Alaska, New York City, Reno, Los Angeles, San Francisco (Strybing Arboretum), and Seattle. The range of climates in which these plants so far have been successfully tested suggests that you'll be able to grow at least several of them wherever you live in the United States.

The Hillside Rock Garden

A hillside turned into a rock garden requires less labor and maintenance time than grass, if the slope is steep and hard to mow. You'll find information on the design and construction of a hillside rock garden beginning on page 54.

While a hillside makes a grand domain for a collector's garden, don't depend on collectors' plants for

Ohme Gardens in Wenatchee, Washington, pictured above and below, started with a barren, stony hilltop bypassed by agriculture, then added alpine conifers, carpeting rock plants, lawns, and ponds. This great landscape achievement commemorates alpine floral zone of many American mountains.

This hillside rock garden contains many of the best elements of rock garden composition. Paths, stones, and plants are in balanced proportion and flowing arrangement. The stones—not too many—are carefully fitted, deeply set, and allowed to enter the paths. Crushed blue-gray shale (¾-inch minus) controls run-off, gives dry footing and the appearance of a mountain scree. Design: William Bogard.

landscape effect. Plants which are rare, minute, fastidious, and labor-consuming should be confined to relatively small areas defined by screes or outcroppings.

Hillside rock gardens should have the greater part of their area devoted to vigorous ground cover plants and tough, spreading shrubs. Use the plants recommended above.

Tilling the soil over the entire bank before planting lets the rain soak in and prevents runoff until the ground covers have formed a protective covering. A scree topping will act as an extra erosion preventative.

Stones are optional on hillsides of 40° or less and on steeper slopes held by deeply rooted, ground-stabilizing plants. The steepest hillside rock garden might exchange definitions with the planted bank.

The Planted Bank

The least expensive way (and often the most attractive way) to hold soil banks is with large scale rock plants without the incorporation of any stone.

The use of plants for retaining purposes has been explored for us by our highway departments. State-by-state, the highway miles of mesembryanthemum, oleander, ceanothus, juniper, arctostaphylos, broom, ivy, pine and other plants make the freeway marathon a little more humane and a little less hypnotic. These plants are also among the best for large jobs of bank retaining in home gardens.

There are many other plants just as good. Read the lists of plants for retaining walls in the section that follows. The plants in the lists will prove equally adaptable to bank planting.

The strongest shrubs for bank plantings are capable of holding banks as steep as 65°, as long as these are composed of reasonably stable soil. This soil category includes compact, glacially deposited sand, "mineral soil" which accumulates about decomposing stone, and porous loam—all of which disperse rather than soak up slide-causing moisture. Clay banks and gravel banks are usually not stable enough to be supported by plants alone.

To facilitate watering and to prevent dislodging, bank plants can be set out in "foxholes" formed by bottomless gallon cans, by circles of aluminum lawn edging, by buried apple boxes with bottoms knocked out, or by sections of railroad ties. At the very least, scoop a foxhole in the bank and form a rim for it with the excavated soil. Reinforce the rim with small stones if they are available.

By the time the metal corrodes or the wood rots, the plants will have plunged their roots to self-service depth and will need only occasional help from you through the driest weather. Soil-rimmed foxholes may require periodic restoring.

Rock Gardening on a Retaining Wall

Retaining walls can be a problem. The average "dry stone" (unmortared stone) retaining wall, as built by a contractor, is an honest, utilitarian pile of roughly stacked stones, thoroughly depressing to the gardener who confronts it. His whole property seems to him as bleak as a prison yard dominated by an insurmountable wall. Sometimes the wall discourages him from even beginning a garden.

Planting is the solution

An ugly stone wall, even the biggest and ugliest, need not stay ugly. There are plants which are capable of covering the largest stone walls with richly textured curtains of foliage. For lower walls there are smaller plants in great variety.

For the lucky few among you whose dry stone walls are things of beauty (probably you built them yourselves), there is no need for plants to do a masking job; a plant tufting here and there from your wall's architecturally beautiful face is all that is needed to bring it to life. Choose plants from the listing under "Cover plants for retaining walls under 6 feet" on pages 46 and 47.

Some rock gardeners build walls just for the purpose of displaying plants. For these gardeners there are plants in infinite variety. The majority of the thousands of species of collectors' rock plants available in North America grow readily in dry stone walls —and appear more at home here than in any other garden situation. Plant collectors with shady walls sometimes use them as display shelves for ferns.

If you're building your own dry stone wall

Building a dry stone retaining wall is plain hard work, but rewarding. You may well turn out a better job of retaining wall construction than you can hire.

By building the wall yourself you may save about 75% of its cost. Moreover, most of us find that building something out of stone is richly satisfying to the stone age man within us.

Amateurs working with hand tools should probably restrict themselves to constructing walls under 6 feet in height, set against reasonably stable soil. Oozy clay soil and gravel banks require larger, heavier retaining stones than can be set by hand.

If you're buying the stone, you probably will find that local stone dealers offer a considerable variety from which to choose. Stones that are gathered or quarried locally are the most harmonious for garden use in your locality. Stones shipped in from other localities may be more colorful but are probably out of relationship with the stone-foliage-atmospheric color harmony of your locality.

Go and see the stone before you decide to buy it. Unless it is to be heavily planted, the wall won't be more attractive than the stones that go into it. You may decide that weathered stone is worth the higher cost.

Estimates of the amount of stone required for retaining walls are usually figured in tons. The required tonnage differs from undressed stone to dressed stone. One ton of quarry stone, field stone, and other types of undressed stone will cover 25 to 40 square feet of retaining wall with an average thickness of 1 foot of stone. One ton of dressed stone will cover about 55 square feet of wall surface, with an average thickness of 6 inches of stone.

Don't be misled by the present day application of the old stoneworker's terms "one man stone," "two

Big jobs of bank planting require big, tough shrubs. For highway at left, a steep cut 60 feet deep and 50° in grade was made in a bank of pure sand. Moonlight broom *(Cytisus praecox)* was planted 6 feet apart. Masses of scented, soft yellow flowers give the bank a special beauty in April and May.

Wood frames support newly planted pyracantha (firethorn), facilitate watering. Entire bank (except within frames) has been covered with black plastic sheeting to kill quack grass, roots of which have densely infested the bank. The plastic sheeting is concealed beneath a topping of crushed rock.

Smaller plants hold smaller banks. The mesh-like growth of a number of our wild strawberries *(Fragaria)* is highly effective. *F. chiloensis* was used on this 55° bank.

It takes planting
to bring a
rock wall to life

Above: In this difficult assignment, small, roundish stones 9 to 12 inches in diameter have been fitted closely and smoothly to form 5-foot retaining walls. Design: E. K. Balls.

Left, above: Stark stone retaining walls like this, placed by building contractors, confront thousands of American home-owners each year. To mask them, use tough, spreading plants.

Left, below: Nearly vertical (80°) wall, 7 feet high, was safely engineered by fitting stones solidly and by facing wall smoothly with slight backward tilt, no gravity-defying bulges.

Below: This two-year-old planting has long-settled appearance which comes at once with use of weathered stone. At top are upright *Thalictrum* and down-draping *Heuchera*.

man stone," and so on. These terms have become imprecise in the extreme. In today's terminology a one man stone weighs up to 400 pounds, two man stones up to 800. When ordering stones, specify the weight range of the stones that you want to use. Placing 250-pound stones will prove taxing but not impossible for two average men working with hand tools. If you're building a smooth-faced retaining wall and plan to lift the stones into position, let the greater part of your load of stone be in 100 to 150-pound range.

Use only one variety of stone throughout the wall. Have plenty of stones on hand, in assorted sizes, so that you won't be tempted for even a moment to fill in the chinks with old bricks, broken pieces of concrete, and other debris.

Field stones of mixed geological character can be used together, because their worn roundness gives them a measure of uniformity, but reject any that are glaringly different in shape or in color—white quartz, for example.

Wherever possible, place the stones flat rather than on end. This is the position in which most stones lie naturally, and in this position stones give walls the aspect of being there to stay for good. Walls built with vertically placed stones unnerve us with their teetery look, and they are actually likely to be unsafe.

Retaining wall styles

There are two major styles of dry stone retaining walls: (1) those built steeply with a straight face, and (2) stepped-back retaining stones placed against moderate slopes.

Terraced rock work, which almost counts as a separate style, is made up of series of retaining walls, usually of the smooth-faced sort.

Straight-faced dry stone walls

The beauty of this style depends on the tightness of its joints and the smoothness of its face. A wall is, after all, a piece of architecture, and if crudely built it seems quite as precarious as a swayback barn.

Skilled stoneworkers occasionally construct dry stone walls steeper than 80°, but amateurs will produce safer results in a more gentle range of from 65° to 80°.

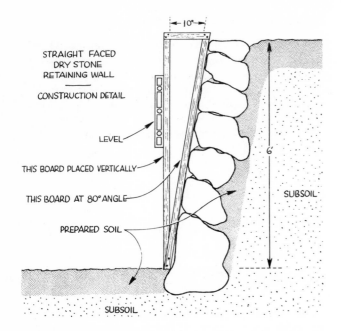

STRAIGHT FACED DRY STONE RETAINING WALL

CONSTRUCTION DETAIL

LEVEL

THIS BOARD PLACED VERTICALLY

THIS BOARD AT 80° ANGLE

PREPARED SOIL

SUBSOIL

SUBSOIL

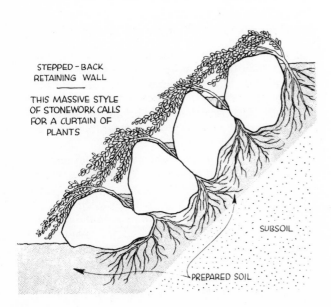

STEPPED-BACK RETAINING WALL

THIS MASSIVE STYLE OF STONEWORK CALLS FOR A CURTAIN OF PLANTS

SUBSOIL

PREPARED SOIL

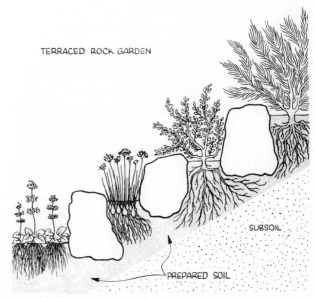

TERRACED ROCK GARDEN

SUBSOIL

PREPARED SOIL

Construction pointers

String guidelines along the base and along the top of the bank that the wall is to follow. But for the neatest wall don't rely entirely on the guide lines; instead, use angle boards. Angle boards are simple to make: Nail together two 2-inch by 2-inch boards (or larger) that are as long as the wall will be high. One board is used in a vertical position. The other is nailed to the vertical board at an angle which corresponds to the degree of slope that your wall is to take.

To use the boards, hold the "vertical board" vertically and place the "angle board" against the face of the wall as you erect it to gauge an even slope for the wall's face (see the sketch on page 45).

Place your largest stones as the bottom course of the wall. Bury about 6 inches of the bottom course of stone to give maximum stability to the wall. Tilt the face of each stone in the wall back so that the stone's weight rests against the hillside.

Planting a wall

If the face of the wall is to be planted, about 6 inches of scree mixture or sandy loam should be firmly tamped into place behind each rock and more scree mixture or loam tamped between the stones.

The ideal way to plant a dry stone wall is to plant as you build. Place the plants along a course of stone with the roots spread out. Cover the roots with about 2 inches of scree mixture or loam and lay the next course of stone over the roots.

Actually, few walls are planted this way. Most builders find the construction of the wall enough to do without undertaking the planting at the same time.

If you're going to plant the wall after building it, use small plants and expect some losses. Scoop out a trowelful or two of soil from between the stones, insert the roots of the plant, and replace as much of the scooped-out soil as will go. Firm the plants into place and sprinkle them immediately if it's a warm day. Water them daily until they begin to grow, and frequently thereafter.

Stepped-back retaining walls

This style of dry stone wall is simpler to build and easier to plant than a smooth-faced wall. Stepped-back retaining walls are the most used—and useful—retaining walls on slopes of from 30° to 65°. But stepped-back walls, except in the hands of a stone artist, become mere jumbles of stone.

In commercial jobs of this style, the stones are usually stacked on top of the ground, or dug in very slightly. The resulting stonework has a massive, disorderly appearance which cries out for concealment by planting. Fortunately the many irregular soil spaces between the stones (called "pockets" by rock gardeners) provide excellent footing for rock plants.

If you are building your own stepped-back retaining wall, you can easily improve on commercial procedure by setting the stones deeply in the ground and organizing them as outcroppings.

Terraced rock gardens

By reason of their architectural feeling, terraces walled with dry stone are especially suited to city gardens. Terrace walls can be of single-stone height on slopes of from 10 to 30 degrees; on steeper slopes, the terrace walls can be constructed of several courses of stone. Series of single-course and several-course walls are interesting to work out.

Cover plants for large retaining walls

The plants in this list are all evergreen shrubs whose prostrate growth and strong habit make them useful as foliage curtains over high walls and massive stones. They are in good scale on walls 6 feet and more in height; with frequent pruning they can also be used on lower walls. Planted toward the top of a wall their prostrate branches trail downward and in time will reach the bottom.

Many of the plants have worthwhile flowers. *Arctostaphylos uva-ursi,* pyracantha, and the cotoneasters have showy fruits. The shrubs in this list will withstand poor soil, lack of water and general neglect, but they will provide fuller, handsomer cover with normal garden care.

Before making your selection, read about each of these plants in the chapter beginning on page 73: *Arctostaphylos media, A. uva-ursi, Cedrus* (prostrate forms), *Cotoneaster adpressa, C. dammeri, Cytisus, Ceanothus gloriosus, Euonymus fortunei* 'Vegeta' (*E. radicans vegetus*), *Genista, Hedera, Muehlenbeckia, Juniperus* (prostrate forms), *Pyracantha, Vinca.*

Cover plants for retaining walls under 6 feet

The plants in the list below are of more restrained growth. They require more water than the plants in the above list. Most of them are evergreen and most of them are hardy to 0°. The exceptions are marked (D) for deciduous; those whose hardiness is questionable are marked with the lowest temperature they can be expected to endure without damage.

Alyssum saxatile, A. wulfenianum, Aubrieta deltoidea, Cerastium tomentosum, Convolvulus mauritanicus (D except in mildest climates) (20°), *Cotoneaster horizontalis, C. congesta* (*C. microphylla glacialis*), *Daphne cneorum, Dianthus gratianopolitanus* (*D. caesius*) and hybrids, *D. deltoides, Dryas octopetala* (D), *Duchesnea indica, Erica carnea, E. purpurascens* 'Darleyensis', *E. p.* 'Darleyensis Alba', *Erica vagans, Euphorbia myrsinites, Ficus pumila* (*F. repens*) (25°), *Fragaria chiloensis, F. californica, F.*

virginiana, Genista pilosa, G. radiata, G. sagittalis, Geranium sanguineum in all its forms (D), *Hebe decumbens* (15°), *H. pinguifolia* 'Pagei' (15°), *Hedera helix* 'Hahn's Self-Branching,' *Helianthemum* hybrids, *Hypericum polyphyllum* (10°), *H. olympicum* (10°), *Iberis sempervirens, Lathyrus splendens* (25°), *Linnaea borealis, Lithospermum diffusum* (10°), *Omphalodes verna* (D), *Penstemon fruticosus, Phlox nivalis, P. stolonifera, P. subulata, Polygonum vaccinifolium* (D) (10°) *Potentilla reptans, Rubus fockeanus, Saponaria ocymoides, Saxifraga sarmentosa, Sedum album, S. rupestre, S. spathulifolium, S. spurium, Veronica catarractae* (15°), *V. pectinata, V. repens, V. prostrata,* (D), *V. latifolia, Viola hederacea* (25°) *Zauschneria californica* (15°) (D), *Z. latifolia* (15°) (D).

(The sedums in this list will grow from branches inserted in the wall with or without roots.)

Some plants can be grown from seed sown into the soil crevices between the stones. These easy-to-germinate rock plants, which are the right size for walls 6 feet high and under, include *Alyssum saxatile, A. wulfenianum, A. argenteum, Corydalis, Eschscholtzia* (California poppy), *Aethionema stylosum, Campanula rotundifolia, Dianthus deltoides, Oenothera riparia, Potentilla nepalensis, P. recta* 'Warrensii'.

Stepping Stones

Stepping stones set two to four inches above the level of the surrounding soil provide a means of close-up display for a rich variety of low growing plants.

In low maintenance gardens let the stepping stones lead through carpet of *Sedum* and *Sempervivum.* In the collector's garden many of the rarest and tiniest alpine plants will be safe between raised stepping stones (if drainage is perfect). They'll benefit from the broken sun and shadow pattern provided by the stones, from a less rapid evaporation of soil moisture, and from the more frequent attention of the gardener who steps over them regularly on his rounds.

Stepping stones set in the usual way—flush with the ground—afford the easiest walking. Enhance them with a planting of perfectly flat mat-making plants — *Herniaria glabra, Thymus serpyllum* in variety, *Acaena buchananii, Mentha requienii, Raoulia, Helxine, Sagina subulata,* and if you live where the temperature doesn't go below 25°, *Phyla nodiflora (Lippia repens)* and *Dichonara carolinensis.* Use a hand clipper to keep these mat-makers from swamping the stepping stones.

Flagstones

Patios of unmortared stone or concrete flags become mellower and friendlier with a planting of mat-makers selected from the list under "Stepping Stones." Buy a

For easy walking, set smooth stepping stones at ground level. Flanking this walk in the Ohme Gardens, Wenatchee, Washington, is Irish moss (*Arenaria verna caespitosa*).

A community of the smallest alpine flowering plants and ferns grows between raised stepping stones. The stones lead to a patio where *Acaena buchananii* grows between paving blocks.

This patterned garden sums up the international influences which have radically altered the use of rocks and rock plants in present-day American gardens. Over all, the garden is a painting of the school of abstract design. The ground color is the blue-gray of granite. The granite is segregated by means of headerboards into river stones, gravel, and sand. In the center is an alpine conifer, an outcropping of weathered stones from the mountains, and colonies of sempervivums and other alpine plants. Behind the conifer, Irish moss forms another design unit. To right of conifer is a design unit of weathered stones and sand which descends from the Ryoanji rock garden in Kyoto, Japan. Design: Tommy Nishimura.

flat or several clumps of any of these plants in the spring, tear them into small rooted pieces, insert them between the flags, firm them with a gentle press of your shoe, and water them.

In Italy the crevices of stone patios and walks are sometimes seeded with rock plants of mounding, foot-high dimension. Meeting an occasional plant audaciously flowering in your way can be delightful or annoying, depending on how hurried you are. *Suggestion*: Confine tallish paving plants to the less trodden corners of the patio.

Plants and Stones in Patterns

The use of ground covers and stones in geometrical or abstract pattern has become widespread in contemporary gardens. Since almost all ground covers are rock plants, pattern making is, in fact, so far the most characteristic use of rock plants in the second half of this century.

By no means does this use of plants bring cheers from all gardeners. Some gardeners consider pattern making too regimented a use for plants—a step backward toward topiary art, formal gardens, and floral clocks. But even those who deplore the style would be hard put to ignore the body of the work. There is a vogue for pattern gardens in many American cities. The pattern garden may soon become passé, or quite possibly it may gain in popularity and become the prevalent garden style in decades to come.

Pattern designs of stones and plants have many qualities in common with painting. It is not surprising that the greatest exponent of plant patterns since the day of Versailles is both painter and landscape architect. He is Roberto Burle-Marx of Brazil. Gardeners who would like to explore the ultimate possibilities of the use of plants in patterns will profit by a trip to a large library where there are pictures and articles about Burle-Marx' work.

Rock plants suitable for making foliage carpets and flower tapestries have the prime characteristic of good fabric: they are slow to become threadbare. Even so, most of them will require dividing and re-planting—or replacing—sooner or later.

Some of the longest wearing, most dependable ground covers for pattern making are named in the following list, grouped according to foliage color. The list is quite arbitrary. There are thousands of plants which might be fitted to this use. Flower colors (in parentheses) follow the plant names. For additional information about these plants, look them up in the plant biographies at the back of the book.

Silver-gray. *Achillea argentea* (white), *Achillea ageratifolia aizoon (Anthemis aizoon)* (white), *Cerastium tomentosum* (white), *Stachys olympica (S. lanata)* (purple).

Gray-green. *Achillea jaborneggii* (white), *Achillea tomentosa* 'Moonlight' (pale yellow), *Cytisus (Genista) decumbens* (yellow), *Dianthus* 'Tiny Rubies' (rose), *Helianthemum* (white, yellow, rose, and pastel shades), *Lotus corniculatus* (bicolored scarlet and yellow), *Paronychia serpyllifolia* (few silvery bracts), *Thymus lanuginosus* (usually none), *Veronica pectinata* (rose or blue).

Dark grayish-green. *Cotoneaster congesta (C. microphylla glacialis)* (white; powdery rose berries), *Sedum album* (white), *Thymus serpyllum* 'Coccineus' (red-violet).

Bluish gray-green. *Hebe pinguifolia* 'Pagei' (white), *Festuca ovina* 'Glauca' (inconspicuous), *Sedum pruinosum* (yellow), *Sedum dasyphyllum glanduliferum* (pinkish white).

Bronzed green. *Sedum spurium* 'Dragon's Blood' (brilliant aniline red).

Purple-green. *Ajuga reptans* 'Purpurea' (dark blue), *Viola labradorica* (violet-purple).

Yellow. *Juniperus communis* 'Aureo-spica' (usually none).

Chartreuse. *Arenaria verna caespitosa,* chartreuse form (tiny, white); *Thymus serpyllum* 'Real Gold' (rose).

Yellowish-green. *Herniaria glabra* (inconspicuous).

Medium green. *Asperula odorata* (white).

Dark green. *Fragaria chiloensis* (white, few), *Gaultheria procumbens* (white, carmine berries), *Hedera helix* forms (inconspicuous), *Ophiopogon japonicus* (white), *Pachysandra terminalis* (white), *Thymus cimicinus* (purple-violet), *Vaccinium vitis-idaea* (white; carmine berries).

Olive green. *Muehlenbeckia axillaris* inconspicuous), *Raoulia tenuicaulis* (tiny, lemon; white seed puffs).

Russet. *Sedum* 'Star Red' (purple-red). Foliage russet in winter, green in summer.

Reddish. *Crassula milfordae* (white) (foliage red in winter; medium green in summer), *Sedum spathulifolium* 'Purpureum' (yellow).

Black. *Ophiopogon arabicus* (white, but scarce). Foliage actually black, but this is still a rare, expensive plant.

Patterned ground covers. Living blocks of *Sedum* and *Ajuga* (lower right) contrast refreshingly with paving blocks. Design: Eckbo, Dean and Williams.

An arabesque of river stones flows past an old maple. *Sedum spathulifolium* 'Cape Blanco' grows among stones; moss is encouraged around tree trunks. Design: Laurence Korsmo.

Building a Rock Garden

Most rock gardens are amateur productions—and are all the more appealing for that. They have a gardener's personality built into them. With love and leisure the rock garden hobbyist spreads the labor and the expense of his hobby over a period of years—perhaps decades. He never really wants to finish. The constant newness of rock gardening sparks his interest: there are always new plants to be tried, changes to be made. There are stones that need turning to show a better face, and plants that deserve to be moved up front.

For the hobbyist who builds his own rock garden, the triumphs of his garden, the subtle stonework, the gentians in flower, are all his own. If he makes mistakes, they also are all his own, and are apt to seem less galling than the mistakes of others that he buys and pays for. They are easier to correct, too. Having made the mistakes himself, he knows better how to unmake them.

Build your own rock garden? By all means, if you have the time and energy.

Six-ton load of selected "surface" stones, dumped from truck and ready to be crowbarred into position. Stones are surface slabs of limestone, fractured by the action of weather from a stone bed of pancake-thin stratification. There is an advantage to using flat stones in rock gardens, especially in the making of outcroppings. Flat stones have more usable surface at less weight than stones which are as thick as they are wide. Two men can handle these stones; the largest are 3½ feet across, only 9 inches thick, and probably weigh under 300 pounds. This load was hand-picked at extra cost. Some suppliers let you do this, and it is worth it. A load of unselected stone may contain many broken or awkwardly shaped stones.

Build a scale model first

It will be helpful to make a miniature scale model of your rock garden before doing the real job. A model will provide an excellent means of visualizing the garden composition and will give you an opportunity to try out revisions. You'll be able to make a reasonably accurate estimate of the number, size and tonnage of the stones you'll need.

Establish a scale for your model. One inch to one foot is convenient. Then with a trowel or with your hands mold a measured patch of ground into the contours that you want the garden to take. Make paths in the model garden if there are to be paths in the actual garden. Place pebbles and small rocks the way you want the final stones to look. Stick in sprigs of evergreens for trees and shrubs. If you plan to build a scree, show the space it will occupy with a handful of sand.

The job takes some engineering...and muscle

At the end of this chapter is an actual case history of the layout and construction of a rock garden (professionally installed). Even if you intend to do all or much of the work yourself, it would be wise to study those pages carefully. You'll readily see the need for planning and a certain amount of physical exertion.

You're in rare luck if the site for your rock garden has both fertile, well drained soil and native stone. Usually the soil must be improved; the stones must be brought in and dumped into piles for you to move by hand.

The only limitation to building a rock garden by hand is in the size of the stones that you can move and set. While low retaining walls and steps can be made of stones weighing as little as 50 pounds, outcroppings should contain stones weighing at least 300 pounds (500 would be better) if they are to be effective reminders of natural outcroppings.

With crowbars and heroic effort, two men can roll 500-pound stones over level ground or downhill. (Take care not to let stones get away from you on a hillside.) If you're going to attempt rolling them into place, make sure that the stones you'll be working with are not too squarish. Squarish stones are much harder to turn over than those with worn, rounded edges.

Rubber-tired industrial wheelbarrows can be used to move stones weighing up to 300 pounds. Turn the wheelbarrow on its side. Roll the stone into it; then, with one or two people helping you, tip the wheelbarrow upright.

Hand trucks are useful for moving stones if their loading arms are long enough to fit under the stone. You might have a steel plate welded to the arms to extend them.

Terraced rock garden of plant collector Arthur Menzies supports a wealth of plant species. On the wall are dianthus, geraniums, lewisias, and ferns. On terrace above are dwarf conifers. Wall is of weathered basalt fragments.

Block and tackle are slow, but safe and effective for moving stones if a large tree or some other object is handy for anchoring the block. Tie a thick padding of gunny sacks around a tree trunk to protect it from the abrasion of the rope.

Before undertaking anything as strenuous as the setting of stone, consider the rock garden alternatives. Could you do without the stone? Granted, stone adds depth of meaning to the rock garden, but except for retaining purposes it is not actually necessary. Almost no rock plant demands to be grown in the company of stones. Soil banks as steep as 65° can be retained without the help of stone simply by a planting of vigorous rock plants. Logs can be used in place of stone for retaining purposes; stumps and driftwood can be used to obtain the sculptural effects of fine, weathered stone.

Still, there is nothing quite like stone.

This contract worker is picking up a truckload of quarried "black granite" a couple at a time in the bucket of the bulldozer and moving the stones to the rockery site.

Stones are dropped along the soil bank that the rockery will contain. The man in the background strong-arms them into position, aided by an iron bar 5 feet long.

Stone setting must be done quickly—if it is to be profitable to the contractor. This rockery wall is being built for retaining purposes, not as a home for plants.

If You Hire Contract Labor...

Stone retaining increases by the mile every year in many of our hilly cities. Where property prices continue to rise, the hillsides are continually cut back. Usually the cheapest means of retaining these soil cuts is with quarried stone. The men who do the work advertise themselves as specialists in rockery construction. Here's a typical listing under the heading "Rock" in the yellow pages of the telephone book:

"Joe Smith"
Rockery design and construction
Large rocks a specialty
Excavating—Bulldozing
All work guaranteed

These men usually work under a duplicate contract which they (the contractor) and you (the client) both sign, stating that the contractor shall install so much retaining at such and such a price, and the client shall pay for the work.

The lowest current price for contracted stone retaining is about $1.50 per square foot of wall surface.

Hired, and on the job, the contractor places the stones as fast as he can chain them up and plop them into position. There is no repositioning. Time is money to the contractor. The faster he works the more he makes. Stonework by contract can be expected to be safe, honest, and serviceable but your contract does not guarantee artistry. In fact, it usually makes artistry impossible. Skilled stone craftsmanship is not a thing that can be accomplished in a predetermined number of hours. But the craftsmen who might accomplish it are hard to find in this day of mechanization.

It is important to consider in advance just how much of the planning and work should be assigned to the contractor.

Should the contractor do the planting?

Some contracts call for the contractor to plant the rockery. This is a most uncertain bargain for the client. Commonly, the contractor looks for nursery overstocks of bushes of some sort or another and plants them out in the rockery as quickly as possible. In time the plants may do the job expected of them, which is to mask the harshness of the rock work—or they may not. They may die from wrong location and inadequate soil preparation. If it is at all possible, do your own rockery planting.

Slapdash rock work and rockery planting is certainly not the universal product of rockery contractors. Many do good to excellent work within the limitations of the system. Ask around and learn who in your city does top-notch work.

Working with a landscape architect

If your aim is to have a rock garden rather than a rockery, it is advisable to have the contractor follow a landscape architect's plan. You can hire a landscape architect to draw up a plan showing the areas to be occupied by stone, the positions and names of plants. (Sometimes the contractor hires a designer for you.) The landscape architect will probably want to use your plot plan as a guide for his landscape plan. Usually he does not come out to see the property unless you pay him to do so.

The contractor may find it necessary to make modifications in the plan, allowing for final soil grades that were not apparent to the landscape architect when he drew from the plot plan, and substituting for any plants specified on the landscape plan which prove unobtainable.

For the landscape architect's fee of $100, more or less, the homeowner gains a more thoughtful positioning of the main lines of the garden (stones, paths, steps) and a more knowledgeable selection of plant material. The stonework probably will still be a quick and commercial job.

If the landscape architect does the supervising...

This is decidedly expensive. Some of the best composers of natural stone spend all day arranging a single truck load of fifteen to twenty-five stones. If the average small rock garden (about 70 by 15 feet) uses two loads of stone and the landscape architect needs two days to compose them, the labor cost for stone setting will be roughly $500 to $800. (This is figured on the basis of one truck and driver and one laborer.) Add to this one landscape plan at $100, two loads of weathered stone at about $200, $100 for soil additives and soil preparation. Approximate cost of constructing a small rock garden (70 by 15 feet) comes to $900 to $1200. Expensive indeed, and we haven't begun to talk of the cost of plant material.

Reasons become apparent for the fact that few landscape architects find enough clientelé for stone composition to make a specialty of it, and for the fact that great works of this specialty are seldom to be seen.

But we do have excellent examples of stone-plant composition in the United States. The desert wash and the planted wall at Rancho Santa Ana Botanic Garden, Claremont, California, are outstanding pieces of work with field stones. The stone artist is E. K. Balls of Carmel, California. In Seattle, the Japanese tea garden contains a masterful stream bed composition, the work of Juki Iida of Tokyo (see the top left photograph on page 9).

Because of their cultural heritage, many of America's best composers of natural stone are Japanese Americans.

Art conceals art in this deceptively simple arrangement by E. K. Balls. The stroller along this path is guided just enough by the open, interrupted stationing of the stones.

Investigate before hiring a landscape architect to compose stones for you. Many landscape architects, however skilled, have no special touch or training for stone composition.

If you design and supervise...

After you prepare yourself by studying this book, you can expect to be able to work as your own designer, and you can expect to work well. As your own landscape architect you save paying professional fees which range from $10 to $30 an hour.

It helps if you have some artistic talent. Find out if you have any before doing the real job by making a model of your proposed rock garden, as we suggested earlier in this chapter.

It would be unusual to find a landscape contractor willing to sign a contract to work under your supervision. If you're going to supervise, he'll probably want to work by the hour. With you working, the job will probably take longer than if he were working at his own pace.

Grading

Improving the soil

From Raw Bank to Rock Garden ...a Case History

This 250 by 100-foot bank, originally cut to make way for a drive, is being sculpted into a classical rock garden. The photo above shows the bank after grading work has roughed in the contours of the rock garden. The designer (the author) stands directing the cutting of paths.

The basic act of building a rock garden is not the placement of rocks or plants, but the contouring of soil. The rock garden designer begins as a sculptor shaping the soil as if it were the bones and muscles that lie beneath the skin of his sculpture. It often happens that after a steep slope, which first seemed to call for retaining, has been reduced and molded into gentle curves, the addition of stones not only becomes unnecessary but undesirable.

Visually, a gentle slope is calmer, more relaxing than a steep one—and practically, it is less likely to suffer rain erosion.

•

After contouring comes soil preparation. The subsoil should be broken up (if hard packed), covered with six inches of humus, and churned up by rotary tilling. If the existing soil of the bank is basically clay, 6 inches of coarse sand should be spread over the already tilled subsoil and humus and the tilling repeated.

The humus can be in the form of rotted sawdust, peat moss, or bog soil known to be free of epidemic weeds (notably Bermuda grass and bindweed). Upland soils are more risky. Once hatched the weed seeds in many of them can defeat your garden efforts

forever after. If the job you're doing requires you to add quantities of soil (in order to bring an area up to grade, for example) be sure of its source and be sure of your dealer.

To find out how much humus you'll need for the job, take the square footage of the area to be covered and divide that figure by 54. The answer will show the yards of soil required to cover the area 6 inches deep.

Example: A 72′ by 15′ rock garden contains 1080 square feet.

$$54 \overline{\smash{\big)}\ 1080} \quad \begin{array}{r} 20 \\ \underline{108} \\ 0 \end{array}$$

Twenty yards of humus will be needed to cover the rock garden 6 inches deep.

If it is important to bring the rock garden surface level up to the level of a walk or some other level, add enough extra humus to compensate for 25 per cent settling by volume.

•

The designer picks out the stones he wants to use. By luck there are field stones aplenty already on the estate where the rock garden is being built. Field stones present design and construction problems; but even so, the native stone of a locality is always more harmonious in gardens in that locality than the most beautiful stone which is geologically foreign.

Deposited by glacial action, these field stones are a motley lot of granite, limestone, sandstone, and chert. Since there is not enough stone of any single variety to complete the job, the various varieties will be used separately in lines suggesting the strata of successive geological epochs.

Selecting stones

Laying a "newspaper pattern"

Laying out newspapers and shifting them to represent pleasing, coherent lines of stone, the designer patterns the entire stonework of the rock garden. It is easier to shift papers about than stones.

•

After measuring the space to be occupied, and then measuring several stones on the truck, a stone of the right size and shape is hoisted off and into position to form a step. Ideally, its shape should form a joint with the step below it and should also lead the next step above it in the desired direction. A

good joint is not always achieved in the first trial. In the lower left corner of the photograph at the bottom of the first column is a stone that has been tried in a certain spot, found unworkable, and put aside until a place turns up for it.

Field stones tend to be smooth, rounded, and lacking in personality. They take especially careful placement to point up their best angles and to bring them into restful relationship.

When setting fieldstones, look for a flattish side on each stone and then set the stone deeply, flattish side up, and with its top surface in the same plane

Hoisting into position

Careful positioning

Grouping large stones

Settling in

with the top surface of every other stone in the garden.

Stone composition is like architecture—a matter of finding related planes and lines. When the stones are carefully related, and all conflicting lines and planes avoided, an aura of repose enters the composition. The greatest composure in stone placement is gained by setting all the stones on a horizontal plane. However, tilting the stones is perhaps a more popular style. Composing stones on a tilted plane gives the garden, at best, a feeling of the cosmic power which has folded the earth into mountains and valleys. At worst the effect is chaotic. It's safer not to make the tilt too dramatic. Ten degrees is not too little and twenty degrees approaches the safe limit.

•

The designer uses a wrecking bar to make fine adjustments in the positioning of the stone. Sometimes he finds that after giving directions such as "Bring this corner out about four inches," or "Raise this end a little," he can save time and temper (both his own and the workers') by lending a hand himself.

Building steps and retaining walls of natural stone is a *tour de force* of stone craftsmanship. The work is hot, heavy, exacting, slow, and exasperating—like fitting together a jigsaw puzzle with 100 to 500-pound pieces. However, the results are worth the effort. Well made steps or walls of stone give us a sense of security and permanence, half fact and half emotion, not to be found in any other material.

•

A granite stone weighing about 2,500 pounds is hoisted by chain and battery-powered boom. The work is hazardous. Aloft, an occasional stone will slip the chain, causing the double danger of crashing dead weight and backlashing chain.

•

A grouping of large stones placed across the drive from the rock garden serves as a visual connection between the rock garden and the other landscape areas. The stones are being set with at least one third their surface buried to give the impression that they lead down to a world of stone lying just below.

Sketches on facing page

After laying out the paths (shown as double curved lines) the garden architect visualizes the rock garden's stone composition as a series of "bar graphs" representing strata (top sketch).

In the center sketch, the stones of the rock garden are in place. Care has been taken not to follow the graphs too obviously. Each individual stone and each group of stones has been placed with its longer dimension following the strata line. Stepping stones carry the strata line across the paths without hindering traffic. Bold groupings of stones at the curves of the paths suggest natural reasons for the curves.

The completed job is shown in the bottom sketch, with dotted lines indicating the major planting areas. Because of the open style of stone placement, the entire job used less than a hundred tons of stone. Old style, close placement of stones would have required several hundred tons for a job of this size.

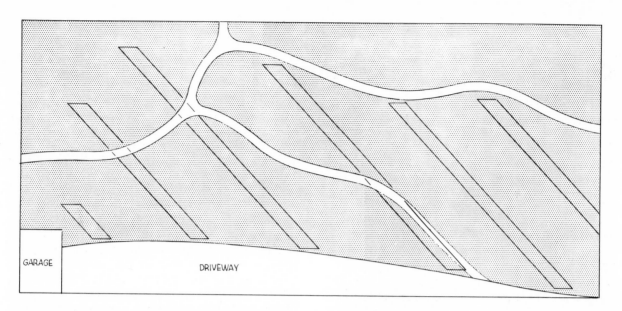

GARAGE

DRIVEWAY

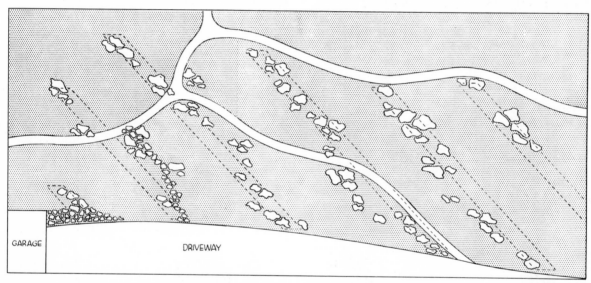

GARAGE

DRIVEWAY

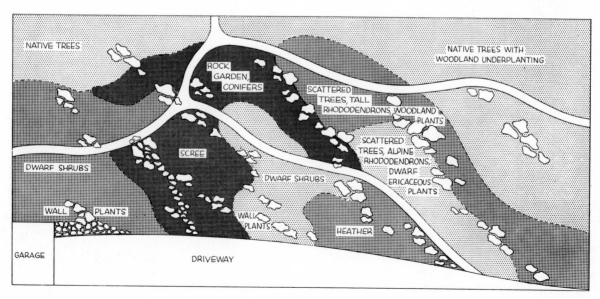

NATIVE TREES

NATIVE TREES WITH
WOODLAND UNDERPLANTING

ROCK
GARDEN,
CONIFERS

SCATTERED
TREES, TALL
RHODODENDRONS, WOODLAND
PLANTS

SCATTERED
TREES, ALPINE
RHODODENDRONS,
DWARF
ERICACEOUS
PLANTS

SCREE

DWARF SHRUBS

DWARF SHRUBS

WALL PLANTS

WALL
PLANTS

HEATHER

GARAGE

DRIVEWAY

Propagating Rock Plants

Do you remember when you planted seeds for the first time? If you're like most of us, your initiation was an epoch of childhood. You began by making the dirt smooth and clean. You gave the seeds their freedom into the dirt, and watered them ceremoniously. Then you went to look each day—at bare dirt. Hope, doubt, and impatience had you in a swivet. Then one morning there it was, your two-leaved, new-green brood pushing through the crumbs of dirt. Chances are that you gave a whoop of delight. Those seedlings were a miracle and you were its activator.

Rock gardeners recapture some of this first thrill every year. The wonder of plant propagation is especially pronounced in rock gardening, where so many of the plants are rare and little-known. Propagating them is one activity that refuses to become humdrum, even for those who are engaged in it professionally. Some rock gardeners base their gardening interest on propagation. For the rest of us, it's always good to have new plants coming along. They are an inexpensive means of filling in gaps in the garden. Propagating a rare and uneasy species is good insurance against losing it. Most rewarding of all, plant propagation is the means by which you'll have plants to give away.

Propagating rock plants is basically simple. But, like any other activity, plant propagation can also be an involved science. Student horticulturists at Kew

These cuttings root best in the open . . .
Shown here—at about 25 per cent of actual size—are cuttings sufficiently large and firm to be planted outdoors. (Several might also be called divisions.) From left to right, with best season for cutting in parentheses: **Top row:** *Geranium dalmaticum* (spring), *Phlox adsurgens* (summer), *Acantholimon glumaceum* (spring), *Thymus serpyllum* 'Argenteus' (summer), *Pterocephalus parnassii* (spring), *Lewisia columbiana* and *L. rupicola* (spring, fall), *Armeria juniperifolia (A. caespitosa)* (late summer), *Saxifraga* 'Polodiae' (summer), *Aubrieta deltoidea* hybrid (summer, fall), *Penstemon barrettiae* (late summer). **Bottom row:** *Hebe pinguifolia* 'Pagei' (fall, spring), *Arabis caucasica (A. albida)* 'Rosabella' (fall), *Phlox nivalis* (late summer), *Dianthus arvernensis* (late summer), *Opuntia aurea* (spring), *Campanula tymonsii* (spring), *Hypericum olympicum* (summer).

and Edinburgh spend years learning its details and alternative techniques. The purpose of this chapter is merely to outline the methods by which you can increase your rock plants. Since most of you will be working without coldframes or other expensive equipment, this chapter tells you how to improvise simple equipment. Finally, we introduce you to the unique vocabulary of plant propagation.

Neither this chapter nor any other account of plant propagation, however exhaustively detailed, can really teach you to propagate plants until you get busy with your own hands. You'll have to improvise your techniques in part to go along with your improvisations of equipment, and you'll have to experience both success and failure before you become a knowledgeable propagator of rock plants.

The plants are eager to help you. The life purpose of plants is to propagate themselves. They carry the ability to do so in their seeds, often in their branches, and sometimes in their leaves and roots. These vari-ous seats of a plant's power of regeneration have given the gardener several methods of propagation: division, cuttings, and seeds.

Propagating by Division

In the simplest terms, dividing plants is accomplished by digging them up, pulling them to pieces, and replanting the pieces. The best type of plant to propagate by division grows as a clump and has roots along underground stems. Clump-making perennials whose roots are many and of equal size, such as the primulas, can be pulled apart by hand or pried apart with garden forks. Perennials which increase by offsets from a central root, such as *Astilbe,* must be cut apart with a sharp knife.

Early spring is the high season for dividing rock plants; autumn division gives equally good results

Root these conifers and ericaceous plants under glass . . . Summer and fall are the best times to start these cuttings, listed from left to right. **Top row:** *Arctostaphylos hookeri* (with heel), *Cassiope selaginoides* (with flower to be removed before insertion), *Calluna vulgaris* 'Foxii Nana', *Juniperus communis* 'Hornibrookii', *Abies balsamea* 'Nana' (heel cutting with lower needles removed), *Cryptomeria japonica* 'Vilmoriniana' (this large cutting of first-year wood can be inserted entire, or a number of smaller cuttings made from it), *Chamaecyparis pisifera* 'Nana'. **Bottom row:** *Vaccinium vitis-idaea* (branched pieces like this inserted in fall will give you a big plant the next spring; or, you could make three cuttings of this branch), *Rhododendron elaeagnoides* (flower shown for interest only), *R. radicans, Gaultheria cuneata* (same remarks as for *Vaccinium vitis-idaea;* remove berries before inserting).

Inserting cuttings. Use stick or pencil to dibble sand, insert base of cutting, firm sand around it. Spacing can be close, but plants shouldn't touch (mold and rot may result).

if you live in a locality where winters are mild enough so that frost won't heave the new divisions out of the ground.

The following plants can be divided in the early spring or in the fall. The names of the plants which are exceptions to this rule are followed by the month when they are best divided.

Acaena, Ajuga, Androsace sarmentosa, Achillea, Armeria maritima, Anemone blanda, Arabis caucasica (A. albida) (October, November), *Arenaria, Asperula, Astilbe* (March and April only), *Aubrieta* (September, October), *Campanula carpatica, Cerastium, Cotula, Dryas, Dicentra* (March, April), *Epimedium, Erigeron* (October), *Gentiana acaulis* (April), *Geranium, Geum, Globularia, Heuchera, Iris* (western American species) (March), *Iris pumila* (June, July), *Mazus, Mentha, Oxalis, Phlox nivalis, P. stolonifera, P. subulata* (October), *Potentilla, Primula juliae, P. vulgaris (P. acaulis)* (September, October), *Sanguinaria, Saxifraga, Sedum, Sempervivum, Thalictrum, Thymus, Tiarella* (March), *Trillium, Uvularia, Vancouveria, Veronica, Viola* (September).

Propagating from Cuttings

Cuttings are detached branches which are capable of forming roots within a week; or, depending on the species, within a year after being inserted in sand in a shady place. The formation of roots on a cutting is called a "strike." For each plant species there is a time of year when an apparent concentration of root-producing enzymes in its stems enables cuttings taken from it to strike better than at any other time. Commonly these enzymes are most active when the plants are growing most actively—during the height of sum-

mer. But this is also the season when plant cuttings wilt and rot most readily. Cuttings taken in June and early July from plants in soft growth are called "soft cuttings." Their tendency to wilt is checked by carefully scheduled watering in the nearly sealed atmosphere of the greenhouse or coldframe. Soft cuttings often strike within 1 to 4 weeks.

Cuttings taken in late July and August are "half-hard cuttings" which may, in the case of many species, root in the open in full shade. Enzymal activity will have slowed by this time. Half-hard cuttings take about 4 to 8 weeks to strike. "Hard cuttings," taken from September to December, will usually root by spring.

The length of the cutting also has vital influence over its ability to root. In general, short cuttings (2 to 4 inches long) will root faster than longer cuttings. But you can take longer cuttings of easy-to-root varieties.

Cuttings taken from non-flowering branches have greater strength and power of regeneration than branches whose strength has gone into the production of flowers and seed.

Morning hours when plants are most full of moisture are better for taking cuttings than the afternoon hours, especially on a sunny day.

Never let the cuttings wilt. Roll them up in wet newspapers as you take them.

How to take a cutting

Cuttings are detached in two ways: (1) they are cut from the plant with a razor blade, a sharp knife or pruner; (2) they are pulled from the plant with a downward tug.

Rooted cuttings ready to be planted out. From left to right: *Leiophyllum buxifolium, Abies balsamea* 'Nana', *Rhododendron radicans, Helianthemum* 'Buttercup'. The leiophyllum, a creeping shrub of the rhododendron family, is shown with soil washed away to reveal characteristic mass of thread-fine roots which plants of this family (Ericaceae) form in sandy, humus-rich soil. *Rhododendron radicans* is shown as it came out of the flat with a ball of sand and peat moss about its roots; its cuttings started in fall will, with luck, be ready to plant out in late spring. *Helianthemum* 'Buttercup' cutting taken in summer is ready to plant out in fall.

Those which are pulled from the plant are called "heel cuttings." They come off the plant with a "heel," a strip of bark at their base. The heel should be trimmed to about ¼ inch. Use a sharp blade in all cutting work. It is important not to mash or fray the cut end of a cutting.

There is a difference of opinion about the relative merits of cuttings taken with a heel and cuttings taken without a heel. Soft cuttings are usually taken without a heel. Larger, half-hard cuttings (4 to 8 inches long) taken with a heel are preferable to heel-less cuttings for open ground propagation. Cuttings of rock plants with hollow stems must be taken with a heel to seal the sap in the stem.

After taking the cuttings, lay them out and cut off lower leaves. Start from severed end of the cutting, as far up the stem as the cutting is to be inserted—but no farther. Leave attached all the leaves that will not be in contact with the sand when you insert the cuttings.

Rooting of cuttings

The surest rooting medium for cuttings of rock plants is coarse, clean sand (builder's sand). You can root cuttings in pots, flats, frames, or beds filled with sand, but they must all be located away from direct sunlight.

Use a root-inducing hormone on the base of the cuttings if you wish. Some propagators are emphatically for the use of hormones; others say the advantage gained by hormones is negligible.

Insert the cuttings about one-half their length in the sand. For the tiniest alpine plant cuttings, half the length of the cutting will be ½ inch or less; for large heel cuttings it will be 4 inches, more or less.

Water the cuttings immediately after inserting them, and every day afterward until they are well rooted. Keep slug bait scattered nearby to lure slugs and snails away.

When cuttings are as well rooted as those shown at the bottom of page 60, they are ready to plant in the garden—if you are prepared to give them extra water and special care. If you don't want to take chances, grow the rooted cuttings in 2 to 3-inch pots until they make well-branched little plants. Then they will be as ready as they will ever be for the open ground.

Half-hard cuttings of most non-woody rock plants root easily in the open. The non-woody category includes the greater range of rock plants, from *Arabis* and *Alyssum* to *Campanula, Dianthus, Geranium, Penstemon, Phlox, Saxifraga,* and *Veronica.*

Cuttings of woody rock plants taken in all stages require a greenhouse or coldframe. The woody rock plants include the rock garden conifers, rhododendrons, *Daphne, Lithospermum, Potentilla fruticosa,* *Spiraea,* and many others. Bottom heat speeds up the rooting of hard cuttings—sometimes dramatically.

A rhododendron which takes 5 months to root without bottom heat may root in a month with heat. Plants which are rooted with heat should be hardened by turning off the heat for a few weeks before they are moved outside.

Some propagators report good results from using polyethylene plastic bags as miniature greenhouses for pots or flats of cuttings. It is, however, extremely easy to have the air and the rooting medium within the bag too wet, which will cause mold and decay.

After watering pots or flats which are to be covered with polyethylene, let them drain for a day, or until the sand has begun to dry. Insert half-hoops of wire in the sand to hold the plastic away from the cuttings. They like as much air space as possible. Keep the plastic-covered containers away from direct sun, because the bag is capable of capturing heat and building it within a short time to 140° or more.

Another substitute for a greenhouse or coldframe is a box covered with a pane of glass or a sheet of polyethylene. Take an apple box or other solid wooden box, and remove the top and bottom. Bury the box with a sidewise slant (about 20° from horizontal). Place sand in the bottom of the box up to the level of the soil outside the box. After inserting the cuttings and watering them, fix a pane of glass over the box (nails on the edge of the box will hold the glass) or tie a sheet of polyethylene over it. The tilt of the box will allow condensation on the inside of the cover to trickle down the side rather than drip on the cuttings.

A few rock plants, among them geraniums and *Anemone pulsatilla,* can be propagated from root cuttings (about 2 to 4 inches long) taken during midsummer. Root cuttings are inserted with their smaller end down, tops flush with the surface of the rooting medium, and treated just as stem cuttings. Geraniums are also increased by seed and division. *Anemone pulsatilla* is one of the easier rock plants to grow from seed, but it may not survive division.

Haberlea and *Ramonda,* two alpine relatives of the African violet, are best propagated from leaf cuttings in July. Detach leaves carefully so that all the stem comes away intact with the vital growing point at its base. Handle them the same as soft stem cuttings under glass. Sedums grow readily from leaf cuttings, but they are so easy to increase by simple division and stem cuttings that leaf cuttings seem a waste of time—except perhaps as a classroom experiment to illustrate this type of plant regeneration. A common forest plant of the West Coast, *Tolmiea menziesii,* propagates itself by forming new plants at the base of the leaf blades. From this habit it takes its common name, youth-on-age. The plant is quietly interesting.

Rock plants to propagate from cuttings

The following plants can be propagated from soft cuttings rooted under cover, or from half-hard and hard heel cuttings rooted in shade in the open. *Exceptions:* Cuttings which usually will root only in greenhouses, coldframes, and other covered structures are marked "glass"; cuttings which have special time preferences are marked with their preferred months.

Aethionema 'Warley Rose' (July, glass); *Alyssum saxatile* (July, glass); *Arabis caucasica (A. albida)* (October, November); *Armeria juniperifolia (A. caespitosa); Artemisia; Aubrieta* (August, September, October); *Cistus; Convolvulus* (glass); *Cytisus* (July, glass); *Dianthus; Erica* (June to September, under glass); *Euonymus fortunei radicans* (April); *Euphorbia* (September); *Fuchsia* (glass); *Gaultheria* (glass); *Gypsophila; Hebe* (October, November, March, in the open); *Helianthemum* (wonderfully easy in July); *Hypericum; Iberis* (glass); *Lavandula; Muehlenbeckia* (glass); *Nepeta mussinii* (heel cuttings, March, April); *Penstemon* (glass); *Phlox nivalis; P. subulata; Polygala; Polygonum vaccinifolium* (glass); *Potentilla fruticosa* (glass); *Rhododendron* (glass); *Rosmarinus; Santolina; Saponaria; Saxifraga* (Kabschia section); *Spiraea; Vaccinium* (glass); *Thymus* (shrubby species); *Vinca* (June, glass); *Zauschneria* (glass).

Propagating from Seed

Rock gardeners have a saying (a harmless braggadocio) which they use when they have especially good results raising a rare plant from seed. They say they have such a plant "coming up like cress."

The cresses are among the easiest of all plants to grow from seed. The family is a very good one for you to know if you're starting your rock garden from seed. The cress (or mustard) family, Cruciferae, includes such vegetables as mustard and cabbage, and such rock plants as *Aethionema, Arabis, Alyssum, Aubrieta,* and *Iberis.* Other rock plants which come easily from seed are *Anemone pulsatilla, Aquilegia, Corydalis, Dianthus, Digitalis, Geranium, Iris* (Western American species), *Lavandula, Oenothera, Polemonium, Potentilla, Scabiosa, Sedum, Thymus,* and *Viola.*

Raising the rare species of rock plants—the collectors' plants—from seed is another matter. The process is fraught with as many hazards as raising turkeys from eggs. That is partly why rare plants are rare. But sometimes you'll get a quick and prodigious germination on such usually reluctant plants as *Lewisia* and *Androsace.* The great fun of this is being able to say that you have them "coming up like cress."

A seed pot needs good drainage. Cut-away pot shows gravel in place for drainage, a soil well mixed with coarse sand, and space left at top to facilitate watering.

Sowing seeds. Shake seeds onto carefully leveled surface of prepared soil. If soil has been sterilized, seeds of rock plants can be sown thickly. When they begin to crowd, separate them.

Seedlings in early stages. Those at lower left are in cotyledon stage. At left center and upper right, seedlings have formed their first true leaves and will soon be ready to separate.

Seedlings ready to be separated. Remove seedlings from pot in a mass by placing one hand over top of pot, turning pot upside-down and rapping it on the bottom with your other hand. Seedlings at this stage have put out enough roots to hold soil together in a block when removed from pot.

Separating seedlings. Remove seedlings gently, one at a time; tease their roots free with a stick or knife. Replant each seedling in a small pot. This method is called "pricking out." Another way is to pull the mass apart into small clumps (lower right), plant them in place in open ground.

No two rock gardeners seem to follow exactly the same seed sowing procedures. One technique that has proved effective for hundreds of species of rock plants in a great range of genera is described below. (wherever the word "pot" appears it can be inferred to mean a seed pan or a flat as well as a flower pot.)

Preparing the soil mix

Have mixed and sterilized soil ready to fill the pots. The soil mixture is composed of one part garden loam, one part coarse sand, and one part leaf mold or other humus. Exact proportions aren't important, but if you change them lean toward more sand rather than more loam. Mix the ingredients with a shovel as demonstrated in the section on scree gardening, page 35. Sift the mixture through "hardware cloth" or other screen with a ¼-inch mesh.

Sterilize the mixed and screened soil by placing it in a covered pan lined with aluminum foil and baking it 20 minutes to a pound in a 300° oven. *Warning:* Soil has a pungent smell while it is baking.

You can also sterilize soil fairly effectively by dumping it into a wooden box (in which you've bored holes) and then pouring boiling water over it. Let it drain and dry for several days before placing it in the pots.

Another method is to apply one of the soil sterilants available in liquid form (you'll only need to buy a small bottle). Check the label to make certain that the product kills weed seeds. Follow label precautions carefully.

Soil sterilization is not completely essential, but it certainly saves later troubles. It destroys weed seeds which will germinate and grow faster and stronger than the rock plants and could fill the pot before you realize that they are weeds. It also destroys newly hatched slugs, snails, and angleworms (which can grow up to bury the seeds with their casts). All of these are so tiny that they will pass through the ¼-inch mesh when you screen the soil.

Garden stores carry packaged mixes of essentially sterile ingredients (sand, peat, vermiculite, ground bark) which are suitable for raising many kinds of rock plants from seed.

Seed sowing and germination

Sow seeds of rare rock plants in November. The sowing of common kinds (*Alyssum saxatile,* for example) can wait until spring.

Use pots at least four inches wide—square plastic pots, preferably. Put in 1½ inches of coarse gravel or hammered pieces of flower pot. This is called "crocking the pot." Tamp the soil in the pot lightly and level the surface; then insert a plastic or aluminum label.

Sow the seeds on the soil surface. Don't sow more

Spores emboss undersides of fern fronds. At left and right are shield ferns (*Polystichum*); in center is hart's tongue (*Phyllitis scolopendrium*), a fern of many garden forms. Spores of hart's tongue and shield fern at right are dark brown, ripe and ready to be gathered. The spores of the other shield fern are pale yellow and not yet ripe.

than one variety to a pot. The germination of rock plants is erratic—some kinds come up in a week, others in one to two years. (There are records of rock plant germination occurring after 12 and 25 years.)

Barely cover the seeds with clean, coarse, dry sand. Most rock plants have pinhead-to-dust-sized seed. A coating of sand of single-grain thickness will cover them. The largest, pea-sized seeds should have ⅓-inch of sand over them.

Water the pots by standing them in a basin of water. Remove the pots when the soil mix is saturated, place them in a shaded coldframe and close it tightly. If you are going to place the pots in polyethylene bags, first set them aside to drain for 12 to 24 hours. Then place them in the bags, tie the openings, and put the bags in a fully shady place.

Seeds sown in the fall and winter must not be kept in a heated room. They will germinate in the heat, grow spindling, and collapse.

Freezing stimulates the seeds of many of the rare rock plants to quicker, more uniform germination. Frost-induced germination often comes the first spring in species which otherwise would not germinate until the second. Let the pots of fall-sown seed receive all the frost that your winter brings. In regions of snowfall, remove the sashes of coldframes which hold sown seeds and fill the frames with snow. This last may sound like witch-doctoring, but many rock gardeners swear by it. When the snow melts in the spring, the seedlings are said to fairly snap out of their shells.

Snow or no snow, keep the pots moist during the days and weeks that you're waiting for germination. Pots sealed in plastic usually require no watering.

Within a week after the germination of seeds in plastic bags, remove the pot from the bag. Sift a thin coating of sand about the stems of the seedlings to help them get their roots down. Place the pot in the open air in a position which receives strong daylight but not direct sunlight. Cover the pots when rain threatens.

After the germination of seeds in coldframes, sprinkle sand among the sprouted seedlings. Raise the sash to let in more light and air, but close the sash if it rains. Water the seedlings once a day or more with the fine spray of the hose nozzle. Never let the surface of the soil go dry.

After the seedlings have developed four true leaves, they are ready to be removed from the pots. (The first two kidney-shaped leaves — cotyledons technically—don't count as true leaves.) Remove the seedlings and replant them.

Congratulate yourself. Relatively little can go wrong now. Keep the seedlings watered and keep slugs baited away from them. If your luck holds, you'll have mobs of flowers next year.

Seeds of rhododendrons, *Gaultheria,* and other ericaceous plants must be handled a little differently from the start. The work is more delicate. Ericaceous seeds are almost microscopic and the seedlings are minute at germination. They grow slowly and may require three years from the time of germination until they are ready to set out in the garden.

Rhododendrons are easy from cuttings. Taken in summer and fall, cuttings are often ready to set out the following spring. However, many American amateurs have created fascinating woodland gardens based on rhododendrons and other ericaceous plants which they have raised from seed. They sow rhododendron seed in pure peat moss and keep the seedlings in cool, shady greenhouses or coldframes until they are strong enough to be placed outside.

The seed sowing of orchidaceous rock plants is work for the plant scientist. The dust-fine seeds of *Cypripedium, Orchis,* and the many other terrestrial orchids is sometimes sown on sterile agar (a gelatinous substance), sealed in jars and kept under close surveillance. Save yourself the disappointment of trying to raise seeds of these plants under less than laboratory conditions.

Ferns from Spores and Cuttings

Some ferns—those which run about by underground stems—take care of their own propagation in the garden. Others stay in a non-divisible clump all their lives. These are ferns which you can increase from spores. You'll find raising ferns from spores simpler than growing rock plants from seed.

Most ferns ripen their spores in the fall. Brown when ripe, the powder-fine spores will waft away when you tap the frond. A sheet of creased paper held beneath the frond as you tap it will catch some of the millions of escaping spores.

Sow the spores as soon as you gather them. Or fold them up in a piece of wax paper and store them in the refrigerator. Spores which are to be germinated indoors (as outlined below) are best sown in February or March.

Fern spores are sown on a mixture of four parts peat moss, one part sand, and one part sterilized loam—all of which should be sifted through a ¼-inch screen. Moisten the mix and then squeeze it as dry as you can with your hands.

Fill pots, clear plastic refrigerator dishes, pyrex casserole dishes, or flats with the mixture. Level it and put in a label. Dust the spores over the mixture.

The pots now go into plastic bags. The lids go on the dishes. Put bagged pots and covered dishes on a north window sill inside the house. If you're using flats, place them in tightly sashed coldframes.

The spores will germinate into scalloped, green, leaf-like growths called prothallia. (The first time you see a prothallium you're apt to mistake it for a liverwort.) Next, tiny true fronds appear. When the first of these have grown half as long as your finger, the sporeling ferns are ready to be separated.

Separate them as you would seedlings. Set them into pots or flats, or plant them out (with care afterward) in the shady garden.

The many and expensive garden varieties of "English ferns" (*Polystichum setiferum*) are propagated from frond cuttings. Detach entire fronds from the plants and cut them in about 5 inch lengths. Insert them in pots or flats of peat moss. Keep them under glass or polyethylene. Frond cuttings taken from August to October will root over winter and send up a clutch of small new fronds. Plant them out in May.

Some of the other Polystichums will root from cuttings. *Polystichum andersoni*, a rare western native, propagates itself by forming new plants along the fronds at the bases of the pinnae. Two other American ferns, *Cystopteris bulbifera* and *Camptosorus rhizophyllus* have developed other means of leaf propagation, discussed under these fern names in the "Plant Biographies" chapter.

If you're keen on ferns, look into membership in the American Fern Society. There are about 900 members, many of whom are distinguished plant scientists. The quarterly bulletin of the society goes to addresses all over the world. Members pay small annual dues and participate in the exchange of spores from 400 species of ferns collected from near and remote places. The treasurer is Richard L. Hauke, Department of Botany, University of Rhode Island, Kingston, Rhode Island. Mr. Hauke enrolls new members.

Germinating ferns in various stages. To left of fingers are ferns in prothallium stage—scale-like growths resembling liverwort. At lower right of photograph, first fronds of sporeling ferns are erupting from prothallia. Directly below little finger are several sporelings large enough to be pricked out and potted or planted out.

Dibbling. Expert Neil Hall uses plant label and practiced hand and eye for dibbling of pricked-out fern sporelings.

Inserting frond cuttings. *Polystichum setiferum* (taken in late summer); firm rooting medium around base of each cutting.

The Rock Garden Conifers

In variety, the rock garden conifers make up a sizable forest which a gardener might explore happily for his entire gardening career. Without guidance, however, this forest would be an easy place in which to get lost. No group of garden plants has more need of some system of division, according to garden value and landscape use, than the conifers which are grown in rock gardens.

Let's discuss these shrubs separately as dwarf conifers, alpine conifers, and prostrate junipers. There are important differences in the values and uses of the trees within these three categories.

Dwarf Conifers

Dwarf conifers have been in cultivation well over a century in Europe and America, long enough to have fallen in and out of fashion twice. They were "in" a century ago; "out" during the late Victorian years; "in" again during the jazz age and the great depression. Since World War II their use has been declining once more. But judging from their past revivals, it seems not at all unlikely that dwarf conifers could be the highest garden fashion in future decades.

What is there about these trees that inspires such fashion or disfavor? Perhaps it is their garden non-conformity. They don't mix well. Dwarf conifers are often precise little trees which shape themselves, with some inborn knowledge of topiary art, into domes, cones, pyramids, globes, and spires. They must be admired—or rejected—for the logic of their geometry.

Our garden era, which has shaken the rigidity out of garden design and returned it to looser, more natural lines, finds less and less use for the more decidedly geometrical of these trees. Their precise forms seem outdated, out of place in almost any position in the garden.

While they no longer belong in borders of mixed shrubbery, or as sentinels stationed along the walk and beside the pergola, on patios they still have occasional place as container plants. The rose garden might make interesting use of them—and the formal garden might, too (if this were a day for formal gardens). But in the rock garden their position is as certain as ever.

How certain is that?

Dwarf conifers can have a value equal to that of the stones in forming the structural frame of the rock garden. In a small rock garden a single dwarf conifer can set the theme and the scale for the whole composition.

Not all—not even most—of the dwarf conifers have structural value in the garden. Some are too small to be more than toys—"Just something to have about," as one diligent collector of these trees phrases it. Others are artificial, or even monstrous in appearance. These, too, are "just something to have about." But with the hundreds of collectors' plants set aside, there are scores of dwarf conifers which rank among the most serviceable, hardy, and trouble-free plants for sunny rock gardens.

Which dwarf conifer to choose is something of a problem. For landscape purposes there are too many varieties, and many of the varieties are only minutely distinct. Also, their names are badly mixed up.

These things are usually true of plants that have been in cultivation a long time. For over a century horticulturists in many nations have been seeking, cherishing, and exploiting these trees. Their enthusiastic, uncoordinated efforts have resulted in a vast reduplication of forms and a hopeless reapplication of names. The forms which have been singled out for mention in the plant biography chapter of this book are outstanding in some way, usually for their beauty and usefulness, occasionally for their oddity. Two or three we mention only to warn you against them.

The names of dwarf conifers are, at present, in an awesome muddle. Some varieties have three or four different names in general usage, and three or four other conifers may be traveling under these same names.

If you're a gardener who worries much over nomenclature, this group of plants is going to be a trial to you. A trip to a nursery may result in more confusion than ever. The dwarfs all seem to be tagged 'Nana' or 'Compacta'—or both. Don't hold the nurseryman responsible. He's a practical man who knows the garden use and the ultimate size of the plants he grows. But he's usually too busy to function as a botanical taxonomist.

When you see a dwarf conifer that you like at a nursery, ask how it is used and how big it will grow. If the answers meet your specifications, buy the conifer, plant it, enjoy it, and try not to worry whether the tag bears the right name. (This, admittedly, will be a difficult thing for many gardeners to do; some of us like plant names as much as we like plants.)

If you insist on the pedigree of a dwarf conifer before you'll buy it, it will be better if you do little

Dwarf conifers show many growth forms in this photograph taken in Strybing Arboretum in San Francisco's Golden Gate Park.

buying and a lot of studying. Many of them are described in the final chapter under *Abies, Cedrus, Chamaecyparis, Juniperus, Picea, Pinus, Taxus, Thuja,* and *Tsuga.*

If you become deeply absorbed and want to know about 500 of the varieties in cultivation, search out a copy of Hornibrook's *Dwarf and Slow Growing Conifers.* The book is out of print and obtainable only with difficulty from dealers in used books—but your library may have a copy. There is no other comprehensive work on the subject.

Much of the information we're using in *Rock Gardens* is based on Hornibrook. His great book is, of course, not without error and omission. The growth rates he ascribes to different trees have proved unrealistic in many instances for trees growing in the open ground. Conifers which Hornibrook lists as growing ½ to 1 inch a year more often grow 2½ inches; those he lists as growing 2½ inches more often grow 4½. Hornibrook's figures may pertain to pot-grown trees.

Three of the largest public collections of dwarf

conifers are at the National Arboretum in Washington, D.C., the Arnold Arboretum in Boston, and the Strybing Arboretum in San Francisco. In 1963 the National Arboretum received a gift of 1500 different dwarf conifers. This collection was assembled in 9 years by Mr. William Gotelli, a contractor from East Orange, New Jersey. Durant-Eastman Park in Rochester, New York, has fine old specimens that were used by Hornibrook as a basis for some of his type descriptions a generation ago. You also can put these public collections to use by comparing their accurately labeled trees with those in your garden or with nursery trees on which you have a buyer's eye.

What makes them dwarf?

An understanding of the dwarfness of dwarf conifers calls for a look toward their origins. Most of them are man-made plants; that is to say, unless a horticulturist had acted as midwife, these trees would never have got a start in the world. He has found them and babied them along either as seedlings, as witches' brooms, or as juvenile forms. These terms stand for some strange and fascinating vagaries of conifer genetics.

Dwarf seedlings

In a large batch of seedling trees grown from the seed of a normal tree, there are slight but perceptible differences. Some grow fast, tall, and openly branched, others grow more slowly and densely. The needles on some are larger than average, on others they are shorter. Tree seedlings are probably as individual as human beings—if only our senses were acute enough to register their individuality. Rarely (once among thousands of seedlings), a tree differs enough from the norm to be usefully or curiously distinct to horticulture. It may grow an inch while the rest of the seedlings grow a foot. This seedling is a dwarf—a weak, recessive form that surely would have been shaded out or crowded out if it had sprouted within a stand of mature trees and normal seedlings. While dwarf conifers are almost never found growing naturally in dense, lowland forests, several of the most interesting and popular dwarfs have been discovered growing naturally among the sparse trees at timberline.

Dwarf seedling conifers are often pyramidal in form—miniature replicas of the normal trees. As such, they are the most generally useful of the three types of dwarf conifers.

Witches' brooms

The dwarfest of the dwarf conifers have an origin so strange that they were once linked with witchcraft. On the branches of otherwise normal mature trees, dense, congested masses of twigs and needles sometimes appear. These gnomish growths may live fifty years or more on the tree, and may stay as small as a cat or grow as big as a bear. Superstitious woodsmen in Old England gave them the name witches' brooms, which we still use today.

Cuttings from witches' brooms will often root readily, and will, on their own roots, retain the dwarf, congested habit of growth that they had on the parent tree.

After a century in cultivation, some of the older witches' brooms have grown 2 or 4 feet across, about as high as wide, and have stayed green and densely branched. The difference in size depends on the variety.

The varieties of witches' brooms number in the hundreds, but in form they tend to be rather similar. The greater number of them are dome-shaped. The differences between many of these varieties are so small that they serve as subjects for scholarly arguments among collectors. These differences are, of course, of little importance to the gardener who is interested primarily in landscape effect.

Juvenile forms

The third origin of dwarf conifers is in the phenomenon of juvenile foliage. Like fawns whose spots echo the existence of ancestral deer, many tree species bear, in their sapling stage, an ancestral kind of leaf, which is replaced in the tree's adulthood by foliage of a different character. The juvenile foliage of conifers is usually softer and more feathery in appearance than that of the mature tree.

Sometimes a tree retains its juvenile foliage through life, never developing adult foliage and always remaining smaller in habit than adult trees of the same kind. Such conifers are called "juvenile forms." Their foliage often gives them an especially graceful bearing, but they are also a little delicate. They do best when well watered and partly shaded, and some gardeners say that they are not as hardy as the seedling dwarfs and the witches' brooms.

Conifers with juvenile and adult foliage mixed together in various proportions are called "intermediate forms." Their garden strength depends on the degree of their juvenile or adult status.

Alpine Conifers

At the edge of the zone of arctic winter, where the ranks of lowland trees break and thin, the alpine conifers—smaller, wirier, and tougher—fill in and fight on for existence several thousand feet higher. These are the trees of the timberline.

The relentless war that snow and wind wage

Alpine conifers (*Abies lasiocarpa*) grouped against a redwood wall have a dance-like rhythm in their sinuous trunks. Eugene Bennett created the totemic redwood-and-nail sculptures. The planting is by George Schenk.

against trees at the upper frontier of tree growth has given them battle scars and individuality. It is for their individuality that these trees appeal to today's expanding school of naturalistic gardening. Contemporary homes, with their surfaces of natural wood and stone, request the complement of a garden of natural-looking, rather than trimmed and tailored trees and shrubs. The highest fashion is for plant material which wears the dramatic stamp of time and the elements. Nothing embodies more of this drama than trees which have struggled for life in the mountains.

The commercial digging of these trees in the mountains of the Northwest began on a noticeable scale about 1950. Each year since the early 1960's tens of thousands of alpine firs, hemlocks, and pines have been dug, trucked out, and channeled through nurseries in western Washington. Carload shipments are now being sent to eastern nurseries.

Because a 5-foot alpine conifer can be collected and sold immediately, the price is appreciably lower than that of a 5-foot dwarf conifer which the nursery man has worked years to perfect. The dwarf conifer market has declined, and the use of the dramatic, alpine conifers has risen to the point of a fad. They're being planted indiscriminately in every setting from the rose garden to the pansy bed.

Fads have a way of receding and leaving boredom in their wake. The time may soon come when alpine conifers will seem as dated for most garden purposes as the topiary dwarfs are today. But like the dwarfs, the alpine conifers will always be at home in the rock garden. Like the dwarfs, they are used as individuals for accent and for the establishment of alpine character in the rock garden. In groups they are used to form a frame for the rock garden. But alpine conifers require more garden room than the dwarf conifers.

Alpine trees grow slowly into forest size. Even after they get settled in the garden and put their roots down deeply, they'll probably only grow 4 to 6 inches a year. For practical purposes they can be considered 10 to 16-foot garden trees.

Most gardeners are misguided as to the potential character of these trees when they are grown under garden conditions. They almost always lose their contorted, open-branched habit. Once they become established in the garden (in 3 or 4 years), the twisted trunk and furrowed bark which are so stylish become lost beneath a dense framework of growing branches and a thick pelt of needles. They soon become what their genetics had always intended them to be—perfectly symmetrical spires or pyramids.

They are certainly not less beautiful this way. Their beauty is only a different cast, which another generation of gardeners would have much preferred. Their wild, weather-torn condition when newly brought down from the mountains would have seemed repellent to gardeners in the 1920's, 30's and 40's—just as it does today when these trees are mistakenly planted near the trim, painted houses built during those decades.

The one satisfactory way to retain the gnarled character of alpine conifers in the garden is to grow them in containers. The trees then behave as large-scale bonsai. The restriction of the roots is matched by a restriction in branch growth. Handled in this way, these trees must also be given the consideration of bonsai. They'll need watering every day during dry weather; for rich green foliage they'll need partial shading.

As container plants, alpine trees remain dramatic entities which have recorded a measure of the time and the unconquerable will to live that move our earth. The Japanese were the first to realize this when they built the art of bonsai around alpine trees.

The Prostrate Junipers

Junipers may be dwarf conifers or alpine conifers. Dwarf or alpine, those junipers of prostrate habit are of such importance to the rock garden that they deserve a separate heading. These are bounding, cascading, widely ramifying shrubs whose qualifications include longevity, hardiness, tolerance of poor soil, resistance to drought and extreme heat, moderate-to-fast growth, compact habit, refined appearance, general freedom from insects and disease, and color variance from green to blue to gray. These qualifications, coupled with an ability to clothe and hold bank or flatland with a restful, unbroken tide of foliage, make the prostrate junipers the most valuable single group of plants for large jobs of rock gardening.

Junipers do a complete enough job of landscaping so that they don't really need the embellishment of stone, except on steep banks that require retaining.

Framing a new rock garden with conifers. At this stage of the work, the stones (few in number) are in place, paths have been outlined, and dwarf and alpine conifers are being planted to give vertical dimension to the composition. The ground will be covered with mat-forming alpine plants. In left foreground is *Picea abies* 'Procumbens' in a bed of *Erica carnea* 'Springwood White'. At center foreground above outcropping stones is an 8-year-old Sargent's weeping hemlock, *Tsuga canadensis* 'Pendula'. The dark, pointed pyramid above and slightly to the right of it is a 20-year-old *Picea abies* 'Nana'. *Abies lasiocarpa* grows in groves on either side of path at right; another one is being planted at far left.

How to Grow Conifers

The hardiness of rock garden conifers depends largely on their geographic origin. Those from warm countries are likely to be tender. Those from northern countries or high elevations are usually remarkably hardy.

American and European alpine conifers *(Pinus mugo, Picea abies, Abies lasiocarpa,* etc.), their seedlings, and their witches' brooms are probably hardy to at least −30°.

Forest conifers from Japanese lowlands *(Chamaecyparis obtusa, C. pisifera)* and their forms are usually hardy to −10°.

Specific hardiness data for many of the rock garden conifers is imperfectly known. Some currently accepted data:

Chamaecyparis lawsoniana and its forms are hardy to −10°. *Taxus cuspidata,* the Japanese Yew, is hardy to −30°. *Thuja occidentalis* forms are hardy all over North America. *Juniperus chinensis* is hardy to −40°.

Alpine conifers do not as a rule take to hot-summer, mild-winter localities. Except for southern gardens at high elevation, these trees are far better off in the northern half of the United States.

The San Francisco Bay area offers a climate agreeable to a greater range of rock garden conifers than any other area in North America. Western Oregon and Washington are a close second to San Francisco. New England and Great Lakes winters are comfortable to many rock garden conifers, notably the *Picea abies* forms.

Keep them healthy

As a class, rock garden conifers are about as easy-going as any plants you can own. They prefer a mildly acid soil (*pH* 6 or lower), the structure of which is of minor importance. As long as drainage is good they'll grow in the worst and the best soils—in loam, sand, clay, gravelly or peaty soils. They'll grow faster in the better soils. Water them when the weather is dry. Don't let the soil dry out—especially during the first and second summer after you've planted them. When they become established and put down tap roots, they will be capable of gathering most if not all of the moisture they need from rainfall, with only occasional watering to carry them through the driest weather. (This is true only if you garden in an area which has at least 30 inches of rain.) *Exceptions:* Juvenile forms appreciate extra water, and the smallest witches' brooms are thirsty plants.

The prostrate junipers are moderately to extremely drought resistant. In areas with at least 20 inches of rain a year, they can be expected to get along, once they are established, on nothing more than rainfall.

In areas where pine shoot moths or Monterey cypress tip moths are prevalent (the San Francisco Bay area) a spray program in February and in August is a necessary safeguard. In all areas watch for aphids on spruces *(Picea)* and red spider on junipers. Spray the tree right away whenever these pests appear (usually during the growing season).

Avoid grafted conifers

The grafting of dwarf conifers is still an unfortunately common practice. Grafted trees grow faster and thus make less expensive nursery plants, but they often lose many of their essential characteristics.

Usually they grow much faster than you would want. Sometimes they abandon their dwarfness altogether, and shoot upward at normal speed into normal trees.

To make sure of their dwarfness, all dwarf conifers except pines and cedars should be obtained only on their own roots. The exceptions are almost impossible to root from cuttings, and usually can be obtained only as grafted plants.

Give them room—or keep them small

The usual mistake made by gardeners who plant rock garden conifers is to forget that they grow. Those winsome little cones and buns fresh from the nursery will double and quadruple in size in a remarkably few years. Often they can outgrow their position, crowd other plants, and upset the balance of the garden composition. None of this is necessary.

If the tree is the right choice and if it is properly spaced, the growth it makes will be welcome. You'll need to anticipate the rate and the accumulation of this growth.

Before you select and buy a rock garden conifer, check the growth rates and ultimate sizes of the conifers described at the back of the book. The annual growth rate of different rock garden conifers varies from ⅓ inch to 1 foot, and their ultimate size varies from 1 to 20 feet. These differences suit the needs of every rock garden.

Here are three planting suggestions that will help keep your rock garden from turning into a conifer jungle:

Don't overplant. One conifer may be enough in a small rock garden.

Keep shrubbery well away from them.

Plant nothing but low carpeting plants near them.

As the garden matures, don't let the leaves of competing plants shade or crowd dwarf conifers. Shaded branches will weaken and finally die, leaving the tree lopsided.

The tricky part of growing plants together in the community we call a garden is foresight about how they are going to get along with each other. Experience helps. But we can't always anticipate which plants will turn into aggressors and attempt to seize more than their share of garden space. When you are in doubt about a conifer's propensities, there is just one thing to do: give it elbow room.

How to keep conifers dwarf

It is the way of trees to keep on growing as long as they live. Many conifers that we consider dwarfs are not really dwarf; they are only slow growing. Eventually—probably within the span of years that you'll be taking care of them—they'll grow up to 4, 8, 12 feet, or more.

Collectors of dwarf conifers often have far more of them about than the size of their property calls for. These collectors have found two effective ways of slowing the growth of their trees: root pruning and pot culture.

Root pruning, if it is to be done at all, should be done every year to prevent the tree from sending out rangy roots. Plunge a spade to its hilt in a circle around the base of the tree. If the tree is a foot high, make the cut 3 inches away from the trunk; for a 2-foot tree make the cut 5 inches from the trunk; for a 3-footer make the cut 6 inches away; for a 4-footer make the cut 8 inches away; for a 5-footer make the cut 9 inches away. For larger trees, cut an inch farther from the trunk for every additional foot of the tree. These operations are only safe to perform on trees which are growing in well-watered gardens. The work should be done during the dormant season—late October to mid-April.

All rock garden conifers can be kept slow-growing in containers. Collectors sometimes plant their conifers in ordinary clay pots, which they bury up to the rims in the rock garden. The pots must be twisted or dug up a couple of times during the growing season to break the roots which grow through the drainage hole.

Neither pruning roots nor burying pots is as sound a rock garden practice as selecting the right conifers for the job and giving them room to grow.

When You Choose
Your Conifers

When we meet a conifer for the first time in a nursery or in a garden, some of our questions are apt to be "How big will it grow? How fast does it grow? How old is it now?" Exact answers to these questions are often not feasible. There are too many local influences, such as varying soil condition, water supply, and summer temperatures. However, you can gain practical knowledge of a conifer's growth rate, its potential size, and its age by making a few measurements and calculations. You may want to do this at the nursery before you decide to buy a conifer, or perhaps you already own a conifer whose age and growth you'd like to know more about.

Make your calculations before the conifer begins to grow in the spring or after the tree's annual growth is complete (usually in July). The latest annual growth on the tree will be marked by a joint where the old growth ended and the new began. Often the needles formed during this latest growth are perceptibly different in size or color from those formed during previous years.

If the tree you're examining is prostrate, dome-shaped, or rounded, its lateral growth will give the best indication of its vital statistics. Select one of its largest and lowest limbs. Measure the latest annual growth of several twigs, including the one on the end of the branch. Take an average of these measurements. The figure you get represents the tree's rate of growth for one year.

If the tree you're examining is upright (columnar, conical, or pyramidal) its growth rate can be determined by measuring the latest annual growth of its leader (tip growth). If there are several leaders, measure them all and take the average. It is likely that a rock garden conifer will equal or exceed its last annual growth each succeeding year.

To determine the age of prostrate, dome-shaped, and rounded conifers, measure the entire length of one of their larger limbs up to its juncture with the trunk. Divide this figure by the annual rate of growth and you'll get a fair idea of the age of the tree.

The age of upright conifers can be determined by dividing the height of the tree by the annual growth of its leader.

There are shortcomings in these age calculations. The majority of the rock garden conifers grow much more slowly for the first 5 or 10 years of their lives than they do afterward. Compensate for this, when you are judging mature trees, by adding about 7 years to your age calculation.

Dwarf conifers are also capable of growth explosions. Until a conifer has remained about 7 to 10 years in one position in the garden, it will not have attained its maximum rate of growth. This is likely to be twice that of its average annual rate of growth for the first several years after you've planted it.

The average annual rate of growth in inches of a prostrate or dome-shaped conifer must be doubled to determine the tree's annual increase in diameter. A prostrate juniper whose annual rate of growth is 8 inches actually grows 16 inches across in one year. The figure of 8 inches was taken from one limb only, growing in one direction.

Plant Biographies

This final chapter lists and describes the best rock plants for American gardens, selected from the overwhelming mass of plant species available to rock gardeners. Some of your favorites may have been overlooked in the crowd (but we hope not many).

The best of the best rock plants—those having beauty, strength, ease of culture, and consequently landscape value—are marked with a star (★). These plants deserve their star only for specific types of gardening which are mentioned in their biographies. A starred bog plant, for example, would be worthless on a dry bank.

Many rock plants possess beauty of unique quality but are at the same time too difficult to grow or too small to be of much landscape value. In the biographies these plants are categorized as "collectors' plants" or as being suitable for the "collector's garden."

The hardiness range of many rock plants is only sketchily known. Plants in the biographies which are assumed (after weighing some supporting data) to be hardy and adaptable to *most* climate zones over temperate North America are initialed: "N.A." But most plants so initialed surely won't winter in the Great Plains, nor will they flower and perform as they should in the southern sections of California and Florida.

Many of the plants named and described in this chapter are as yet little known in American gardens and scarcely available from American nurseries. They are here because the hope of this book is to project itself into the future of American gardens—where these plants will have eminent value.

ABIES BALSAMEA 'NANA'. The wood of balsam fir (*Abies balsamea*) is known to every boy who builds model airplanes. Balsam fir grows in eastern North America from the tundra south to Virginia. 'Nana' is a flattened, compact form with the dark, lustrous needles of the species. Grows about 2 inches a year and will suffer if it gets hot and dry. Shade it lightly.

★**ABIES LASIOCARPA.** This is the alpine fir, which grows in valleys or on slopes up to timberline over most of the mountain ranges of western North America, forming forests of Gothic spires. In the different parts of its range it may share the timberline zone with western larch, mountain hemlock, white fir, noble fir, whitebark pine, and lodgepole pine, but always the alpine fir is the slenderest spire among the alpine conifers. The color of the spire is variable. Dark green trees and blue-green trees grow side by side.

A. lasiocarpa is the mainstay of commercial collectors, who dig it to supply a ready market for alpine conifers. In the Northwest its demand has eclipsed that for Colorado blue spruce and every rock garden conifer. The commercial collectors have also begun to cut alpine firs by the thousands for Christmas trees. (In California the more accessible white fir, red fir, and noble fir are more often cut for the Christmas tree market.)

Fashions in trees are as transitory as the garden fashions they reflect, but *Abies lasiocarpa* will always be an outstanding rock garden conifer. Expect it to put on 5 inches of growth a year after it becomes established. (This takes about 5 years.)

· **ABIES PROCERA.** (*A. nobilis.*) Young noble fir trees have stiff, straight, spokelike branches around a pole-like trunk. While the tree acquires more interesting form with age, the blue-gray color is good from the start.

★**ACAENA BUCHANANII.** One of the most traffic-resistant ground covers for sunny places, acaena has been used in its native New Zealand to cover a country airfield. *A. buchananii* has densely silky, pale-gray, inch-long leaves, toothed and divided rather like those of roses (to which acaenas are related). Height: 1½ inches.

ACAENA MICROPHYLLA. This ground cover is tolerant of a wide range of conditions—dry or moist soil, sun or half shade. Its leaf color is a blend of purple, gray, and green. It has the only worthwhile flowers among the acaenas —red-spined globes that look much like little sea urchins. Height: 1½ inches.

ACANTHOLIMON GLUMACEUM. A mound of dianthus-like leaves which grows on Ararat, the Biblical mountain, and also with perfect willingness in a warm, sunny spot in the rock garden. Height 15 inches. N. A. *Acantholimon echinus* and *A. venustum* are also in cultivation in North America, although precariously. When these Near-Easterners are eventually tried in gardens in the hotter sections of America's Southwest, they are likely to prove runaway successes. At present they must be considered collectors' acquisitions. All have starry flowers in various shades of pink on short stems which thrust from mounds of sharply pointed leaves.

★**ACANTHUS MOLLIS.** Architectonic plants with 2-foot leaves, deeply slashed, dark green and polished; and in the late summer, 5-foot spires of beak-like flowers of dull white, lilac, or rose. They like mild climates winter and summer, a well-drained soil in shade, and the company of large ferns, hellebores, and francoa. But they are bold enough to stand alone against massive stones or against walls or fences.

Like many other architectonic plants, acanthus has served as an inspiration to the architecture of men. The capitals of the Corinthian columns were stylized after the leaves of acanthus.

ACERANTHUS DIPHYLLUS. A Japanese woodland plant, dwarf and clump-making, with two leaflets to a stem and 4 to 6 drooping flowers of white or lilac. The names *Epimedium diphyllum* and *E. diphyllum* 'Roseum' are in well established but improper usage for this plant.

Grow aceranthus in cool, moist soil in shady places with hepaticas and primulas for company. It is hardy to below zero. Height: 9 inches.

ACHILLEA AGERATIFOLIA AIZOON. (*Anthemis aizoon.*) A tough, permanent, spreading mat of narrow, silvery-gray leaves in rosettes covered over in May by brilliant white daisies with a whitish eye. The white-on-white ensemble gives this flower special beauty. Grows readily in light sandy soil in a sunny location. Height: 10 inches. N. A.

★**ACHILLEA ARGENTEA.** Silvery yarrow. Clusters of white flowers on thick mats of silver leaves; a high return in beauty for as small an investment of care as can be made in the garden. Sun and well drained light soil. *Achillea jaborneggii* and *A. tomentosa* (yellow flowers) are of similar habit, appearance, and value. Height: 9 inches. N. A.

ADIANTUM PEDATUM. The maidenhair or five-finger fern has black stalks as thin as wires supporting a fan of fragile leaves. All that is graceful and airy in woodland plants is found in this fern. Easily established in shady places, even in dry shade, but it has a special liking for ravines and banks dripping with spring water. Height: 18 inches. N. A.

★**AETHIONEMA.** The aethionemas grow in the arid mountains of Lebanon and Turkey, across into Armenia and down into Iran. They are thus fully equipped to grow in the hotter and drier parts of California and the Southwest. They are also at home in the Northwest and along the eastern seaboard.

Those commonly in cultivation are all of fairly equal value and similar appearance. The mark of the desert is in their leaves, narrowed to needles and colored gray to repel the sun. In April and May long clusters of pink, fragrant flowers open on spiky stems.

★**AETHIONEMA GRANDIFLORUM.** (*A. theodorum.*) Larger clusters of darker rose-pink than the other species. The plants may live twenty years if cut back after flowering. (This is good practice with all aethionemas.) Height: 18 inches. N. A.

★**AETHIONEMA SCHISTOSUM.** About 14 inches high and has large pink flowers in short clusters on unbranched stems.

★**AETHIONEMA STYLOSUM.** Sends seedlings up by the score—which may be desirable or pesty depending on where it is placed. In the sparse turf beneath native oaks or in desert areas, this free seeding propensity can be turned to good use, giving a meadow effect. *A. schistosum* and *A. grandiflorum* also seed about, but rather sparingly. Height: 11 inches. N. A.

★**AETHIONEMA 'WARLEY ROSE'.** Thought to be a sterile seedling of *A. pulchellum* (although there is some argument about its parentage). This famous rock plant is considered by many British gardeners to be one of the 10 best, even though it strains itself in its heavy production of flowers and may die after 4 years or so. Height: 10 inches. N. A.

AJUGA GENEVENSIS 'BROCK-BANKII'. Rich blue labiate flowers densely produced on a column in May and June. Clumps of spatula-form leaves low on the ground. A refined, non-running plant easily grown in any reasonable location. Height: 9 inches. N. A.

★**AJUGA REPTANS.** A great plant, modest in its demands, generous with its runners and its deep blue flower spikes in May. It can substitute for a grass lawn under shade trees and in odd, smallish areas. *Ajuga reptans* 'Purpurea' has a dark, metallic purple-tinged green in the leaf. The variety 'Jungle' is larger and leafier than typical *A. reptans*. Height: 9 inches. N. A.

ALLIUM. Onions in the rock garden? Many are as worthy of space as scilla, dwarf narcissus, and the other small bulbs of spring. Onion flowers come later —in May and June—and have no nasal offense about them unless you try to pick them or otherwise bruise the plant. White *Allium neapolitanum* is altogether scentless. *A. giganteum* sends up 3 to 5 foot stems, each topped with an enormous globe of rosy flowers. These are everlasting and can be used in dried arrangements.

Twelve inch *A. moly*, with yellow flowers in May, is more scaled to the average rock garden. This old favorite is hardy throughout North America. *A. schoenoprasum*, known as chives in the kitchen, is also an attractive garden plant. Globular flower clusters of light purple. *A. cyaneum, A. narcissiflorum*, and *A. ostrowskyanum* are three miniatures valuable enough for the front rank of the collector's rock garden.

ALYSSUM MURALE. (*A. argenteum.*) Broad, flattened clusters of yellow on a foot or more of bare stem. The flowering season extends from late May into July, and the seed clusters last into winter as handsome, silvered reminders of summer. The plant seeds about magnificently, so it should be kept to wild rocks and meadows. It is from the Mediterranean, which should make it especially suitable to California and the Southwest. Height: 24 inches. N. A.

★**ALYSSUM SAXATILE.** The baskets of gold of Victorian gardens is no less rich as bouquet nowadays. The color is a bit crass and mustardy for some tastes, but this is completely alleviated in the soft, creamy yellow form *A. s.* 'Luteum' (*A. s.* 'Citrinum'). Both are available from major seed houses, and both come easily from seed. Spreading plants with gray leaves. They prefer well drained soil and a sunny location. Height: 15 inches. N. A.

★**ALYSSUM WULFENIANUM.** A prostrate creeper, covering an area the size of a card table. The leaves are small and gray; the flowers are as rich and yellow as *A. saxatile*. *A. alpestre, A. serpyllifolium, A. idaeum* are similar in habit, but smaller and on the temperamental side. Height: 8 inches. N. A.

ANDROMEDA POLIFOLIA. A peat bog shrublet in nature, adaptable to much drier upland conditions in the rock garden. Pink globes in arching clusters over springy, 15-inch high mats of gray-green narrow leaves. 'Nana Compacta' is about 9 inches high. *A. p. minima* from Hokkaido, Japan, is about 4 inches high.

ANDROSACE LANUGINOSA. *Androsace* stands close to *Primula* and repeats the precisely formed flowers of primroses, but in smaller scale. The soft lilac flowers of *Androsace lanuginosa* are arranged in clusters above silvery mats.

The plant is not free growing enough to serve as a ground cover, and yet when it is well established it may form mats 3 feet across. 'Leichtlinii,' white flowered with a distinct eye of crimson or yellow, has an even greater appeal to many rock gardeners. This species and the next have value unexcelled in the collector's garden. Height: 8 inches. Adaptable to Western Washington, Oregon, California south to the Monterey Peninsula, and to the northeastern states.

★**ANDROSACE SARMENTOSA.** Mouse ear tufts of felted leaves spreading by short stolons; shell pink primrose-like flowers in April and May. With a little favored attention, the plant can compete with aubrieta, alyssum, and the other muscular rock garden plants. 'Chumbyi' is much smaller, suited to the collector's garden. *A. carnea, A. lactea, A. primuloides, A. sempervivoides* are inch-high plants that all good collectors sigh for.

★**ANEMONE APENNINA.** 2 inches in the 5 of this plant are used up by the flowers, which are starry in form and tender blue in color. These appear in late March and April for many years after you plant the dry, black, worthless looking tubers. These you can order in the autumn from bulb dealers. Nothing in the spring garden gives a greater thrill of discovery than these absurdly big, blue stars opening in the first days that are warm enough to bring the bees out. N. A.

★**ANEMONE BLANDA.** Similar to *A. apennina* in value and appearance, but has darker blue and more regularly formed flowers. These two anemones like nothing better than a woodsy soil beneath Japanese maples, azaleas and other light shrubbery. Height: 4 inches. N. A.

ANEMONE HUPEHENSIS JAPON-ICA and **A. HYBRIDA.** Japanese anemone. Under these two names are included plants sold as *A. japonica*, a September-flowering group of well-known border perennials with white or pink single or double flowers. The Japanese anemones are equally harmonious among shaded rocks, where they can be used to form a transition from the rock garden to the woodland garden. Height: 30 inches. N. A.

★**ANEMONE NEMOROSA.** This plant, in its various named shades of blue, is so permanent, self-sufficient, and widely ramifying in shady places — whether among rocks or beneath trees—that it must qualify as a plant with landscape value. Height: 9 inches or a foot. N. A.

ANEMONE PULSATILLA. Upright cups of violet, wine, or white; ferny leaves; showy heads of plumy seeds. A special plant deserving pathside placement in the woodland or in the rock garden. Sow the seeds for increase. Height: 14 inches. N. A.

ANEMONE SYLVESTRIS. A white-cupped woodlander from Germany's Black Forest. Deserves a place both for the beauty of its large flowers and for the free running ease of its growth. Height: 10 inches. N. A.

ANTENNARIA. Almost any of the North American alpine "cats' paws"—aptly named for the form of the flower clusters—will grow into pleasant, silver mats in the rock garden. *A. rosea (A. microphylla)* is a rather good species (none is really exciting) common in our mountains. *A. dioica* from the Alps has richly rose-colored flowers which are genuinely pretty. A collector's item. Height: 3 inches. N. A.

ANTHEMIS AIZOON. See **ACHILLEA AGERATIFOLIA AIZOON.**

ANTHYLLIS MONTANA. Usually available in its selected form 'Rubra.' The typical bloom is washy pink; even 'Rubra' lacks brightness. Tidy mats of gray-green; pea-shaped flowers in rounded clusters. Worth a place for the fact that it flowers in late June and July. Height: 8 inches. N. A.

AQUILEGIA. There are several dozen wild columbines in the northern hemisphere. Some are plants of the lowland forests; others are sub-alpine plants, inhabiting elevations where forests break up and give way to meadows. A few are high alpines which root deeply in the crumbling stone of America's Rocky Mountains. The higher the plants range, the smaller they become. The lowland species grow as much as 3 or 4 feet, the high alpines as little as 3 or 4 inches.

As a rule the small columbine species are short-lived in the garden. Give them a scree mixture and sun and expect at best three good years from them. However, most of the columbines are generous with seed. If you are lucky, they may self sow.

The columbine species possess a grace of simplicity which the parti-colored border columbines can never impart to the rock garden and, after all, it is to capture and hold this quality of graceful simplicity that we build rock gardens. Height: varying. Range of adaptability: throughout temperate North America.

AQUILEGIA CANADENSIS. A forest plant, from 1 to 2 feet high, with orange-red flowers. Common in woods and foothills east of the Rocky Mountains. Seedlings transplant readily into the garden, and wild seed (sown fresh) will provide plants aplenty. *A. c.* 'Nana' is 9 to 12 inches high, otherwise similar to the type.

AQUILEGIA CHRYSANTHA. From New Mexico and Arizona. A 3 to 4-foot plant, yellow flowered, with spurs about 2 inches long. Long spurs are characteristic of the American columbines. When this feature is present in the border hybrids, it is the mark of American ancestry.

AQUILEGIA ECALCARATA. *(Semiaquilegia ecalcarata.)* A small Japanese plant with spurless flowers of a color like claret and creme de cacao stirred together. Oddly appealing in the collector's garden.

AQUILEGIA FLAVESCENS. Similar to *A. canadensis* but with yellow flowers. *A. formosa* is the Western American counterpart of *A. canadensis,* and just as easy to handle in the garden.

AQUILEGIA LONGISSIMA. From southwest Texas. A tall plant (to 3 feet) with yellow flowers. The 4-inch spurs are the longest among aquilegias.

AQUILEGIA VIRIDIFLORA. Himalayan. A winsome, smallish plant quite worthless for show. The flowers have petals of dark chocolate, sepals of chartreuse, and spurs which are a blend of the two. A collector's delight.

AQUILEGIA VULGARIS. Common—but never vulgar — in wooded places from England across Europe. It is a 2-foot plant, violet-flowered, with short, clubbed, incurving spurs. This is the stout parent which has contributed longevity to the garden hybrids.

The taller columbines hybridize freely on their own, aided by the bees, so that it is hardly possible to keep the species distinct. *A. alpina* and *A. jucunda* are sometimes listed in seed catalogues, but almost anything is likely to come up from seed purchased under these names.

The real *A. alpina* is an 18-inch plant with clear, dark blue flowers, yellow-stamened and short-spurred. *A. glandulosa* (also called *A. jucunda*) is much the same plant, but with soft blue sepals and white petals. *A. flabellata* is a Japanese sub-alpine, a stocky plant with thick leaves (rounded in the lobes) and stubby flowers of lavender blue. *A. flabellata* 'Nana Alba' has white flowers on a huddled plant.

ARABIS BLEPHAROPHYLLA. A Californian species which grows as a native in pine duff. Suited to well drained, sunny places in the rock garden. It forms rosettes of large, dark green leaves and 8 to 10-inch clusters of bright magenta crucifer flowers, which appear with *Anemone blanda* and *Narcissus cyclamineus* in the earliest spring. N. A.

ARABIS CAUCASICA. *(A. albida.)* Billowing white mounds of wall rockcress date far back in the history of the English rock garden. In our country, the wall rockcress is part of the syndrome of durable rock garden antiques comprising arabis, alyssum, aubrieta, and iberis.

A. caucasica is somewhat out of fashion now, but old-fashioned flowers have a way of coming back to fresh use after a generation or two, and when they have as much intrinsic value as this plant, they are never far behind.

The great values of wall rockcress are that it grows unfailingly in almost any rock garden, forming ramping masses of felty and notched leaves in rosettes; and that it flowers unfailingly, with clusters of white, four-petaled flowers. These four-petaled ally arabis, aubrieta, and mustard in the gigantic family of the *Cruciferae.*

There is a rose colored form of this known as 'Rosabella'; and the typical white flowered plant has a variegated foliage form, *A. C.* 'Variegata', of limited value and use. Height 9 inches. N. A.

★**ARCTOSTAPHYLOS HOOKERI.** A creeping manzanita with glossy russet bark; small, pointed leaves, and clustered pink flowers in the form of amphorae.

Anemone apennina

Androsace sarmentosa 'Chumbyi'

Astilbe chinensis 'Pumila'

It may grow to 3 feet. *A. H.* 'Monterey Carpet' and *A. H.* 'Wayside' are superior selections of denser, lower habit, useful covers for banks and rocks. Hardy to 0°.

★**ARCTOSTAPHYLOS MEDIA.** This name covers a group of natural hybrids of *A. columbiana,* a manzanita native to the Pacific Northwest and northern California, and *A. uva ursi* (kinnikinnick) of circumpolar distribution. *Arctostaphylos media* grows to about 5 feet across in 5 years and makes a bank cover of outstanding value. Prefers sandy, acid soil; sun or half shade. Blends well with madrona, salal, evergreen huckleberry, ninebark, and tall, leggy rhododendrons, under which it can be used as a protective cover. *A. m.* 'Grandiflora' is a larger flowered selection. Height: 24 inches. N. A.

★**ARCTOSTAPHYLOS UVA-URSI.** Kinnikinnick is one of the most valuable prostrate shrubs for holding sandy soil cuts and for big jobs in rock gardening. It grows in any acid, well drained soil in sun or shade. The branches root down as they grow, and gain about a foot a year. If you want a solid cover in a hurry, buy plants in gallon cans and set them out as closely as 18 inches apart. If you are in no hurry, space them 6 feet apart.

Kinnikinnick has small, oval leaves, glossy and dark green; the pink, urn-shaped flowers are followed by clusters of red fruits half hidden among the leaves. Height: 10 inches. N. A.

ARENARIA GRANDIFLORA. White flowers on a small mat of lax, green needle-like leaves. Very good and easy in sandy soil and sun. Height: 8 inches. N. A.

★**ARENARIA MONTANA.** Combines vigor and refinement in its mats of small grayish leaves and white, saucer-shaped flowers which are large compared to the rest of the plant and numberless in the month of June. Grow it in the sun. Height: 10 inches. N. A.

★**ARENARIA VERNA CAESPITOSA.** Irish moss is one of the most useful of carpeting plants. It grows well in moist shade and even better in moist, sunny areas. Foliage in the type plant is a rich green; there is a golden-green variant sometimes called Scotch moss. The tiny white flowers are pleasing but not significant. Use the green form between stepping stones or paving blocks, as a small scale ground cover or bulb cover. This is the only plant that can give a close approximation of the softness and velvety quality of true moss. Unfortunately, the carpets are not long lived. Replanting may be necessary in 2 or 3 years. N. A.

ARMERIA. Most of the thrifts grow among rocks on the coasts of Europe and America, but *Armeria juniperifolia (A. caespitosa)* grows in the dry Spanish Sierra above Madrid. This makes a 4-inch-high pincushion studded over with almost stemless pink or white flowers; 18-inch *A. maritima* of England's coast makes large tussocks of grassy leaves, from which arise tall-stemmed, ball-shaped flower clusters of white or rose. The selection called 'Laucheana' has deep rose flowers. *A. pseud-armeria (A. cephalotes)* is about intermediate in habit between these other species. N. A.

ARNEBIA ECHIOIDES. The prophet flower, once popular in America but now seldom seen and difficult to obtain. A foot-high plant with narrow green leaves and rounded yellow flowers marked with a black spot at the base of each of the five lobes. N. A.

ARTEMISIA. These are gray shrubs for gray borders and dry, sunny banks.

ARTEMISIA ABROTANUM. Southernwood grows typically to 5 feet, spreading by underground stems. There is an 18-inch form which brings the exquisitely dissected, Brussels-lace foliage down to rock garden height. N. A.

ARTEMISIA ABSINTHIUM. Common wormwood. In boulevardier days in Paris, this was the destructive ingredient of the now forbidden absinthe. Many Italian-Americans keep this silver Mediterranean shrub in their gardens, perhaps for its medicinal properties, perhaps for purely nostalgic reasons. Height: 36 inches. N. A.

ARTEMISIA DRACUNCULUS. This is tarragon, whose odorous gray leaves flavor salad vinegar. Height: 20 inches. Not hardy in the colder sections of America.

ARTEMISIA FRIGIDA. Western native, widespread over plains and dry mountains. The dissected silvery leaves were used in tonics by pioneers in the Rockies. Height: 12 inches. N. A.

ARTEMISIA TRIDENTATA. The sagebrush of western American ballad and legend can be dug from the prairie when it is no more than 9 inches high and grown on a large bank among lavenders and other drought-tolerant shrubs. Height: 3 to 15 feet. N. A.

★**ASPERULA ODORATA.** Sweet woodruff makes running carpets either in sunny places or, with special charm, in the woodland. There it sends out tufts of narrow, whorled leaves endlessly, binding the leaf mold, making carpets over rotting logs and under old shrubbery grown lank in the half light. Sweet woodruff has a high tolerance of sunlessness and soil acidity. It will even grow beneath fir trees under the acid rain of needles. The tiny white star-like flowers grow in clusters at the ends of the branches. The flowers and leaves have a subtle fragrance which led vintners in old times to infuse sweet woodruff in white wine and call the product "May wine" in honor of spring and flowers. May wine is still popular in Germany. Height: 4 inches. N. A.

ASPERULA HIRTA. An alpine woodruff of palest rose flowers from the Pyrenees Like an *A. odorata* reduced to half size, but slow and compressed in its growth. Deserves a high rating among alpine miniatures. There are other alpine woodruffs just as deserving as *A. hirta* but not so hardy. *A. suberosa* is slow, touchy and insecure in northern climates. California, however, may prove as hospitable to it as its native Mt. Athos in Greece. Foliage like tufts of gray moss and long-tubed trumpet flowers of soft pink. Scree conditions in sun. Height: 5 inches. All these collector's plants are hardy to about —5°.

ASPLENIUM TRICHOMANES. Maidenhair spleenwort grows in cliffs and old rock slides over much of North America. The fronds have dark, thin stems (stipes, technically), lustrous like lacquered wires. Along the stems are opposite rows of roundish ¼-inch leaflets (pinnae to botanists). The overall impression that the plant gives is of fragility impossible to bring into the garden. Actually this fern is easy to grow in half shade. Height: 4 inches. N. A.

ASTER. Flowers of great beauty in plants ranging from ankle height to man height. Asters prefer deep, rich soil that is well watered and well drained, and a place in the sun or in light woodland.

It is hard to know where to draw the line separating asters for the rock garden from those for the border. The size of your rock garden sets the only practical limitation. The following are some middling to small-sized species of outstanding value.

ASTER ALPINUS. Lavender or white with a gold center. Short lived. Divide frequently or sow the copious seed. Constant flowering. Height: 12 inches. N. A.

ASTER DUMOSUS. The genuine plant is a 2-footer which has been developed into many color forms. Also going by this name are a number of dwarf hybrid asters, ranging from 5 inches to 2 feet. One of the 5-inch dwarfs is 'Niobe', white flowered in September. N. A.

★**ASTER FRIKARTII.** A form of this hybrid aster known as 'Wonder of Stafa' shows pure lavender-blue daisies about 2½ inches across from July until late summer. Height: 24 inches.

ASTER KUMLEINII. Native to the Great Plains. Masses of blue-violet or pink or rounded bushes in September and October. Height: 30 inches. N. A.

★**ASTER PURDOMII.** Long violet rays and a richly orange colored center in May. (*A. farreri* and *A. souliei limitaneus (A. forrestii)* are other Asiatic kinds of similar appearance and value.) Height: 12 inches. N. A.

ASTER SUBCAERULEUS. Large lilac blue flowers with orange centers. May to September. Height: 15 inches.

ASTER YUNNANENSIS. Clear, soft blue rays around an orange center. June. Height: 18 inches. N. A.

★**ASTILBE.** The species are hardly known, having been supplanted in gardens by a legion of hybrids. These are indispensable plants in moist or wet soil. They have ferny leaves and flowers in plumy clusters appearing in midsummer. New and ever more highly touted varieties are introduced every season. Buy them by color rather than by name. All are good. The range of color extends from white to salmon, rose, and carmine. Dwarfs and giants are both available. Height: 6 to 72 inches. N. A.

Propagate astilbes by dividing clumps every 3 or 4 years in early spring or fall.

★ASTILBE CHINENSIS 'PUMILA'. The plant distributed under this name is distinct from the other garden astilbes. It sends out stolons and makes a mat a yard across in four or five years. Clear pink plumes a foot high in August and September.

★ATHYRIUM FILIX-FEMINA. Lady fern. Majestic plumy fronds, light green in color, soft in texture, unroll to a full 6 feet in rich wet soil. Even with all its size, lady fern seems one of the most fragile ferns. Actually, it is as tough as bracken. Lady fern will grow practically everywhere along our west and east coasts, even in dryish soil in full sun (where the fronds are smaller and stiffer). An indispensable plant for bogs, woodlands, and north walls. One disadvantage: the fronds die down in the winter.

Hundreds of varieties have been selected and catalogued in England. Of these, *A. f.* 'Frizelliae' has been in cultivation over a century.

★AUBRIETA DELTOIDEA. One of the great rock plants. Low, widely flowing mats of green, notch-leaved rosettes; and, in May, a profusion of 4-petaled cress flowers. Varieties are white, rose, lilac, or violet. For the sunny hillside garden, the dry stone wall, or as a ground cover. Shear the stems halfway to the ground after flowers fade. Hardy to zero or below. Water it well. Height: 6 inches.

BELLIS PERENNIS. The English daisy of lawns and border edging is both a beloved and a reviled plant depending on individual sympathies. The big, blowsy double forms are too coarse for the rock garden, but there are dwarf doubles of refinement: 'Dresden China' (pink) and 'Boutonniere' (white). Height: 4 inches. N. A.

BELLIUM MINUTUM. This Grecian is about the smallest daisy in size, and the largest in elfin charm. Irresistible plant for the collector. Height: 1 inch. Not overly hardy.

BERGENIA. Saxifrage relatives from the Himalayas and Siberia. Tuft-forming perennials with thick roots and crowns which support huge leathery leaves, dark green, glossy, round or oblong, long stemmed, and up to a foot long in the blade. Inch-wide white, rose, or purple flowers in tousled clusters open in January (if weather is mild), February, and March.

Bergenia looks cabbage-coarse on rock work. Use it as a ground cover beneath large trees, or, in the city garden, along the dark and narrow strip which divides your house from the house next door. Bergenias are tough plants, hardy to 10°, drought resistant, tolerant of the poorest clay or sand soil, and of sun and deep shade.

Remove old battered leaves and divide the plants in the fall every two years to keep them from becoming overgrown. Discard the older portions of the plants. Keep slug bait around the crowns at all times. Height: 12 to 18 inches. N. A.

★BERGENIA CORDIFOLIA. The most common species. Rose-pink flowers grow in nodding clusters, nested and sometimes half hidden among the vast cabbage crowns.

★BERGENIA CRASSIFOLIA. Rose, lilac, or purple flowers in erect clusters held well above the leaves.

★BERGENIA LIGULATA. Smaller, lighter green leaves than the other two, and white flowers.

BRODIAEA. Any of these western American bulbs is worth garden space. Most come in shades of blue and violet, but there are other colors as well. They transplant easily, and if there is a question of conservation, seed-grown bulbs of many of the best species are available from Dutch suppliers.

CALCEOLARIA POLYRRHIZA. The hybrid calceolarias are old-fashioned favorites of conservatories. Their curious, pouched flowers occupy a space in Americana shared by Sunday band concerts in the park. *C. polyrrhiza* is no glasshouse shrub, but an 8-inch creeper with pouches of yellow. Best in moist places in sun or shade. No other calceolaria is safely hardy or perennial in the northwestern states. *C. darwinii* and *C. biflora* can be attempted in the open on the coast of California.

★CALLUNA VULGARIS. Scotch heather varies from 6 feet down to 4 inches in its various named forms. The best for rock gardens are: 'H. E. Beale', with long spikes of silver pink from July to October; good for cutting; makes a lank 3 to 4-foot shrub which needs hard pruning. 'County Wicklow', 2 feet with flowers similar to those of 'H. E. Beale'; August to October. 'J. H. Hamilton', 1 foot; double coral pink; August to October. 'Foxii Nana', negligible flowers, dark, mossy foliage on a slow-growing rounded shrub up to 1 foot high. 'Nana', dark green carpet 9 inches high; valuable ground cover. 'Dainty Bess', a rock garden shrublet of great charm; gray-green mat 4 inches high; double silvery pink flowers in August and September; will stand —10° or more, but dislikes high temperatures and low humidity.

CALOCHORTUS. The globe tulips, *C. albus* (white), *C. amabilis* (clear yellow), and *C. amoenus* (deep rose) are perfectly amenable to garden culture in sun or half shade almost anywhere in North America. Their flower ensemble is something like a string of paper lanterns hanging from a rod. These three will be found in the bulb trade.

The calochortus species known as cat's ears or pussy ears—*C. tolmiei* (*C. maweanus*) (white or cream), *C. coeruleus* (bluish), and *C. elegans* (greenish-white)—grow along the coast, in mountains or on high plains. They can be coaxed into showing their down-filled flower cups in the scree or coldframe.

Most splendid are the big flower bowls of the mariposa tulips—orange and ochre, yellow, lavender, or white, often intricately marked. But the mariposa tulips will not grow in climates where the winter soil is wet or frozen. If they grow wild near your home, you can expect success with them in your garden. Let the bulbs go dry after they have flowered.

CAMPANULA. The bellflowers would be reason enough for the rock garden, even if saxifrages, sedums, and sempervivums did not exist. All the appealing qualities of miniature plants—the absurd smallness of body and bigness of flower, the glowing colors and fragility which challenge the products of the Venetian glass blowers—are found in this genus. *Caution:* In gardens where slugs and snails abound, campanulas will not.

★CAMPANULA CARPATICA. Upright blue or white cups 2 inches across above a clump of toothed green leaves. It is tough enough to be used for edging in the perennial border, and refined enough to star in the rock garden. June to October. Height: 12 inches. N. A.

CAMPANULA CARPATICA TURBINATA. A form of *C. carpatica* but lower, grayer in the leaf, and more open in the flower. Far less vigorous than *C. carpatica.* Height: 8 inches. Other campanulas, equally deserving, are *C. barbata, C. betulaefolia, C. collina, C. glomerata, C. pilosa, C. pulla, C. sarmatica, C. tommasiniana, C. tridentata,* and *C. waldsteiniana.* N. A.

★CAMPANULA CEPHALLENICA. Graceful panicles of starry violet flowers which press against and creep over the contours of boulders in retaining walls. the plant is strong enough to be useful almost anywhere. Height: 7 inches. N. A.

CAMPANULA COCHLEARIFOLIA. (*C. bellardii.*) Makes running mats of little scalloped leaves and pendant bells of shimmering violet or white on an inch of threadlike stem. It is a vagrant growth which will romp through dianthus and run beneath alpine rhododendrons one year, completely disappear from that area the next and come up from seed ten feet away. The performance is lively and harmless if large plants are grouped with it. Sun, half shade. Height: 4 inches. N. A.

★CAMPANULA ISOPHYLLA. In nature a rare plant restricted to a few sea cliffs near Genoa; in gardens, as common as hanging baskets, from which it cascades in masses of green or frost-gray foliage and wide, flat stars of ice-blue or white. Height: 9 inches. Hardy to 20°.

★CAMPANULA PERSICIFOLIA. Peach leaf bluebell. Excellent border plant—so graceful, in spite of its demitasse-sized cups of china blue and white, that it is just as admissible to the large rock garden. For the meadow it is ideal. The same case may be made for *C. medium,* the Canterbury bell.

C. persicifolia 'Nitida' (*C. nitida*) is an odd dwarf of *C. persicifolia,* a Mendelian recessive no more than 6 inches high. Seed of this dwarf invariably grows up into normal, 4-foot peach bells.

★**CAMPANULA PORTENSCHLAGI- ANA.** (*C. muralis* in many catalogues.) By either name it makes tufted green mats completely covered with deep cups of dark violet in June. In Europe this campanula is a famous plant of mellow old dry stone walls. *C. elatines* and *C. elatines garganica* are similar plants, though somewhat smaller and a bit frail. Height: 6 inches. N. A.

★**CAMPANULA POSCHARSKYANA.** A most useful introduction from Yugoslavia. Big enough, strong enough, and showy enough to rank with alyssum and aubrieta among the great rock plants which are able to form curtains of foliage and flowers on the starkest stone bulwarks. It grows and flowers after the manner of *C. cephallenica,* but more vigorously. Can be used as a roughly textured ground cover in shady corners and woodlands. Height: 16 inches. N. A.

★**CAMPANULA RADDEANA.** A stout, hardy clump of green; glossy flowers of purple-violet. Sun or light woodland. No problems. Height: 11 inches. N. A.

★**CAMPANULA RAPUNCULOIDES.** A glorious weed, tall (up to 5 feet) and stately, with fountains of rich deep violet funnel-shaped flowers in the wild border or woodland from June until September. N. A.

★**CAMPANULA ROTUNDIFOLIA.** The masses of nodding violet goblets which this plant produces tirelessly all summer would be sufficient to make *Campanula rotundifolia* one of the great rock plants —if it were not at the same time one of the all-time great weeds. You will never get rid of its invasive seedlings unless you move away. Only for wild rocks and woodland acreage. There it *is* great. Height: 14 inches. N. A.

★**CAMPTOSORUS RHIZOPHYLLUS.** The walking fern of eastern American woods. The fronds are heart-shaped and undivided; they taper to a long slender tip. The tips of the fronds arch down, touch the forest mold and form roots. An entire new plant springs from each frond tip. This "walking" ability accelerates to a gallop in favorable places, so keep the fern well away from choice plants. Yet walking fern is not always easy to establish. It must have deep shade and deep leaf mold. Height: 6 inches.

★**CASSIOPE LYCOPODIOIDES.** This Asiatic alpine and *C. selaginoides* from the Himalayas are about the strongest of these white-belled alpine "heaths." They respond to conditions suitable for alpine rhododendrons—full sun or light shade and a moist, spongy, yet well drained soil. The American species, in the company of *Phyllodoce,* form the "heather" gardens of our mountains, but never do the same at low elevations. Collected plants rarely do more than sit still.

CASTILLEIA. Impossible—virtually impossible. All the flaming Indian paint brushes of orange, scarlet, yellow, and vermilion tend to be parasites on grasses and other meadow plants. They will not transplant, but seed gathered ripe and scattered in a wild meadow (if you own such) has possibilities.

★**CEDRUS DEODARA 'PENDULA'.** Gray-green branches cascade over rocks at a rate of about 7 inches a year. The branches and needles can be left alone to form a curtain, or they can be thinned to expose the gray-barked trunk which becomes thick, heavy, and ancient-looking in a gratifyingly few years.

CELSIA ACAULIS. This Grecian alpine is a low, tufted, woolly-leafed plant, yellow-flowered all summer. Considerable potential for gardens in California and the Southwest. Height: 10 inches. Hardy to 5°, but dislikes wet winters.

CENTAURIUM. (*Erythraea.*) *C. scilloides* (*C. massonii, C. diffusum*), has little pink gentian-like flowers with trailing stems of glossy leaves. Good with *Houstonia* in cool, peaty places. Frost-damaged at 20°.

★**CERASTIUM TOMENTOSUM.** Snow-in-summer makes an irrepressible silver-gray ground cover, best in sunny, dry places. In the rock garden it can get out of hand and throttle everything that is smaller than a cistus, a helianthemum or a mugho pine. With these, however, it will make beautiful company. *C. biebersteinii* and *C. grandiflorum* are similarly beautiful and dangerous. *C. alpinum lanatum* is an alpine, small and safe in the rock garden. Height: 10 inches. N. A.

★**CERATOSTIGMA PLUMBAGI- NOIDES.** The name is so unwieldy that it has never really replaced the older, less proper name, *Plumbago larpentiae.* Brilliant cobalt blue stars in September and October. Needs a warm sunny spot. Height: 15 inches. N. A.

CHAMAECYPARIS LAWSONIANA. The Port Orford cedar is one of the most graceful conifers—a slender 100-foot pyramid of bluish foliage in open, plume-like arrangement. *C. l.* 'Fletcheri' is a 12-foot juvenile form with ascending branches. ★*C. l.* 'Ellwoodii' is smaller, narrower and slower in growth (6 to 8 inches annually). *C. l.* 'Minima' is a broad, blunt pyramid about 4 feet high in 20 years. There are several globular dwarfs sold under such names as *C. l.* 'Nana'.

CHAMAECYPARIS OBTUSA. The Hinoki cypress of Japan, a splendid, solemn green pyramid to about 100 feet. There are many dwarf forms of which the Japanese make favorite use.

CHAMAECYPARIS OBTUSA 'CAES- PITOSA'. The "golf ball" cypress is one of the smallest, slowest witches' brooms ever found, a bun-sized, bun-shaped mound of dark green, moss-fine foliage. A 35-year-old specimen grown in the open ground is a foot high, 15 inches across. Annual rate of growth: about ⅓

inch. As a container plant, *C. o.* 'Caespitosa' grows even more slowly, makes a delightful pet that will stay green and will grow (infinitesimally) for as many decades as you take care of it. This means daily watering when the sun shines, light shading, persistent weeding, and fertilizing with nothing more capacious than an eye-dropper.

The "tennis ball" cypress, *C. o.* 'Tetragona Minima', is much the same plant but not quite so slow or small; a number of other *C. obtusa* witchlings might vie for the names "golf ball" and "tennis ball."

★**CHAMAECYPARIS OBTUSA 'NANA GRACILIS'.** Grows about 3 inches a year and for practical purposes can be considered a mature tree at 6 feet or so. In habit it is a pleasantly uneven pyramid of black-green scale-like leaves in sprays like cupped, upturned hands. *C. o.* 'Nana Gracilis' is often sold as *C. o.* 'Nana', which is slower, smaller, and actually much rarer than its catalogue listings indicate.

★**CHAMAECYPARIS PISIFERA 'FILI- FERA'.** Threadleaf false cypress. Makes a fountain of branches which first ascend, then arch and fall in long green streamers. On hillsides the branches cascade 2 or 3 feet below the base of the trunk. The open habit of this shrub is one of its great attractions. This openness can be encouraged and developed into a grace of individual character by using pruning tools with thought and care.

CHAMAECYPARIS PISIFERA 'FILI- FERA NANA'. Smaller than *C. p.* 'Filifera' and about as broad and tall. On its own, *C. p.* 'Filifera Nana' does not develop as much grace and lightness as the bigger edition, but it can also be pruned for line. A 35-year-old specimen is 6 feet by 6 feet. Annual rate of growth: about 2 inches.

CHAMAECYPARIS PISIFERA 'SQUARROSA'. A period piece much planted in this country in the 1920's and 30's. Seldom offered by nurseries today, it is often seen in older gardens. These notes are included mainly for the benefit of gardeners who have grown (or have inherited) a mature specimen of this tree and who are puzzled whether to keep it or cut it down.

This juvenile form of Sawara cypress (*C. pisifera*) with fluffy, gray-green foliage, makes an irregularly pyramidal 35-foot tree at a rate of about 5 inches a year. Left to its own devices, this tree soon collects a mass of dead foliage on the older parts of the branches. It needs an annual clipping of old foliage. Branches can be pruned back to keep their youthful firmness. But with an eye for classic oriental spareness, Japanese gardeners encourage this tree's natural openness by pruning out fully half its branches. Grown in light shade and well cared for, this conifer will always be one of the most graceful small trees in the garden.

CHAMAECYPARIS PISIFERA 'SQUARROSA MINIMA'. A globular growth of gray-green, enlarging at a rate of about 1½ inches a year. Landscape use limited, by reason of its geometry, to geometrical gardens. Other forms of similar growth and use are 'Squarrosa Intermedia', 'Nana', 'Filifera'.

CISTUS. The rockroses have flowers like single roses, often with a spot at base of petals. Mediterranean shrubs, 2 to 8 feet in height and wider than tall. They have great value on large slopes or flats of light soil in hot sun. At their best in southwestern gardens, where they are perfectly at ease in desert drought and in coastal winds and salt spray.

Good investments are *C. albidus* (rose-lilac), *C. cyprius* (white), *C. ladaniferus* (white) and its variety *C. l. maculatus* (white, blotched blood-red), and *C. purpureus* (reddish purple). They combine well with helianthemum, although the color associations can be circus bright if you are not cautious. Then again, this may be just the effect you like.

CISTUS 'DORIS HIBBERSON'. Clear pink flowers with crinkled silky petals. Gray-green leaves. 3 feet.

CISTUS HYBRIDUS. (*C. corbariensis.*) This is 3 feet high, with gray-green crinkled leaves and large white flowers.

CISTUS LAURIFOLIUS. Grows to 8 feet. Dark, leathery leaves, clusters of white flowers with prominent golden stamens. Combines well with ceanothus, manzanita, madrona. Hardy to 0°.

CISTUS SALVIFOLIUS. A flat grower 18 inches to 2 feet high, spreading to 5 or 6 feet. It has white flowers in profusion.

COLCHICUM. The foliage of most autumn crocuses is too huge and tropical in appearance for the rock garden. But their great chalices of luminous lilac, claret, and white are unforgettable in autumn when they thrust up through the fallen leaves of dogwoods or cherries. Plant the bulbs in light woodland or in front of large rhododendrons to provide backing for their prodigious leaves.

CONVOLVULUS. There are good morning glories and bad ones. The bad ones are all-too-well-known weeds. The good ones are pure of any weedy tendencies. They like lean soil, little water and hot sun. The best ones are described below.

★**CONVOLVULUS CNEORUM.** A shrub, growing 2 to 4 feet high. Narrow leaves with a sheen of silver and large satin-white morning glories with bands of pale rose. Flowers in May and again in September. Many uses: against houses and other structures, in borders of shrubbery; in dryland plantings with cacti, santolina, artemisia. Kills back if the temperature drops below 20°.

★**CONVOLVULUS MAURITANICUS.** Gray-green trailing plant. Grows about 18 inches high and 5 feet across. Produces lilac-blue or violet-blue morning glories in abundance from June to November. Excellent cascading over rocks and dry banks. Combines well with tall herbs, and with native coastal or desert plants. Hardy in California and the Southeast; touchy in the Northwest; tender in the Northeast.

CONVOLVULUS NITIDUS and **CONVOLVULUS CANTABRICA.** Beautiful, but too small except in the collector's garden.

COPTIS LACINIATA. Glossy, evergreen leaves, three-parted and much-scissored in their outline. For the forest floor community and also as an underplanting for rhododendrons. Height: 4 inches. N. A.

★**CORNUS CANADENSIS.** A creeping dogwood found in woods from Alaska to the Mendocino coast, and eastward across America. The ivory-colored, petal-like bracts which surround the flowers are about an inch across. The flowers are followed by scarlet berries, brightly lacquered and bead-like. Use as a ground cover in cool, moist woods. Slow to establish, but then goes ahead rapidly. Height: 5 inches. N. A.

CORYDALIS. Fumitory. Graceful, fern-leafed plants for mossy rocks and open woodlands. Spurred flowers, usually yellow. Many good species. *C. lutea* makes a haze of yellow on the rock terraces of Italian orchards and vineyards and on many of the older rock gardens in the United States. The plant seeds about, perpetuates itself, and is as good a choice as ever for areas under casual cultivation. About 15 inches high. N. A.

COTONEASTER ADPRESSA. Deciduous, flat mat with red berries. Needs space, prefers starvation soil. Height: 10 inches. N. A.

★**COTONEASTER CONGESTA.** (*Cotoneaster microphylla glacialis.*) Tiny rounded evergreen leaves, winter berries of powdery rose on a fairly slow growing (about 8 inches a year) prostrate shrub. Rock hugging. Will grow in sand or hardpan and makes a thriftier shrub if not overly fed or watered. Height: 10 inches.

★**COTONEASTER DAMMERI.** Very flat mats of evergreen, glossy leaves; white flowers, followed by scarlet berries. This should be given big jobs to do. The prostrate branches root as they grow, and in time one shrub may cover as much ground as there is to be covered. For practical purposes, plants should be set out at 5 or 6 foot intervals. Especially good clothing for massive retaining walls of concrete or stone, covering the contours of either with tidy blankets of green. Height: 6 inches. N. A.

★**COTONEASTER HORIZONTALIS.** A deciduous shrub laden through the winter with masses of scarlet berries. Grows in time to about 4 feet high and 10 feet across in fan-shaped branching habit; can be grouped to form a ground cover over large slopes. Height: 48 inches. N. A.

COTONEASTER MICROPHYLLA THYMIFOLIA. Grows to 3 feet high, 12 feet across. Tiny, dark, evergreen leaves; small, dull rose berries. N. A.

★**CRASSULA MILFORDAE.** (Known for years in the nursery trade as *Crassula,* species Basutoland.) A South African succulent fully hardy to zero in light,

Ceanothus gloriosus

Chamaecyparis pisifera 'Filifera Nana'

Cassiope lycopodioides

Cymbalaria muralis (below)
Hedera helix (above)

Convolvulus mauritanicus

Crocus asturicus
Mat below: Paronychia nivea
Leaves above: Artemisia absinthium

sunny soil. Rapidly expanding mats (to 18 inches across in one year) of pea-green rosettes which turn rich brownish red during a frosty winter. Small pinkish flowers in terminal clusters.

CROCUS. The wild crocus of Mediterranean and Asian mountains are much sprightlier in the rock garden than the puffed-up Dutch hybrids. Wild crocus are readily available from the same bulb suppliers who sell the hybrids. Some of the best and longest lived are: *C. asturicus, C. balansae, C. chrysanthus, C. etruscus, C. sieberi, C. speciosus, C. susianus, C. tomasinianus, C. versicolor.* They like sun and they enjoy having the soil bake dry after their foliage begins to turn yellow. Height: 4 inches. N. A.

CRYPTOMERIA JAPONICA 'VILMORINIANA'. This is one of a number of similar witches' brooms from Japan's cryptomeria forests. The witchlings have their parents' foliage of clubmoss-like form, but reduced in size and compressed into ball or bun shapes. *C. j.* 'Vilmoriniana' takes on a bronzy tint in the winter. Similar forms are *C. j.* 'Monstrosa Nana', *C. j.* 'Globosa Nana', *C. j.* 'Nana', *C. j.* 'Pygmaea'. (There probably are not five different plants to go with these five different names.) *C. j.* 'Bandai-sugi' is a distinct form with gnarled, irregular branches of bluish-green foliage.

The cryptomeria witchlings appeal mostly to collectors. They are, however, valuable bonsai subjects, tolerant of pot culture and transformable by artful pruning into oldish little trees. In pots they may grow as little as a ½ inch a year, compared to 2 or 3 inches in the open ground.

CYCLAMEN. Bun-shaped tubers which give rise to marbled, heart-shaped leaves (typically) and winged flowers of pink, carmine, rose, lavender, or white. They like the filtered shade of oaks, Japanese maples, dogwoods, and other trees whose roots are not greedy. Cyclamen get along well with other refined woodland plants such as deer fern, trillium, and tiarella.

The soil for cyclamen should be rich in leaf mold or peat moss. Plant the tubers with the slightly indented side upward; the tops should be barely covered.

C. neapolitanum is the hardiest species (to 0° or lower). Sows itself; if you are lucky (or skilled) it may develop into a colony. Rose or white flowers, September to November. Several other species are nearly as hardy as *C. neapolitanum* but do not increase as freely. Among them are: *C. atkinsii*, deep green, slightly mottled leaves; light rose pink flowers from January to March. *C. coum*, black-green, round and glossy leaves, without marking; deep crimson-rose flowers in February and March. *C. europaeum*, rounded leaves with a fluted edge; bright crimson flowers with a faint fragrance in July, August, September. *C. persicum*, the florists' cyclamen; hardy in coastal California, but too formal in its cultivated forms for the company of wild flowers. *C. repandum*, ivy-shaped leaves marbled with silver-white; flowers tipped

with deep rose (paler on the wings) in April and May.

CYMBALARIA MURALIS. (*Linaria cymbalaria*.) Kenilworth ivy is a tender little trailing plant with clinging stems of ¾-inch kidney-shaped leaves, edged with round scallops. The tiny but bright lilac-blue flowers hover over the leaves on nearly invisible stems.

Kenilworth ivy is a perennial which behaves as an annual in the North. If frost takes it, seedlings will carry on year after year. A plant of 19th century gardens, it still grows in the cracks of old walls and in the dark shade cast by high old houses.

The seed is not often sold these days, but if you find Kenilworth ivy growing in an old garden, pinch a few pods of seed and scatter them on cold, shady rock work and in the darker corners of your garden. You will enjoy the vagrant self-sufficiency of this plant.

CYPRIPEDIUM. Only collected plants of the ladies' slipper orchids are offered for sale. Growing them from seed would be almost a laboratory procedure. Collecting and marketing these plants, several of which are quite rare, is a dubious economy. Another argument can be advanced that these plants are doomed to extinction, anyway, by agency of the bulldozer and the suburban developer. The arguments of both conservationist and liberal have weight. The plants are on the market. You can decide for yourself.

Cypripediums are not easy to grow under garden conditions. They much prefer (may even demand) natural, leaf-mold soil which is cool, moist, shaded, and untainted with insecticides and fertilizer. There are two species which are comparatively tractable: *C. calceolus pubescens* and *C. reginae* (*C. spectabile*). There are several more which are reasonably impossible.

CYSTOPTERIS BULBIFERA. Berry bladder fern. Narrow divided fronds 2½ feet long of lettuce green. Reproduces itself prolifically by forming bulblets (actually infantile ferns) along the underside of the fronds, which detach themselves and take root. Easy to grow in shady situations. Deciduous. N. A.

CYTISUS. Most brooms are Mediterranean shrubs, conditioned to hot and hungry soil and strong sun. Grow them on large banks with the shrubby convolvulus, lavender, artemisia, hypericum, and helianthemum. Only a few (out of many) are in general cultivation in North America.

★**CYTISUS KEWENSIS.** Wiry green branches to about 6 feet across and 2 feet high. Clusters of cream-white flowers.

★**CYTISUS PRAECOX.** Rounded, gray-green shrub building up to 5 feet in 15 years. A mass of soft yellow flowers in May. Unexcelled for retaining steep banks of sand or gravel, refined enough for a close-up position in the garden. Once established, this broom requires no watering (except in desert locations), stands up to weeds until you find time to pull them. Hardy to approximately 0°.

CYTISUS SCOPARIUS. Scotch broom. A beautiful yellow plague that has engulfed thousands of unguarded acres in the west coast states. But selected forms of it set little seed and offer masses of brilliant, usually parti-colored pea flowers. Occasionally they can be used on large banks and rock works. To avoid a color contest, the different varieties should not be used together. Some varieties and their colors: *C. scoparius* 'Andreanus'—yellow with crimson wings. 'Donard Seedling'— rich reddish-pink and orange. 'Dorothy Walpole' (lacks vigor)—rose-pink with velvety crimson wings. 'Lord Lambourne'—scarlet and cream. 'Pomona'—orange and apricot. 'San Francisco'—red. 'St. Mary's'—pure white.

DABOECIA CANTABRICA. Irish heath. Upright evergreen shrub, to 3 feet. Leaves are dark green and elliptic—much broader than the needle leaves of other kinds of heather. The flowers are globes of purple or white—or a bicolored combination of the two. They nod above the leaves on threadlike stems from June until fall. This graceful plant requires rich, moist, peaty soil. Kills back at 15°.

DAPHNE. Shrubs with sweet scented tubular flowers in the spring. Try them in deep, rich, soft soil—perhaps at the fore of the rhododendron bed. They are said to like lime, but they will grow without it (if they grow at all). Unpredictable plants—sometimes easy, sometimes temperamental.

DAPHNE BLAGAYANA. A flattened shrub which roots along its branches and wanders about for a few feet. Scented white flowers in early spring. Temperamental. Seems to prefer part shade. Has a wayward appeal. Evergreen.

DAPHNE CNEORUM. This is often one of the greatest rock garden shrubs, making itself into a 3-foot high, 5-foot wide mound of deliciously fragrant, vibrant pink flowers in April and May. Just as often it is a bad job, turning pale and sickly after a year or two and then dying off branch by branch. It is not a matter of care—or the lack of it. The *D. cneorum* that is set out on the hardest, driest bank and left to fight with the weeds is often as good (or as bad) as the one that receives every advantage. A great plant for gamblers. Set it out anywhere in the sun or half shade, and hope for luck. Hardy at —20°. Evergreen.

DAPHNE COLLINA. A rounded, clipped-looking evergreen. Attains about 3 feet at a rate of 4 inches a year. Light lilac fragrant flowers. Full sun or afternoon shade in hot areas. Hardy to about 0°.

DAPHNE COLLINA 'NEAPOLITANA'. (*D. neapolitana.*) A hard-to-come-by evergreen which makes a smoothly rounded 3 to 4-foot growth of black-green leaves and fragrant lilac-purple flowers in April. Plants on grafted roots are impermanent. Hardy to about 10°.

DAPHNE MEZEREUM. Poker-stiff stems of magenta flowers in February before the leaves appear, followed by poisonous summer berries of lacquered scarlet. Immensely popular for its early flowers. 3 to 4 feet. Hardy to about 0°. Sun, half-shade.

DAPHNE RETUSA. Dwarf shrub of especially slow growth, lilac flowers and dark sullen foliage. Distinctive. Hardy at 10° below zero. Evergreen.

DELPHINIUM CARDINALE. Stately scarlet flowered perennial for sunny rocks and meadows. Blooms May to July. Not hardy north of its native California. 3 to 6 feet high.

DELPHINIUM CHEILANTHUM 'FORMOSUM'. (*D.* 'Belladonna.') Nothing more blue or more beautiful exists for the rock garden than this 3-foot perennial larkspur. It makes slim stems and airily spaced leaves and flowers. Not long-lived but an easy plant to start and to renew from seed. Light shade. Combine it with light yellow *Aquilegia chrysantha*, white *Campanula persicifolia*. N. A.

DELPHINIUM GRANDIFLORUM. (*D. chinense.*) This is similar to *D.* 'Belladonna' in value and use. Comparatively easy to raise from seed. Height: 24 inches. N. A.

DELPHINIUM NUDICAULE. A 10 to 18-inch scarlet flowered plant from California. (There are also yellow, buff, and brownish-red forms.) Blooms March, June. Start this from seed and give it penstemons and oenotheras for company in the sunny rock garden. Hardy to 10°.

DENNSTAEDTIA PUNCTILOBULA. Hay-scented fern. A vigorous, creeping fern with upthrust, fresh green fronds. Easily established in the woodland and also in sunny places. Deciduous. Height: 18 to 36 inches. N. A.

DIANTHUS. Pinks. Plant for blue-gray foliage, for the scent of cinnamon and clove in ragged-edged flowers, and possibly for remembrance—since they are very old-fashioned flowers. Plant them in sunny soils on either acid or limy soils. All those listed are hardy to below 0°, except the cottage pinks.

The dianthus species are very much confused in both collections and catalogues. Plants or seeds obtained as *D. alpinus, D. glacialis, D. neglectus,* etc. are apt to prove to be hybrids or even to be as far off the mark as *D. deltoides.*

DIANTHUS ALPINUS. A collector's plant with inch-high tuffets of dark, glossy green leaves and practically stemless big and rounded flowers of bright rose in mid- and late summer. Do not confuse with *D. allwoodii* 'Alpinus'. N. A.

★DIANTHUS ARVERNENSIS. An alpine reduction of the Cheddar pink. 3-inch-high mats.

★DIANTHUS DELTOIDES. One plant is capable of seeding itself into a crop 30 feet across in several years. This makes *D. deltoides* inadmissible among the small alpine plants, but a glorious thing for rough rocks and meadows. Its mounds of fine, grassy leaves are about 2 feet across and 16 inches high, covered from May until September with starry, dark pink flowers. Hardy to 0° or lower.

DIANTHUS GRANITICUS. This is like *D. deltoides,* but about half the size, and half as rambunctiously growing and invading.

★DIANTHUS GRATIANOPOLITANUS. (*D. caesius.*) The Cheddar pink, with its trim mounds of blue-green and fragrant, rosy pinks in May and June is a familiar staple of sunny rockeries. One parent of many hybrids, none of which quite equals the rock garden appropriateness of the simple-flowered parent. However, such hybrids as *D.* 'Little Joe' (single red flowers from April to November) and 'Tiny Rubies' (½-inch bright rose carnations) are hard to resist. Height: About 10 inches. N. A.

DIANTHUS NEGLECTUS. Collector's plant. Green tufts of fine grass-like leaves 4 inches high. Flowers are cherry pink on upper side of petals, buff colored on the underside. Blooms June to September. The true plant can always be told from its many imposters by turning the flowers over. Hardy to 0° or lower.

★DIANTHUS PLUMARIUS. This is one parent of the cottage pinks. It is a forgotten plant in gardens, having been displaced by its glamorous offspring. The cottage pinks form masses of spiky blue-gray foliage and white to rose spice-scented flowers, familiar to rock walls and flower beds in most North American towns. The doubles seem rather dressy for inclusion in a garden of wild flowers (if you agree that this is what a rock garden should be). Hardy down to —15° or lower. Height: 12 to 18 inches.

DICENTRA. The bleeding hearts are in keeping with ferns, Solomon's seal, and other vigorous woodland plants in cool, shady places. Their foliage is finely cut, and each flower is shaped like a heart with a drop (formed by the tiny petals) at its tip.

★DICENTRA EXIMIA. A clump-maker without stolons. Seeds about and makes a good show with Virginia bluebells and trilliums. Clustered flowers, bright rose; blue-gray foliage. Height: 12 inches. N. A.

★DICENTRA FORMOSA. The only safe place for this native western forest plant is in a forest, especially beside a creek, where it can be allowed to go its own way and form 50 foot colonies of ferny leaves and light lilac hearts. Blooms from April to June.

For large work in the wild garden, the plant is unbeatable. But keep it far away from anything shyer than bracken. To establish a colony of *Dicentra formosa* quickly and easily, gather seed from wild plants in midsummer, mix it with sand, and broadcast it where you want it to grow.

★DICENTRA OREGANA. Cream-colored hearts tipped with purple; silver-plated foliage. Grows high in the Siskiyou Mountains in old rock slides chinked with humus. In the garden it establishes readily and makes 3-foot mats in sun or shade. Height: 12 inches. N. A.

If *D. oregana, D. formosa,* and *D. eximia* are brought within a bee's flight of each other, hybrid seedlings will come up and will often crowd out their parents. This may be as much a gain as it is a loss. These hybrid plants are stronger than either of their parents (they possess "hybrid vigor") and have a new range of brighter or softer rose and strawberries-in-cream colors. Dr. Marion Ownbey has been selecting and reselecting these hybrid dicentras for many years. His best plants are destined for a place among America's finest contributions to gardening.

★*Dicentra* 'Bountiful' (a Wayside Gardens hybrid) has carmine flowers all summer. Clump-forming, with dark blue-green foliage. For the border as well as the woodland. Height: about 15 inches.

★*Dicentra* 'Bacchanal' originated in England. It is a running, reveling plant, opening cluster after cluster of its rich grape red flowers from spring until fall. Height: about 13 inches.

★**DICENTRA SPECTABILIS.** Bleeding heart. Beloved old-time border perennial. Noble, frond-like leaves and chains of red lockets hanging from horizontal stems in April. For deep, rich soil and part shade. Good with lady fern and sword fern. Height: 48 inches. N. A.

DICHONDRA CAROLINENSIS. (*D. repens.*) Perennial mat of small round leaves, rich dark green and neat. Hardy to 20°. Used in warm climates as a standard substitute for grass lawns.

Flowing up against a composition of stones, dichondra has the restful quality of moss. Start from seed or divisions.

DICKSONIA PUNCTILOBULA. See **DENNSTAEDTIA.**

DIPLACUS LONGIFLORUS. See **MIMULUS.**

DISPORUM. Woodland plants related to lilies. They spread slowly from underground stems, have pendant flowers of chartreuse or ivory and showy berries of orange or red. *D. hookeri* is the showiest in flower. Height: about 9 inches in a sunny spot; about 16 inches in the shade. N. A.

DODECATHEON. The shooting stars are American relatives of *Primula*. Leaves are in basal rosettes, and the shooting star flowers are borne in clusters at the top of naked stalks. Early spring. They require primula conditions in the garden—moist soil, coolness, and half shade. *D. meadia* from the eastern states is pale rose and is the strongest growing, to 16 inches. *D. dentatum* (7 inches) is white. *D. vulgare* (*D. pauciflorum*) 'Red Wings' (9 inches) is bright rose. N. A.

★**DORONICUM.** Big yellow daisies in April and May on low growing masses of dark green leaves. Easily grown in half-shady places. Hardy to 0° or less, but won't take to regions with hot, dry summers. *D. cordifolium* is 9 inches high; *D. clusii* and *D. pardalianches,* 2 feet. N. A.

DOUGLASIA. High alpine cushions for the hopeful collector. *D. vitaliana* has

the strongest constitution, but is chary with its little yellow primroses. N. A.

DRABA. Yellow-flowered pincushions for sunny screes and other areas of especially good drainage in the gardens of most careful gardeners. *Draba olympica,* the strongest of them, makes small mats of dark green, moss-like leaves sprinkled over in April with dainty 4-petalled flowers which tell of mustardy kinship. N. A.

DRYAS DRUMMONDII. The pointed yellow buds never open into flowers. It is justly rare in gardens, but a hybrid of *D. drummondii,* and *D. octopetala,* called *D. suendermannii,* is the Dryas in common cultivation in North America. This is unfortunate. *D. suendermanii* picks up practically none of the yellow color of *D. drummondii* but it does have *drummondii's* coarse elongate pistil and other interior parts. (The *D. drummondii* listed in North American nursery catalogues is almost always *D. suendermannii.*)

DRYAS INTEGRIFOLIA. (*D. tenella*) is a smaller, much more slowly growing *D. octopetala* with smooth-edged leaves.

★**DRYAS OCTOPETALA.** A flat shrub with tiny, half-evergreen oak-like leaves. The June flowers, small white anemones on 2-inch stems, are followed by globes of silvery-tailed seeds as attractive as the flowers.

Will grow 10 feet across in as many years. The flat growth habit makes this a valuable cover for utilitarian stonework. Takes any well-drained, reasonably fertile soil, but will not survive drought. Hardy to —0°.

★**DUCHESNEA INDICA.** This is practically a strawberry, with rampant, loose-growing mats of strawberry leaves, yellow flowers, and attractive but tasteless red strawberries held point-uppermost above the leaves. An easy, dependable cover for wild, shady banks. Height: 9 inches. N. A.

EDRAIANTHUS. Tuft-making plants with violet flowers in clustered heads. Closely related to campanulas. Better than good for the collector's garden. Sun. N. A.

EPIGAEA REPENS. The well-remembered trailing arbutus of eastern American woods. Mats of egg-sized, egg-shaped leaves and, in the early spring, clusters of pale pink stars, exhaling an innocent sweetness which might be distilled into a perfume for debutantes.

Trailing arbutus is not really difficult to establish in cool, shady places in soil which is more leaf mold than mineral. Hardy to 0° or below. *E. asiatica,* with larger, pinker flowers can be seen in the temple gardens of Japan and in a few Seattle gardens. Hardy to about 10°.

EPILOBIUM. Either too big and weedy or too small and fragile to be of much account in most gardens. *E. angustifolium* (the fireweed) can, however, be established in wild acreage for its mantall stems topped with long, loose clus-

ters of rosy flowers. Bees turn these into a most delicate honey. N. A.

E. fleischeri is well worthwhile to the collector for its summer flowers of satiny rose on foot-high stems. Hardy to 20°.

★**EPIMEDIUM.** Shade plants of graceful, airy aspect, with divided leaves and strange-lovely little four-part flowers in open sprays in spring. These are conspicuously spurred in the case of *E. grandiflorum* (*E. macranthum*) and star-like in the case of *E. pinnatum*. Their flowers, and especially their handsome foliage, make exceptionally long-lived cut material. Leaves picked close to the ground when mature will last 2 months in water.

Epimediums make graceful ground covers in shady places. Under the shelter of evergreen trees, their leaves stay fresh all winter. N. A.

EPIMEDIUM ALPINUM RUBRUM. Small, dark red flowers with short, reddish-white spurs.

EPIMEDIUM DIPHYLLUM. This will be found listed under its more proper name, *Aceranthus diphyllus.*

★**EPIMEDIUM GRANDIFLORUM.** (*E. macranthum.*) Grows 9 to 16 inches high—lower in sun and dryish soil, higher in moist soil and shade. Reddish-violet flowers. Variety 'Niveum' has pure white flowers. Variety 'Violaceum' has reddish-violet flowers with shorter spurs. New forms or hybrids of this species with larger flowers of white, bright rose-violet, and pale yellow have come recently from Japan where several enthusiasts are devoting their best gardening efforts to *Epimedium*. Two new epimediums are *E.* 'Snow Queen' and *E.* 'Violet Queen'.

EPIMEDIUM PINNATUM. Small, roughly star-shaped flowers of bright yellow. Variety 'Elegans' has larger, more numerous flowers. (*E. sulphureum* of catalogues probably is *E. p.* 'Elegans'.)

★**ERICA CARNEA.** Spring heath. A dense, finely branched mat of dark green needles covered from January to March with clusters of bottle-shaped flowers of white, rose-pink, and bright rose. Best used as a ground cover in sunny, well-drained soil rich in humus.

A massed planting of *Erica carnea* in the rock garden recalls the meadows of wind-clipped *Cassiope* and *Phyllodoce* in the mountains of Western America. *Erica carnea* is a community plant in nature and needs to insulate its shallow roots with a solid mass of branches as soon as possible.

Obtain small plants and space them closely enough so that the foliage will interlock in a season or two. This will mean planting the rose colored varieties about a foot apart and the vigorous variety, 'Springwood' ('Springwood White') 18 inches to 2 feet apart.

As a ground cover *Erica carnea* tends to die out in its older portions after 15 years or so. This tendency can be alleviated by clipping the branches immediately after flowering and topdressing with mixed sand and peat moss.

'Springwood' is the strongest-growing, longest-lived variety. It is a prostrate grower, requiring very little pruning. The flowers are large and white with brown tips. 'King George' and 'Ruby Glow' are among the best of the richly rose-colored varieties. 'Vivellii' is often short lived. 'Snow Queen' is a slow-growing white dwarf. *Erica carnea* sustains frost damage at about 10°, but requires a cool winter rest.

ERICA CILIARIS. A leggy, gray-leafed heather, 2 or 3 feet high. Spiky summer flowers of white, pink or rose. Needs much water. Prune in early spring. Hardy to 10°.

Erica 'Dawn' is an entertaining hybrid between *E. ciliaris* and *E. tetralix*. In the spring the new foliage comes out carmine, lightens to orange and yellow, then turns green. The dark rose flowers appear from June to October.

ERICA CINEREA. Summer-flowering heathers of soft, finely textured, dark green foliage and flowers ranging in color from white through soft pink and bright rose to magenta-purple. There is a remarkable foliage form, 'Golden Drop'—a compact 6-inch-high shrub, golden yellow during the growing season, rich orange in fall, deep copper-bronze in winter. 'Golden Drop' and the rest of the many named selections of *Erica cinerea* are often seen in poor condition after they reach an age of only 5 to 7 years. To avoid this premature old age, give them extra water and a heavy pruning immediately after flowering; this pruning actually seems to strengthen weakly shrubs. Frost-damaged at 10°.

ERICA PURPURASCENS 'DARLEYENSIS.' (*E. darleyensis*.) A hybrid of *Erica carnea* and *E. mediterranea*, this old-time, washy-lilac, flowering shrub blooms from November until April, the strongest and hardiest of the winter flowering heathers, and has the longest flowering season of all. Unfortunately, its flower color lacks warmth in comparison with the selected forms of *E. carnea*. Use it for its great toughness under poor growing conditions. It will grow in clay soil or sand and once it is established it will get along with practically no watering. There is a white flowered hybrid of *E. carnea* and *E. mediterranea* called ★*E.* 'Darleyensis Alba' which has the same toughness, and long-flowering season, plus good, pure white flowers.

ERICA SUBDIVARICATA. (*E. persoluta*.) Two feet. White or rose flowers. This and all the heathers which follow are safest in the orange belt. *E. cruenta*: 3 feet. Tubular, blood-red flowers in fall and winter. *E. hyemalis*: 3 feet. Inch-long tubular flowers of white-tipped pink in winter. There is a white variety, 'Alba'. *E.* 'Felix Faure': Low, compact plant with rose-pink flowers. *E. mammosa* 'John McLaren': Compact growth, pink flowers.

ERICA TETRALIX. Two feet of woolly gray-green foliage, and pendant pink bells of luscious sugared or iced appearance. The shrub is not strong, requires very moist peaty soil, afternoon shade, and pruning in April. Flowers constantly from June until frost. Hardy to 0° and below.

★**ERICA VAGANS.** The Cornish heath flowers from July to October. There are three well-known varieties, sturdy shrubs of rounded habit and dark green needles. 'Mrs. D. F. Maxwell' grows to 3 or 4 feet, has clear dark pink flowers. 'St. Keverne' grows to 2 feet or so and has clear, medium pink flowers, 'Lyonesse' is white flowering, 4 to 5 feet high. All three will take hard shearing in April. If this is done every spring they can be kept at half their usual height, but with a considerable loss of grace. Hardy to 0° or lower.

ERIGERON. Distinguished from *Aster* only by the attachment of the rays (the petal-like outer flowers of the blossom head), which are in several rows like double eyelashes. Those of *Aster* are in one row. *Erigeron* is a large genus containing a number of summer-blooming alpine daisies which are collectors' plants of the first quality. N. A.

ERIGERON COMPOSITUS. A 6-inch dome of split and lobed leaves, lavender or white daisies.

ERIGERON GLAUCUS. A plant of sea cliffs and sea sands in Oregon and California. It is a succulent, foot-high tuft with violet daisies, whose free-seeding propensities make the plant especially suitable for the meadow garden. It blooms from April to August.

ERIGERON LEIOMERUS. A Rocky Mountain alpine 4 inches high. Pale blue flowers of watery purity and freshness.

ERIGERON PINNATISECTUS. A high alpine from Colorado with cut leaves and large violet daisies. Height: 8 inches.

ERIGERON SPECIOSUS. Two feet high, with lilac-blue flowers. Turned loose in the alpine meadow, it will seed about, making friendly company with tall columbines and oenotheras.

ERINUS ALPINUS. Four-inch high tufts of small spatulate leaves and racemes of purple, rose, or white in early spring. Likes crevices between shady rocks in a garden of miniatures. March-April. Hardy to 15°.

ERODIUM. Plants closely related to pelargonium and geranium with filigree leaves (typically) and expressive flower faces, reminiscent of gibbons. They like sunny hot rocks and southern gardens. Several of the perennial species grown by collectors in North America find their way into the trade from time to time.

ERODIUM CHAMAEDRYOIDES. From rocky islands in the Mediterranean. An inch-high mat of tiny scalloped leaves and white or pink flowers with rose veins. A slow, refined ground cover in southwestern gardens; a scree plant in the Northwest. Frost-damaged at 20°.

ERODIUM MANESCAVII. Foot-high ferny tufts and large, bright magenta-rose geraniums. Erodium has a catapult device for slinging its seeds into new and surprising places. *E. manescavii* is representative of that huge category of rock garden plants—the benign weeds. This is a group of untamable, unconfinable plants including many of the stalwart potentillas, columbines, evening primroses, aethionemas, and a hundred others.

If the rock gardener will accept these plants on their own terms, letting them come up where they will and pulling those that he does not want, he will find them among the most satisfactory plants for the large rock garden. He may be chastened to learn that the plants which plant themselves usually look more comfortable and harmonious than those he himself set out with all his art and craft.

ERYNGIUM. Huge architectonic or sculptural constructions of rigid, spiny leaves (like Mexican sun-discs of tin) mounting in geometrical order on stiff, dividing and redividing stems and surmounted by teasel-like flowers. The whole plant—stems, leaves and flowers—is steel blue, amethystine, or silver, depending upon the species. Eryngiums are best grown from seed and set out when small in sunny places in deep light soil. First-rate for dry land gardening. The following two species are hardy to 0° or below; *E. amethystinum*—3 feet of blue; *E. giganteum*—a silver 4 to 6-footer with especially broad leaf discs.

ERYSIMUM KOTSCHYANUM. A mat-forming wallflower about 6 inches high with dark yellow four-petaled flowers. Successfully tried in Southern California, the Northwest and the Great Lakes District.

ERYTHRAEA. See **CENTAURIUM.**

ERYTHRONIUM. The dog's-tooth violets are woodland corms. Their strap-shaped leaves are glossy green, often with lighter and darker marbling. The flowers are lily-like and nodding. The European species, *E. dens-canis* (rose or purple flowers) is the best adapted to gardens, seeding about and also increasing by corm offsets. Of the American species, *E. revolutum* (rose pink), *E. hendersonii* (lavender), and *E. oregonum* (*E. giganteum*) (yellow) will make flower-rich colonies in the gardens of skillful growers, and *E. tuolumnense* (deep yellow) will make large but sparse flowered clumps. *E. montanum*, the magnificent white fawn lily which covers acres in Western mountain pastures has so far proved impossible to grow in lowland gardens.

EUPHORBIA. This genus includes not only poinsettia but also a host of succulent, deserty-looking plants, verging on the grotesque as desert plants do but brilliantly yellow with unreal-looking flowers (which are actually floral leaves). They are not harmonious plants in green, forested landscapes, but they look just right in dry, stony areas.

EUPHORBIA MYRSINITES. A blue-leaved, 15-inch, running plant with flattened flower heads. N. A.

EUPHORBIA WULFENII. Grows to 4 feet high. Flat clusters of chartreuse-yellow in early spring. In a container placed against a wall it is fully as arresting as a contemporary sculpture. Hardy to 0°, but does best in warm climates.

★**FELICIA AMELLOIDES.** (Often sold as *Agathaea coelestis.*) Blue daisies all summer (into the winter in warm climates) on a 3-foot upright bush of dark green leaves. Frost-damaged at about 20°.

★**FESTUCA OVINA 'GLAUCA'.** Blue fescue. A fine-bladed blue-gray grass; forms tufts but does not spread. Use it as a ground cover, in pattern planting, as an underplanting beneath blue and gray needled conifers, as a container plant, or in combination with stones and desert plants. Thrives in both coast and desert climates. Give it full sun or half shade and perfect drainage. The tufts build up to a shaggy 16 inches if they are left alone. Shear them occasionally to keep them lower and neater. Divide in the early spring. Hardy at 5°.

FICUS PUMILA. (*F. repens.*) The creeping fig has adhesive branches which will climb rockwork and walls of concrete, brick, wood, or stone—pressing broad, pointed leaves tightly against any of these surfaces. In season, large inedible figs hang from the vine. On a starvation diet, creeping fig makes a tracery of branches. Well fed, it becomes a heavy, rather coarse curtain. Native to Japan, where the tiny-leafed variety 'Minima' is set to climbing stone lanterns. Winter damaged at 20°-25°.

★**FILIPENDULA PURPUREA.** (*Spiraea palmata.*) A bog and woodland plant with large maple-like leaves in a clump, and 2½-foot flower stems spraying at the top into a hand of raspberry rose flowers in July and August. N. A.

★**FRAGARIA CHILOENSIS.** Wild strawberry. This dark green strawberry, native to sand beaches on the west coast of North and South America, is one of the most useful—and most used—ground covering plants. The glossy, 3-part leaves form dense carpets 3 to 6 inches high in sun, 8 inches high in shade. White strawberry flowers dot the carpet in the spring. The fruit is produced sparingly, if at all.

Foliage texture has a great affinity for woodland settings and for wood itself. Wild strawberry can be used in place of a lawn at the edge of a grove of trees, or in beds against wooden steps or fences. It serves stone just as well. On steep clay banks it can be used to form a mesh of growth protective against washouts. On sea sand it is a natural binder. All told, this strawberry is probably the most widely useful of all the plants classified as "rock plants" in the broad definition of this book.

Start wild strawberry from divisions set out in fall or early spring 12 to 18 inches apart and watered frequently until growth begins. The closer spacing will produce a solid carpet at the end of the first summer; the wider spacing

will take two years to fill in. Although *F. chiloensis* is adaptable to various climates, its limitations are set by extreme summer heat and dryness, and by winter temperatures of about 10°.

F. californica, F. virginiana, and the other wild strawberries can be naturalized in woodland gardens for their three-part evergreen leaves and tangy fruit.

★**FRANCOA RAMOSA.** A lushly leafed evergreen plant related to saxifrage. Two to 3 foot stalks of pink or white flowers in long, narrow clusters. Grows easily in shade and spreads into large clumps. Combine with acanthus, tall ferns, and foxglove. Frost-damaged at about 15°.

FRANKENIA. Close and wiry carpets with tiny gray leaves and starry pink flowers all summer. The two species in cultivation, *F. capitata* 'Laevis' (*F. laevis*) and *F. thymifolia,* are much alike. *F. capitata* 'Laevis' forms broader, stronger carpets. Both like sun and dryish (but not droughty) soil. Hardy to about 10°. Height: 2 inches.

FRITILLARIA. Our native species are hardly growable under garden conditions. *F. meleagris,* the guinea hen flower of Europe with checkerboard-patterned, chocolaty-maroon flowers is as curious as any, and as easily grown as scilla in the spring woodland. Height: 12 inches, N. A.

GALANTHUS. The snowdrops are spring bulbs, white-belled with a rim of green. They flower in earliest spring and can be planted beneath deciduous shrubbery where their bells open before the shrubs come into leaf. Hardy to below zero. Height: 8 inches. N. A.

GALAX APHYLLA. Wand flower. A handsome foliage plant for cool woodland conditions. The leaves are about 4 inches across, rounded and leathery with a high gloss. In the winter they turn russet. The flowers which give the plant its common name are not brilliant, but dainty. They are small, white, and densely produced in a narrow cluster. Height: 12 inches. N. A.

GAULTHERIA. Mat or mound-making shrubs, smallish relatives of rhododendron and often planted beneath their taller kin to form a protective ground cover. Gaultheria, however, can hold the garden stage all by itself. These are handsome plants with polished leathery evergreen leaves, delicate urn-shaped or orbed flowers, and berry-like fruits of white, scarlet, blue, or blue-black.

★**GAULTHERIA CUNEATA.** A mat of procumbent branches 8 inches high. Narrow, inch-long leaves widen from their base for three-quarters of their length, and then close in to a sharp but abrupt tip. Wine red stems. White urns in June and white berries. Full sun or half shade. Hardy to 0° or a little lower.

GAULTHERIA ITOANA. Like a half-sized *G. cuneata,* with ½-inch-long leaves. Forms procumbent mats 4 inches high. Full sun or half shade. Hardy to 0°.

★**GAULTHERIA MIQUELIANA.** Spreads about strongly by stolons and comes up with twiggy 8-inch tufts of small olive green oval leaves, deeply netted with a crackle pattern like the glaze of old pottery. White or pinkish urns in April; white, corrugated fruits in the summer. Hardy to 0°.

GAULTHERIA NUMMULARIOIDES. Small, heart-shaped leaves carried flat in alternate rows along prostrate branches 4 to 6 inches long. The plant is reminiscent of certain ferns—the common house plant, *Pellaea rotundifolia,* for one. Pink flowers in June, then black berries. Morning sun, afternoon shade. Frost-damaged at 15° or 20°.

★**GAULTHERIA PROCUMBENS.** Wintergreen. Two to 6-inch-high mats of roundish, stiff, leathery leaves. Pink urns followed by scarlet fruits from fall until mid-spring. The leaves yield oil of wintergreen. A woodlander of wide distribution in our eastern states.

★**GAULTHERIA SHALLON.** Salal. Native from Southern Alaska to California, on the westward flanks of the mountains and along the seacoast. The dominant undergrowth from Western Oregon northward through its range, this bush of large, deep green, roundish leaves grows a windclipped 16 inches along the coast, an open, angular 6 feet in the Douglas fir and coast redwood forests. Salal has showy loose clusters of orbed flowers carried in pendant rows. Blue-black berries follow a month later, in June and July.

In the garden, salal has top value as a ground cover and as a masking shrub for massive rockwork. Planted in full sun, salal grows to its coast height; in deep garden shade it becomes head-high as it does in the forests. In an exposed position salal may sustain frost damage at 0°, even in its native range.

"Brush pickers" on Washington's Olympic Peninsula, in northern California, and in the Northwest harvest salal branches for the nation's florists. Carload shipments go east to New York and other markets, where they are sold as "lemon leaves". You may find salal in a Miami hotel dining room or in the salon of an ocean liner.

GAULTHERIA WARDII. Grows 4 feet high in its native Tibet. Long cane-like stems come arching out of the ground, lengthening as much as 16 inches a year. The bark, yellow-green when new, has a coat of light brown down. Sun turns the bark wine red. The dark green leaves are willow shaped, 3 to 4 inches long, ¾-inch wide, with a long tapered point. White urn flowers and azure fruits.

Best suited to shade gardens in the azalea belt of the Southeast and the fog belt around San Francisco. In the north *G. wardii* kills to the ground at 15° or 20°, but comes back strongly.

GENISTA. Broom. (Also see *Cytisus.*) The brooms come in a range of sizes to suit any rock garden. They prefer deep, sandy soil into which they drive 6 feet of cord-like roots. Hot sun helps them set masses of golden yellow pea flowers.

They must have a little moisture in the soil—but never much. Hardy to 0°. Generally adaptable over North America. Ideal for southwestern gardens.

GENISTA DELPHINENSIS. A diminutive of *G. sagittalis,* 4 inches high and 24 inches across in 10 years.

GENISTA HORRIDA. Wicked spines on a gray-green mound 15 inches high, 30 inches across in 10 years. As golden yellow as the others, but needs heat for best bloom.

★**GENISTA PILOSA.** Perfectly prostrate carpets. Branches are long and thin, gray-green, decently leafy, and spineless. Along these spidery branches, yellow flowers come out all at once, explosively, in May.

Let this shrub trail limply over large rocks or use it as a ground cover. Occasional foot traffic will not hurt it. Grows about 4 inches high and 7 feet across in 10 years.

★**GENISTA RADIATA.** A soft and plumy looking bush, rounded, finely branched, and gray-green. About 3 feet high and 6 feet across in 10 years. Golden yellow flowers in May. Can be planted to form solid bays of foliage on poor, dry soil. The billowing softness of this shrub imparts the qualities of calm and composure to the severest landscape.

GENISTA SAGITTALIS. Odd flat leafless branches make foot-high masses that resemble a coarse grass. The abundant, showy flowers appear in June in the south, July in the north. Valuable in a desert setting. Spreads about 9 inches a year.

GENISTA SILVESTRIS 'PUNGENS'. (*G. dalmatica.*) A foot-high mound of prickly green wires completely hidden in June by golden yellow flowers. Twelve inches high, 28 inches across in 10 years.

GENISTA VILLARSII. On the order of *G. pilosa,* but procumbent instead of prostrate, and much slower. Nine inches high and 24 inches across in 10 years.

GENTIANA. Gentians are blue-flowered perennials that serve as a measuring standard for the color. But the masses of gentian blue that are the autumn fame of gardens in Scotland are almost unknown in North America. We lack the necessary summer dullness and coolness over much of our country. Gentians demand constant moisture in the ground, on the surface of the ground, and in the air—all through the growing season. The areas in North America that can meet these conditions are limited to the fog belt along the Pacific coast from the Monterey Peninsula northward to Alaska, and to mountainous areas inland where there is high rainfall and prevailing coolness. Even here, gentians appreciate light shade and extra water during the rare hot days.

Sometimes the essential climate conditions of coast or mountains exist elsewhere in microclimates—in especially favored gardens or natural acreage protected from the prevailing climate of the area. A microclimate to the liking of gentians exists in a sunny glade in a woodland garden where the surrounding trees help keep the humidity high. If a small stream runs through the glade, moistening the soil, conditions may be optimum for the robust growth and flowering of gentians and a great variety of rare primulas, saxifrages, and other hard-to-please wild flowers. But the moisture in the soil must never be stagnant—these plants want fresh water percolating through the soil.

Special devices and structures have been invented for the growing of gentians, primulas, and other even more delicate plants in unfavored climates.

GENTIANA ACAULIS. Ground-hugging tufts of dark green, glossy leaves, and stubby stems bearing huge flaring urns of deep, yet glowing, cobalt blue. In the scree gardens in the full sun of Edinburgh these can be seen 500 at a time in May, and in scattered numbers during the summer and fall. In gardens where the plant grows and flowers with extravagant ease, it is even used to make carpets of blue at the edge of flower borders. Yet in other gardens next door to these, *Gentiana acaulis* may grow well but never flower. Why, no one really knows—everyone who grows it seems to have a contradictory theory. Most of these theories are sound and will grow good gentians—which may or may not flower. According to Farrer there are also some really inventive schemes for success with *G. acaulis,* such as burying an old leather boot under it. (Remember that this is a famous plant which has accrued a whole parcel of legends and lore.) However, the standard procedure is to grow *Gentiana acaulis* in rich loam on the acid side, give it a sunny place, and water it well.

GENTIANA ANDREWSII. The closed gentian of damp woods in the northeastern United States and Canada adapts fairly easily to lightly shaded gardens over much of the United States. It is tall growing, with typical dark, glossy green gentian foliage. The dark blue flowers in July and August are attractive but not fully satisfying. They stay closed, never getting beyond the state of budhood.

GENTIANA CALYCOSA. Type of the western American gentians. Often seen in mountain meadows at the edge of icy streams. The plant is upright growing to 1 foot, with dark blue, bell-shaped flowers, singly or several in a cluster atop the flower stems from July to September. In the garden it needs much water, but good drainage. *G. oregana, G. bisetaea,* and *G. setigera* are similar westerners.

GENTIANA DECUMBENS. The namesake of a distinct group of Himalayan gentians, all closely related and much alike in appearance. They have a single rosette of long, elliptical leaves, flower stems about a foot high, and bell-shaped flowers of dark purplish-blue from June to August. They are relatively easy to grow and to flower, adapting to much hotter, drier conditions than other types of gentians. *G. olivieri* (*G. dahurica*) and *G. gracilipes*

Gaultheria miqueliana

Genista sagittalis

Erigeron glaucus

are other members of this group. In the United States *G. gracilipes* is usually distributed as *G. purdomi*.

GENTIANA SEPTEMFIDA. Offers hope for gentian blue over much of America. It has been tested with full success in San Francisco, Seattle, and New York. Almost any soil and position in the garden will suit it as long as it receives plenty of water.

In July and August a well-established *G. septemfida* sends up dozens of flower stems about a foot high, each holding a clutch of bells which break and recurve at their rims into five starpoint lobes. The bell of the flower is dark blue outside, dilute blue inside. The starpoints are liberally covered with small green dots.

G. septemfida will grow in full sun in soil pockets in the rock garden or in primula conditions (half-shaded, peaty beds).

GENTIANA SINO-ORNATA. Heads a group of Himalayan species which have narrow, grasslike leaves in divisible clumps, and trumpet-shaped autumn flowers with conspicuous bands of green and darker blue on a blue ground.

G. sino-ornata is not difficult in a cool, moist loam. Its relatives, *G. farreri*, *G. veitchiorum*, and others are touchy plants which you can attempt in the foggy dew of the West Coast.

GERANIUM. Cranesbill. These are the true geraniums; the garden plant called geranium is in the genus *Pelargonium*. True geraniums include 4-foot meadow plants, 3-inch alpine scree plants, and plants of every size between.

The taller geraniums are easy to grow in sun or shade in almost any soil. They exhibit considerable independence about planting their own seedlings, which makes them most useful in woodlands or wildish places, or in not-too-exact groupings of tall perennials.

The smaller geraniums are among the most rewarding plants that grow in rock gardens. All those listed here (with noted exceptions) are growable across North America wherever the temperature does not drop much below 0°.

GERANIUM CINEREUM. An alpine tuft of gray-green foliage with lilac-veined white flowers in June and July. This will endure frost to about 0°, but prefers a warmer winter. The related *G. argenteum* (silver leaves) and another alpine, *G. napuligerum* (pink flowers) need a dryish winter with only light frosts to be at their best. All three are collector's plants of distinction.

GERANIUM DALMATICUM. An outstanding plant for small gardens of almost any character. It makes a 6-inch-high clump of small glossy, lobed leaves. Rounded flowers of clear shell pink open in June and July. Not fussy about soil or shade-sun relativity, but likes a fertile loam and a sunny spot. Divide the plant every 3 years in early spring.

★GERANIUM MACRORRHIZUM. Bright rose-pink flowers from May to July, maple-like leaves. It is 2 feet high and seeds itself into hundreds among rocks and in woodlands.

★GERANIUM PYLZOWIANUM. A rose-flowered summer blooming miniature which runs about forming dense mats of little tubers underground and delicately cut leaves above. The leaves and tubers invade every plant in their path, and soon have a large area to themselves. These are habits to be condoned and to be made use of only as we might condone and use *Dicentra formosa*—in the wild garden.

GERANIUM RENARDII. Beautiful broad leaves, netted and felted. Summer flowers are white with pale blue veins. Likes southern winters better than northern.

★GERANIUM SANGUINEUM 'ALBUM'. Stands an open, wiry 18 inches; has small leaves of birdfoot cleft and white flowers from May to September. Easy and hardy in rock gardens, woodlands, and borders.

★GERANIUM SANGUINEUM 'PROSTRATUM'. (*G. s.* 'Lancastriense'.) From the windy coast of Lancashire. Makes a dense, rounded bush about 1 foot high and 2 or 3 feet across. Flowers (June to August) are crepe-textured, white with rose-pink veining.

GEUM CHILOENSE. An evergreen perennial with handsome compound leaves, lobed and corrugated. It is often sold as *G. coccineum*, which is a smaller, hardier species with red, rather than red-orange flowers. Most modern geums are hybrids between the two. Orange-scarlet flowers appear periodically from May until frost, but their color is too commanding to combine with the majority of flowers. A harmony can be made of this and the apricot-tinted yellow of *Meconopsis cambrica* in the sunny border or woodland. *G.* 'Waight's Brilliant' is a 4 to 6-inch rock garden dwarf with the flowers of *G. coccineum*. The two famous geums of the Alps, *G. reptans* and *G. montanum*, are of little account in the garden. N. A.

★GLOBULARIA. The globe flowers of Mediterranean Europe are distinctive for their puffs of gray-blue flowers. *G. cordifolia* is the strongest species, a mat maker over warm, dryish rocks. It carries countless globes in May and June. Hardy to 0°.

★GYPSOPHILA REPENS. The rock garden representative of the mist-fine bloom clouds known as baby's breath. *G. repens* is compressed into mats of grayish leaves; these are topped in summer by airy, 6 to 9-inch high clusters of tiny pink or white stars.

The deceiving delicacy of its appearance, combined with the actual stoutness of its constitution, places this species among the great rock plants. Flowers from May to September in the sunny rock garden. N. A.

HEBE. New Zealand shrubs formerly classed with *Veronica*. Farrer, in one of his best passages, blasts them to perdition: "repellent leathern bushes with hard dead-looking foliage often of a metallic cast-iron look, or else with no apparent leaves at all, but scaly stiff branches and tentacles like gigantic club-mosses on some pantomime scene of the Lower Regions . . . . . plants that are no plants, but lifeless imitation of living things, forged by Hephaestus out of dark metals in the underworld."

But before Farrer's poltergeist sends Charon around to claim all these plants from our midst, let's examine them objectively. Some of the *Hebes* are strange indeed to our eyes, but there is a beauty in this strangeness which is the norm in their wonderful world of Australia and New Zealand, where birds, plants, and animals have evolved in isolation into living forms which turn our thoughts these days more to outer space than to the Lower Regions.

The other-worldly beauty of *Hebe* fits well into the American southwest setting of bright stones and sky. They like the heat and winter dryness there, but require watering through the growing season.

The following species and varieties are hardy enough to grow in our northern states as well as our southern, as long as the winter temperature does not drop below 0°. The hebes must have sun and alpine drainage.

HEBE BUXIFOLIA. A rounded 18-inch to 3-foot shrub with glossy yellow-green leaves approximately the size and shape of the leaves of some boxwoods. The May and June flower clusters are small, white, and disappointing. *H. buxifolia* is a fast-growing, fast-deteriorating shrub. Prune it after flowering to slow down its progress toward legginess.

HEBE CUPRESSOIDES. Balloons up to 5 or 6 feet in as many years, and then falls apart. But it has a dwarf of much better habit, *H. c.* 'Nana' (*H. c.* 'Minima'), a scaly-leaved, gray-green shrub like a witches' broom of some unknown cypress. The branches even have a resinous smell when rolled between the fingers. Grows rounded, matures at 7 years, and is then 16 inches high, 24 inches across. Grown for foliage rather than for the insignificant flowers. Renew it from cuttings taken in July and August.

★HEBE DECUMBENS. Similar to *H. pinguifolia* 'Pagei', but the flowers come about 2 weeks earlier than those of 'Pagei' and the clusters are not quite so ample.

★HEBE ELLIPTICA 'AUTUMN GLORY'. A pale green foliaged shrub, usually about 2 feet high and 3 feet across. Purple flower spikes from July to November—a welcome time.

HEBE LYCOPODIOIDES. One of the "whipcord hebes." Like other members of this group (*H. hectori*, for instance), it is an upright 1- to 2-foot shrub with scale-leaved branches which closely resemble tightly braided leather, such as riding crops are made of. Starry white flowers push forth from the branch tips in New Zealand, but not in the northern United States (we can expect better in the Southwest). *H. lycopodioides*, 15 inches high with brownish yellow-green branches, is sometimes sold as a dwarf conifer—to cover up for its lack of flowers, perhaps.

★**HEBE PINGUIFOLIA 'PAGEI'.** A spreading shrub with ½-inch blue-gray leaves edged with chalky rose. June flowers in showy white masses. Grows 4 feet across, 9 inches high in 5 years. Adventitious roots appear along the stems during the fall and winter. Cut self-rooting branches into 6 to 8-inch lengths and insert them where you want them to grow. You can increase one shrub into a bank-covering carpet in a few years.

HEBE TRAVERSII. Dark green leaves and poker-stiff branches in a sheared-looking dome. In summer the white flowers, carried in full and gracefully loosened spires, redeem the shrub's topiary primness.

★**HEDERA HELIX.** The many forms of English ivy make larger or smaller clothing for banks of soil and walls of brick or stone, for woodlands, and for dark awkward strips of ground between houses and property lines. The plant is undemanding, tolerant of a great range of soil and exposures, and forgiving of neglect. It requires only an annual pruning in the spring to keep it from mounding up.

The type with dark, hand-sized leaves is rather too coarse in growth and texture for close-up areas, but some of the smaller forms such as *H. h.* 'Hahn's Self-Branching' are easily contained as edging along walls and steps. For really small work there is *H. h.* 'Conglomerata Nana'. Ivy is hardy to 0° or lower.

★**HELIANTHEMUM NUMMULARI-UM.** The garden sun roses are foot-high, mat-forming shrublets, rather like *Cistus* in miniature. The leaves are sometimes grayish, sometimes dark green and glossy, always small and refined. There are many forms; the cup-like flowers come in colors as bright and variable as a scoop of hard candies—lemon, peach, apricot, rose, terra cotta, white, burnt orange, scarlet. They are produced in extravagant quantities in April, May, or June, depending on climate. If the shrubs are cut back severely after flowering, there will be a floral encore in the fall.

Use *Helianthemum* to cover sunny rocks or as a ground cover on meager soil. To avoid garish effects, don't plant too many of the color forms together. One may be adequate. Hardy to 0° or below.

★**HELLEBORUS.** Winter flowering woodland plants with broadly palmate leaves divided into wide-spread fingers. The leaves are evergreen and of definite landscape value beneath trees and under shrubs. They have white flowers of noble size (*H. niger*), large maroon, wine, rose or pinkish flowers (*H. orientalis*), or small greenish yellow flowers in clusters (*H. corsicus*).

A rich, sandy loam produces the largest flowers. Plants should be set out when small in their permanent position, since their massive roots resent disturbance. Dividing the hellebores is an experiment which can be conducted in the earliest spring. Hardy to 0° or lower, but best adapted to cool summer areas.

★**HELLEBORUS CORSICUS.** Three-foot stems of saw-edged leaves. Yellow-green flower cups last from March to May and bring the bees. The foliage is striking. There are three leaflets arranged in a palm about 6 inches across. In various lights these leaflets seem to have tints of yellow, gray, or blue overlying the basic green. They are leathery and waxen to the touch.

HELLEBORUS FOETIDUS. The leaves of this hellebore are divided into very slender leaflets. Eighteen inches high. Clustered flower cups of green, rimmed with rose, from February to April.

★**HELLEBORUS NIGER.** Christmas rose. A strong plant of this grows 18 inches high and 2 feet across. The dark green leaves are divided into toothed leaflets. The buds come up white, one or two to a stem in December or January. They open to cup form and then to plate-like flatness. These big platters light up the dull winter days for about 6 weeks, slowly changing from white to rose to green. Variety 'Praecox' has smaller flowers which open in the fall. The names *H. niger* 'Maximus', *H. n.* 'Altifolius', and *H. n.* 'Major' are applied to plants of the typical form with especially large, pure white flowers.

★**HELLEBORUS ORIENTALIS.** Lenten rose. Large open flowers, several to a stem, in February, March, and April. The numerous varieties and hybrids of this vary in flower color from greenish white to pink, rose-purple, and maroon.

HELXINE SOLEIROLII. Baby's tears. A ground cover for shady, ferny places. In texture, *Helxine* is like a fragile *Selaginella* moss and in form it is a rapidly spreading mat 2 or 3 inches high. The plant is in keeping with watersides and woodlands. It can't take foot traffic, however, and because of its extreme invasiveness it must be kept far away from small plants. Probably not hardy below 20°.

HEPATICA ACUTILOBA and **HEPATICA AMERICANA.** (*H. triloba.*) These two Eastern American mountaineers and woodlanders are easily established in damp, shady places in the garden. They may scatter their seeds about and form colonies of considerable size from a couple of original plants. White and pink seedlings show up along with the usual rich blue. Height: 8 inches. Temperate N. A.

Collected plants of the European hepatica. *Hepatica angulosa*, are occasionally marketed in this country. This is a larger, showier hepatica, but a difficult one to flower.

★**HERNIARIA GLABRA.** One of the best green mats for use between stepping stones and as a substitute for lawns of table-top size. An inch high—with tiny, dense leaves which stay freshly green the year around and take traffic nearly as well as grass. Adaptable to both sunny, dry soils and well-watered areas in half shade. Barely in the trade these days. N. A.

HEUCHERA. The heucheras, evergreen leafy perennials in the saxifrage family, are exclusively North American plants. The roundish leaves grow in basal clumps. They may be lobed or toothed along the edges. Of the more than 30 species, one has received the lion's share of attention: coral bells (*H. sanguinea*). This has become one of the most planted border perennials over all but the coldest sections of the United States and Europe, while the other species are grown almost entirely in botanical gardens and collectors' gardens.

The group as a whole deserves a better reception. Many heucheras are beautiful foliage plants (two of them have marbled leaves). Several bear a thousand flowers at once in tall, striking open clusters. One of these species has been crossed with coral bells to produce *H.* 'Santa Ana Cardinal', a new hybrid which is one of the most promising garden plants ever developed from western American wild flowers.

Heucheras are delightful material for the hybridist. Any of the species will cross if given the slightest chance. Where the ranges of the species overlap, intermediate forms are found in abundance. In cultivation this natural willingness can be aided by simply planting different species close together and letting the bees exchange their pollen, or they can be hand pollinated. You aren't apt to get a plant as good as 'Santa Ana Cardinal', but after sowing crossed seed it is fascinating to see a new plant emerge which resembles both parents. If seed of this first generation cross is sown, the second generation of plants will divide up in Mendelian fashion into an astonishing variety of heucheras, large and small.

Heucheras are tough. You can grow and flower them in sun or shade almost anywhere in the garden—in the border, woodland, or rock garden. The woodland species enjoy cool, ferny places.

HEUCHERA AMERICANA. Alum root has pale green marbling on darker green leaves which turn bronze red in winter. Some forms show marbling only on the young leaves, others retain it the year around. Hardy to below 0°. Clusters of greenish white flowers.

HEUCHERA BRIZOIDES. A horticultural name for a list of hybrids with open clusters of pink which seem intermediate between those of *H. micrantha* and *H. sanguinea*, the reported parents. Hardy to 0°.

HEUCHERA MAXIMA. Thousand-flowered clusters 3 feet high. From the Channel Islands of California. Damaged at 10°.

HEUCHERA MICRANTHA. Small whitish flowers in open, tiered clusters on 2-foot-high stems. Blooms from May to July. Hardy to 0°.

★**HEUCHERA SANGUINEA.** Coral bells grow wild in Arizona and northern Mexico but are hardy over most of the United States. Bright coral rose flowers, held 15 inches high in slender panicles,

Iris cristata

Iris douglasiana

Hebe pinguifolia 'Pagei'

appear in May, June, and July. The one disappointment about coral bells is that the flower color, beautiful in itself, is hard to combine with most other flower colors. However, the plant is worth a place of its own if you can't find anything to go with it.

★HEUCHERA 'SANTA ANA CARDINAL'. Hybrid between *H. sanguinea* and *H. maxima.* A strong growing plant which seems to possess hybrid vigor. Produces immense (but graceful) clusters of rich rose on 32-inch stems. The showiest of the heucheras. Its peak of bloom is in April, May, and June.

HEUCHERA VILLOSA. Leaves are deeply scissored at the edges into a maple-leaf pattern. The globed flowers are pinkish or whitish and tiny, but they open in abundance. Hardy below 0°.

HOUSTONIA. Bluets are made of little spoon-shaped leaves densely packed in dwarf mats. In the two best species, *H. caerulea* and *H. serpyllifolia,* the flowers are four-rayed stars of clear, watered blue with an eye of gold. From moist, meadowy places close to the nation's capital and down through southern woods. Grow houstonia beneath rock garden rhododendrons or on the half-dry fringes of the bog garden. Hardy below 0°.

HUTCHINSIA ALPINA. A dwarf mound-maker not unlike *Houstonia* in its density of minute, green leaves. The leaves are divided into lobes like mustard leaves; if you nibble one you get the sharp taste and odor of mustard to which hutchinsia is related. The flowers are white, in little spikes, and four-petaled (cruciform) like those of mustard. Grow hutchinsia in cool, half-shaded soil. Increase the plant by tearing it to pieces in the spring and replanting in the open garden. N. A.

HYACINTHUS. Hyacinth has better things to offer the rock garden than the Dutch garden varieties, with their elaborately coiffured and heavily perfumed heads. Two species hyacinths which possess the grace and simplicity that have been bred out of the garden varieties are: *H. amethystinus,* with 6 to 10-inch stems strung with china blue bells; *H. azureus (H. ciliatus),* which has even dwarfer stems of darker blue flowers. Both are in the bulb trade.

HYPERICUM. St. John's wort contains some of the most valuable shrubs for warm, sunny rock gardens. They are at their best in California and the southern half of the nation. In the northern states many of the species are liable to frost damage at 10°.

Hypericum flowers are five-petaled, flat, rounded, and yellow (blazing golden yellow or paler), but always with a prominent boss of many stamens. The flowers of many hypericum species cover the plant like a cloth of gold in May.

HYPERICUM ANDROSAEMUM. Sweet Amber. Taller than most (about 3 feet) with handsome, dark green, oval leaves, but smallish flowers from June to September. The great attractions of this plant are its aromatic sweetness and its blackish berries which last into the winter. No other hypericum has fruit of any garden consequence.

HYPERICUM CALYCINUM. Rose of Sharon or Aaron's beard was formerly one of the most planted ground covers. It forms a long-lived, all-enduring, stem-rooting mat of foot-high arching branches set with dark oval leaves and, in summer, large hard-gold flowers whose stamens are tipped with red. Always useful on rough banks under semi-cultivation. Hardy (below ground at least) to below 0°.

HYPERICUM CORIS. A little clump of thready stems, needle-like leaves, and airy clusters of pale gold. A collector's delight.

HYPERICUM MOSERIANUM. A widely grown hybrid of *H. calycinum* and *H. patulum,* between the two in height and with the red-tipped stamens of *H. calycinum.*

HYPERICUM OLYMPICUM. Forms a deep, stout cord of a root topped by a flattened basket of wiry stems and blue-gray leaves. Flowers are Byzantine in their golden lavishness (and the plant comes from Byzantine lands).

HYPERICUM PATULUM. An evergreen spreading shrub, 18 inches to 3 feet high and rather like a taller *H. calycinum.*

HYPERICUM POLYPHYLLUM. A near duplicate of *H. olympicum*—a little smaller, but just as golden.

HYPERICUM RHODOPAEUM. From dry Yugoslavian hills. Gray-felted leaves on radial stems which emerge from a central rootstock and creep flat over the ground. Flowers are as good as the best for their brilliant goldness and abundance. Damaged at 10°.

IBERIS SEMPERVIRENS. Evergreen candytuft is one of the big four of American rockeries and wall gardens. (The other three in this quadrumvirate of popularity are *Arabis caucasica (A. albida), Alyssum saxatile,* and *Aubrieta deltoidea.*)

Evergreen candytuft is a 2-foot,rounding, dark leafed plant with the appearance of a shrub. It is extremely easy going in sunny places, and flowers from April to June with masses of bright white flowers in flattened clusters.

Shear evergreen candytuft after it flowers to keep it compact and to induce reflowering the same summer. This is one of the easiest rock plants to grow from seed. A packet should provide plants aplenty. Available in numerous smaller or more floriferous garden forms such as 'Little Cushion', 'Purity', and 'Snowflake'. 'Little Gem' is flat growing and like *Iberis saxatile* in winsome littleness on the rock garden scree. N. A.

INCARVILLEA DELAVAYI. A perennial with painted, tropical looking flowers of carmine, purple, and yellow. This and the other Himalayan species are not safe in wet winter soil. Coldframe culture recommended. Hardy to 0°.

IRIS. Sword-like iris leaves are effective foils for stones. Most of the hundred-plus iris species available in America and the thousands of varieties within those species are suitable for larger or smaller rock gardens, but the big, many-splendored border iris is too much for the rock garden.

★**IRIS CHAMAEIRIS.** Has been the mate of ★*Iris pumila* in a union which has produced scores of dwarf bearded iris, ranging in height from 6 to 12 inches and in color from white and yellow to violet purple in endless combinations. These early dwarfs are easy and delightful in rockeries, borders, and rock gardens. A well drained, loamy soil and a sunny position suits them best. Divide every third August in cool northern summers, every third September in the South. Hardy at —15° and probably lower.

IRIS CHRYSOGRAPHES. In nature a Himalayan bog plant. Readily adapted to upland garden conditions. Stout masses of 2-foot, sedge-like leaves. The narrow flower segments of lilac or dark purple have a faint scent of ripe plums. Hardy at —10°.

★**IRIS CRISTATA.** This woodland dwarf from eastern America has broad little daggers for leaves, a running habit of growth, and early flowers of light blue with yellow at the base of the beard. The leaves die down in the fall, after which the plant can be divided easily into many sections. Hardy to —10°.

IRIS DOUGLASIANA. Big tough clumps of sword-shaped leaves. Flowers (from March to May) vary from cream through lavender to deep red-purple. Grows along the coast from southern Oregon to California's Santa Barbara County, where colonies of its clumps elbow out the toughest grasses for room on the hills which go down to the sea. It is just as strong and tenacious in the garden. Grows equally well among stones, in woodlands, or in perennial borders. Divide as you would *I. tenax*. Hardy to 0°.

★**IRIS DOUGLASIANA 'AGNES JAMES'** and **I. D. 'PEGASUS'.** These similar albinos retain the strength of typical *I. douglasiana*. The flowers have the white lightness of terns. Hardy to 0°.

★**IRIS GRACILIPES.** This iris of upland places in Japan is one of the most graceful of all rock plants. Its leaves are like a clump of slender, arching grass about 8 inches high. Flowers have a ruffled texture and a dissolved pale-blueness, with darker markings of gold. They poise, mothlike, on their stems just over the leaves. There is a double-flowered form of *I. gracilipes* which is actually as pretty as the single, and an albino (*I. g.* 'Alba') which is exquisite. Best in light woodland shade and light woodland soil. Hardy to 0° or lower.

★**IRIS INNOMINATA.** A graceful native of the Siskiyou region of southwestern Oregon. Leaves are narrow, dark, leathery, and evergreen. Typically the flowers are rich yellow with darker pencilling on the petals, and ruffles along their edges. Where the range of *Iris innominata* overlaps the Oregon ranges of *I. tenax* and *I. douglasiana,* hybrid iris

appear in abundance. Their flower colors break into pastels—ivory, buff, chamois, orchid—in May, June. Grows rapidly and flowers abundantly in rich, well-watered gardens, but soon exhausts itself from the effort. The plant is more permanent if naturalized in light woodland and watered sparingly. Height: 12 inches. Damaged at 10°.

★**IRIS RETICULATA.** A little, bulbous species with leaves as straight and thin as bullrushes and small, intensely blue flowers marked with gold. Blooms very early. Divide every second or third fall.

★**IRIS TENAX.** Makes clumps of slender leaves in meadows and open woodlands in western Oregon and Washington. Large, abundant flowers, pencilled along segments. The flowers (May to July) are typically lilac purple, sometimes violet-purple or white. Adapts easily to garden conditions, sun or shade, and stays permanently. Hardy to 0° or below. Divide in earliest spring every 4 years. Height: 15 inches.

IRIS VERNA. An eastern American with 6-inch, clump-making evergreen leaves and rich, violet-blue early flowers, orange-yellow on the inner falls. The garden hardiness of this species is suspect below 15°.

JASIONE. Meadow plants from the Alps. Clear blue flowers in ball-shaped clusters with numerous spiky extensions which give flowers considerable resemblance to sea urchins. *J. perennis* and *J. humilis* are available and recommended for light soil and open places. Midsummer bloom. Height: 12 inches. N. A.

JEFFERSONIA. Named for Thomas Jefferson. Members of the barberry family with large 2-lobed leaves, fleeting, round-petalled flowers, remarkable seed capsules like archaic clay pipes and the yellow, wavy roots of barberries. There are only two: white flowered *J. diphylla* from eastern American woods and pale blue *J. dubia* from the woods of Manchuria. Both bloom in spring. Distinctive plants for the woodland garden. Both are rare in cultivation. N. A.

JUNIPERUS CHINENSIS. There is considerable difference in opinion concerning which names go with which junipers. With the exception of *J. c.* 'Pfitzeriana', the *J. chinensis* forms offered in the trade are often wrongly labeled, or even casually rechristened. If the names you see in the nursery are correct, the appearance of the shrubs should tally with the descriptions below.

★**JUNIPERUS CHINENSIS 'ARMSTRONGII'.** This is like a small Pfitzer juniper with low, arching branches. To 4-by-4 feet.

★**JUNIPERUS CHINENSIS 'HETZII'.** (*J. c.* 'Hetzii Glauca'.) Spreading shrub with a short, exposed trunk and graceful arching branches of gray foliage. Grows about 4 feet high—and more across—in 10 years. (Eventually it is 12 feet high.) A specimen plant for a bank or a box on the patio. Can be pruned into a definite tree form.

★**JUNIPERUS CHINENSIS 'PFITZERI-**

ANA'. Pfitzer juniper is an indispensable spreading shrub for clothing large dry banks and masking monumental rock work. The feathery gray-green branches are arranged in open sprays so that air and light fill half the space occupied by the shrub. Since the rate of growth is fast (about 1 foot a year) and relentless, this is no shrub to plant in a bit of rockery facing the sidewalk or in narrow beds between the house and lawn. It reaches a height of 5 or 6 feet and a spread of 15 or 20 feet in a surprisingly few years. Hardy to below 0°. There are green, glaucous and gold-tipped Pfitzers. Gray-green *J. c.* 'Pfitzeriana Compacta' attains about half the spread at about half the speed of the typical form.

★**JUNIPERUS CHINENSIS SARGENTII.** A 10-foot-wide mat which grows on the shores of Hokkaido, Japan's northern isle. It is as cold as Maine there, which indicates that this juniper should be hardy anywhere in the United States. A favorite with gardeners in Nevada.

★**JUNIPERUS COMMUNIS 'AUREOSPICA'.** (*J. c.* 'Depressa Aurea'.) A tussock of low-angled branches, bright golden in their new growth, bronze as their foliage matures. Slow growing (4 to 6 inches a year). Use it for a stimulating spot of color or in pattern planting.

★**JUNIPERUS COMMUNIS 'COMPRESSA'.** A narrowly conical tree with closely pressed, upward-growing branches. In the open ground under ideal conditions, a 15-year-old tree is 4 feet high, 9 inches wide at its broadest mid-section. The tree, which resembles an Italian cypress in miniature, is sometimes used by the English in miniature formal or alpine gardens in antique stone basins.

In containers the growth of *J. c.* 'Compressa' may slow to ½ inch a year, yet the tree stays gray-green and healthy. It is sometimes tender when the temperature drops to 0° or lower.

★**JUNIPERUS COMMUNIS 'HORNIBROOKII'.** A gray-green mat about a foot high, of light and springy appearance due to the thinness of its branches and foliage. Spreads widely at a rate of about 6 inches a year.

JUNIPERUS COMMUNIS 'JACKII'. This shrub of Western American mountains is variable in form. In its most distinctive form it grows as a single, limp, whip-like branch which trails over the ground for yards. Fun to have in a rock garden which has space for curios.

★**JUNIPERUS CONFERTA.** Shore juniper makes a low mat of blue-green with a pleasantly ruffled surface. An excellent choice for the seaside, where salt spray and even occasional submergence will not bother it. Shore juniper does not take to hot inland summers.

★**JUNIPERUS HORIZONTALIS.** The creeping juniper ranges over Canada, the Great Lakes country, and New England. There are a number of named forms differing mainly in the gray and blue tints of their foliage. All are ground-hugging and carpet-making. Their growth rate is moderately fast—about 8 inches a year, to an ultimate spread of 15 or 20 feet.

(Remember that this 8-inch growth rate represents just one branch growing on one side of the mat. The branch on the opposite side also grows 8 inches a year. Therefore, the diameter of the juniper increases 16 inches a year.)

Waukegan juniper (*J. h.* 'Douglasii') has soft blue summer foliage, purplish winter foliage. This is a fully prostrate form, uncommonly drought resistant, and one of the best covers for large areas of sandy or gravelly soil. Andorra juniper (*J. h.* 'Plumosa') is slightly mounding to 18 inches, has feathery gray-green foliage which turns bronzy in the fall. 'Bar Harbor' is an excellent gray-green selection.

★**JUNIPERUS PROCUMBENS.** This is a slow growing mat (4 to 6 inches a year) of bright blue-green juvenile foliage. There are some unnecessary forms with splotches of yellow variegation here and there among the branches. None of the *J. procumbens* forms is as strong or drought-resistant as the bank-covering junipers. *J. procumbens* itself makes a valuable specimen plant for the small rockery, equally attractive grown as a dense mat or with its branches thinned to show the bark and the branch habit.

★**JUNIPERUS SABINA 'TAMARISCI-FOLIA'.** "Tam" in the nurseryman's language—an admiring name for one of his best sellers and best bargains. Usually less than 2 feet high, tam juniper is a compact mat of dark green. The rate of growth is about 8 inches a year.

A bank of this even, flowing green has a most restful effect. Tam can be allowed to flow right up to the ground-sweeping branches of spire-form conifers such as alpine fir and Norway spruce, or, in really large areas, Douglas fir and Colorado spruce. Together, the flat and vertical masses create a complete landscape of alpine character.

J. sabina, the typical species of this European native, is rare in American cultivation. It is a more or less upright shrub, 6 feet high or so. A bright blue selection of it is appearing on the market as *J. s.* 'Blue Danube'.

JUNIPERUS SQUAMATA MEYERI. A gawky but popular shrub; resembles a bunch of spiky branches which have been poked into the ground at odd angles. The color is splendid—metallic blue in summer, coppery purple in winter. Placed against a wall of darkly stained wood this shrub has striking value. In such a position it is best along with a ground cover. Too much of a scene-stealer to be a good companion for other shrubs. As a free-standing specimen it is of formidable appearance, on the order of yucca. To 8 feet in about 10 years.

JUNIPERUS VIRGINIANA 'GRAY OWL'. First an upward-growing, then an arching shrub. One of the coolest-looking gray-green junipers, and equal to the better-known *J. chinensis* 'Hetzii' in size, habit, and value. To 9 feet in 12 years. Not readily obtainable as yet.

LATHYRUS. The wild peas are little grown in gardens. One of them, *Lathyrus splendens,* the Campo pea of hillsides in California's San Diego County, deserves to be much better known. Its clusters of large, brilliant crimson pea flowers on 6 feet of climbing, twining stems, make it one of the most spectacular American wild flowers. Blooms from April to June. For warm southern gardens.

LAVANDULA. All lavenders are worthy of the hot, sunny rock garden for their herb-scented brush of gray leaves, and their spikes of violet or purple summer flowers which are long-lasting and attractive to bees. Old-fashioned lavender, 3-foot *Lavandula officinalis* (*L. vera*) and its 9-inch dwarf variety, 'Compacta' ('Compacta Nana' of nursery catalogues) are as good as any. *L. latifolia* (*L. spica*) and pinnate-leaved *L. stoechas,* in their wild forms, are not much different in general appearance from *L. officinalis,* but there are a number of horticultural varieties with darker flowers and more compact habit.

Lavandula lanata is extraordinarily alone. This is a crevice plant from the dry, stony Spanish Sierra. It makes a low mound whose leaves seem thick with blue-white hoarfrost. California gardens accommodate this Spaniard perfectly. It is half hardy in the north. Rare in American gardens and plant catalogues.

LEDUM. *L. groenlandicum, L. glandulosum,* and *L. columbianum* are peat bog shrubs which can be transplanted easily and grown in the bog garden or among rhododendrons and heathers. Leathery little evergreen leaves and small, clustered, five-petalled star flowers of white in summer. Prune them hard to keep them compact.

LEIOPHYLLUM BUXIFOLIUM. Sand myrtle. A dwarf shrub related to rhododendrons. Has every qualification for admittance to the first row of the rhododendron bed. Leaves are ¼ inch ovals of dark shining green. Flowers are equally tiny, but numerous enough to cover the plant with a haze of pink, flaky-fugitive petals and stamens. Grows wild in the New Jersey pine barrens and down through southern mountains, taking various forms along the route. Height: 8 to 30 inches, increasing at a rate of 1 to 3 inches a year. Evergreen. N. A.

LEONTOPODIUM. The edelweisses (there are several, much alike) have much more fame than actual beauty. All have flowers like starfishes cut out of gray flannel. The edelweisses are meadow plants which appreciate meadow conditions in the rock garden—light, well drained, well watered soil, and a sunny position. *L. alpinum,* the typical species, is short lived. Other closely related species are more safely perennial. *L. a.* 'Stracheyi' of the Himalayas is larger and showier in flower than *L. alpinum* and lives about 4 years. *L. a.* 'Soulei' of the Alps is a dwarf edelweiss which is permanent in the garden if it is divided every second March. The edelweisses are easily grown from seed. Hardy to 0° or below.

LEUCOCRINUM MONTANUM. Sand lily is an American prairie plant whose 6-inch tufts of gray leaves hold at their center a clutch of fragrant waxen white, long-rayed stars in April and May. One of our best natives and easily established in deep, warm, sandy garden soil. Winter climates where frosts, rains, and thaws occur alternately will not keep it long. Pot and coldframe culture in wet-winter climates.

LEWISIA. *Lewisia cotyledon, L. tweedyi, L. rupicola, L. columbiana, L. nevadensis,* and *L. oppositifolia* are western American mountain plants with flat, ground-hugging rosettes of narrow leaves and 6-inch stems of silken-petaled flowers of white, rose, apricot. *L. rediviva,* the bitter root, makes a 3-inch tuft of round fat leaves which dry up in May when huge rose-colored cactoid flowers open. Leaves reappear with the fall rains. Roots are still gathered by the Indians who found long ago that peeled dried bitter roots are a palatable source of starch. Lewisias are much-sought collectors' plants. The different species respond to garden conditions with varying success. Four-inch *L. rupicola* can be kept permanently on a half-shaded scree. *L. columbiana* is also easy and permanent, but has small, unshowy flowers. The rest live 3 or 4 years—occasionally longer in the gardens of the green-thumbed. All species enjoy scree conditions and all except *L. rediviva* do best in part shade. Hardy to 0° and below.

★**LIMONIUM LATIFOLIUM** (*Statice latifolia*) is a yard-tall sea lavender from Russia, well known in perennial borders for its antennae-like constructions of wire-like stems lined with lavender starlets in summer. The deep roots suit this and other sea lavenders for coastal sand or for cactus gardens inland. N. A.

LINARIA CYMBALARIA. See **CYMBALARIA MURALIS.**

★**LINNAEA BOREALIS.** Twinflower grows as a mat of long thin branches which creep and root over soft, humus-deep woodland soil. These are set on either side with rows of rounded, glossy evergreen leaves, held flat against the ground. Above them rise 4-inch stems, thin to invisibility at a little distance. The stems fork at the third inch, and end at the fourth in the twin pendant bells. Bend close to catch their scent of almond.

Twinflower in slightly varying form grows around the boreal world, and throughout its range is one of the most beloved wildlings. Linnaeus, the tireless scientist who invented the binomial system by which we apply Latin names to plants and animals, and who himself named and described thousands of plants and animals, had a special fondness for twinflower. He asked that it be named after him, and he had himself portrayed holding a sprig of its twin bells.

In hot summer localities, use twin-flower as a ground cover in cool woodland shade. In western Washington and Oregon it will grow in full sun (if well watered) and in a sunny position will turn bronze in the leaf through winter. N. A.

LINUM. Flax. Foot-high *L. alpinum* and 2-foot *L. narbonense* and *L. perenne* have spidery branches of narrow leaves tipped with bland blue stars. *L.*

flavum is a squat tuft of rounded, dark green leaves and richly yellow flowers, fuller in the petal than the others. Summer blooming. Grow them on sunny, well-drained soil and expect three years or so of abundant flower from them. Flax is easy to grow from seed, but is neither long-lived nor oak-hardy.

★**LIPPIA REPENS.** See **PHYLA NODI-FLORA.**

★**LITHOSPERMUM DIFFUSUM.** Sends trailing stems of narrow deep green leaves radiating from a central trunk and root. In May the plant blazes with a thousand little trumpets of deep, gem-pure blue, followed by minor flares of trumpetry all summer. Sun and good drainage. Questionably hardy below 15°. *L. d.* 'Grace Ward' with larger and fewer flowers and *L. d.* 'Heavenly Blue' with smaller, more numerous flowers, are two selections in the trade.

★**LOBELIA CARDINALIS.** Cardinal flower. Four to 6 feet of slim upright stems flocked with bird-like flowers of flame red. Cardinal flower grows in bogs and wet meadows in eastern North America from Canada to Florida. Readily started from seed and grown in bog gardens and moist borders.

★**LOBELIA SIPHILITICA.** Has blue flowers on a smaller plant than *L. cardinalis.* Grows in bogs and moist places over much of the same range as cardinal flower.

★**LOTUS CORNICULATUS.** Bird's-foot trefoil. A mat-forming perennial with little clover leaves and bright yellow pea flowers stained with scarlet. There are 2 or 3-inch-high forms which make tidy evergreen ground covers, in flower from May until October. (There are also rank 2-foot-high forms better used as horse fodder.) Variety 'Flore-pleno' is a dwarf double with quarter-inch leaves and showier flowers which still seem refined enough for the best rock garden company. Bird's-foot trefoil grows best in sun and sandy soil. N. A.

LUPINUS. The "tree" lupines, *L. arboreus, L. longifolius, L. littoralis,* and others can be sown on dunes and sand banks to act as anchors for the soil. Their big spikes of yellow, violet, or lavender pea flowers are scented and attractive to bees. The first two bloom in spring, the third in summer. Damaged at 20°.

★**LYSICHITON AMERICANUM.** A western native with hooded yellow flower bracts rising like huge candle flames over cold marshes in March, when the frogs are singing. Afterward come tropical-looking elephant-ear leaves. Easy to establish in the bog garden. Height: flowers 14 inches, leaves 28 inches. Similar, but with white bracts, is *L. camtschatcense* of Japan and Siberia.

★**MAHONIA.** Close relatives of barberry. The American species are 1 to 10-foot evergreen shrubs of top landscape value. The green-leafed mahonias enhance stonework, harmonize with nearly all green-leafed plants. The gray-leafed mahonias work as well with desert stones and plants.

★**MAHONIA AQUIFOLIUM.** The Oregon grape has cane-like branches 1 to 6 feet high; dark, glossy evergreen leaflets, crimped, stickery and holly-like, in 5 to 9-part leaves; bright yellow little May bells, densely packed along short rods; currant-size, blue-black berries with a blue-gray bloom, tart and flavorful and excellent in jelly (follow a recipe for barberry jelly).

This native of the Pacific slope from British Columbia to northern California is perhaps the Northwest's most valuable shrubby contribution to gardening. England appreciates Oregon grape as much as we do. Our eastern states grow it as far north as Boston.

Oregon grape is a shrub of many garden uses: in foundation planting, in mixed shrub plantings, in the woodland garden, as an informal hedge, beneath coniferous trees, on massive rockwork.

The divided foliage of Oregon grape combines something of the form of all leaf types—and something of the impression that each of these types makes on our senses. For that reason Oregon grape blends with practically all other garden shrubs, perennials, and trees. Oregon grape leaves are elegantly displayed like the leaves of some forest plants and bamboos; at the same time they are substantial in texture, like rhododendron leaves. This same blending quality is present in the leaves of other mahonias.

★**MAHONIA DICTYOTA**. Grows on chaparral hillsides in the interior of California—a tall shrub with pale green leaflets, deeply toothed, twisted and wavy along the edges, and long-spined. Light yellow flowers and gray-blue berries.

★**MAHONIA FREMONTII.** A desert shrub, 3 to 10-feet high. Small bluish-gray leaflets, strongly spined. The yellow flowers in May and June and blue berries are in small scale with the leaves.

★**MAHONIA NERVOSA.** Low-growing Oregon grape. A dwarf shrub with a strong will to spread underground and make colonies in upland woods. This species has the glossy holly leaflets of mahonia grouped in a leaf of fern form: as many as 10 pairs of leaflets line both sides of a quill-like stem, and one more extends from the tip.

The leaves are arranged in a loose cluster, and are tilted upright so that the plant as a whole resembles a fern clump. Flowers and berries are like those of *M. aquifolium*. The vertical growth is extremely slow. Twenty-five-year-old colonies in shade have slender, 30-inch-high branches, 18-inch-long leaves. In full sun *M. nervosa* makes healthy growth, but it is even lower. Fifteen-year-old colonies in sun have branches 8 inches high, leaves 8 inches long.

M. nervosa shares the natural range of *M. aquifolium* and has proved hardy wherever the taller Oregon grape is grown. In the garden, let *M. nervosa* tuft up through drifts of *Erica carnea* or between stones in a dry wall. *M. nervosa* makes a drought-resistant ground

Lewisia tweedyi
Matted plant above: *Sedum spurium*

Oxalis oregana with ferns

Juniperus communis 'Compressa'

cover beneath conifers or a refined foundation plant. This distinctive shrub deserves much more attention from American gardeners.

★**MAHONIA NEVINII.** Grows wild only in the eastern end of California's San Fernando Valley. This 3 to 7-foot shrub has small, narrow gray-green, spine-tipped leaflets, saw-edged and twice as long as broad. The flowers are yellow in late March to May; the berries bright scarlet or yellowish.

These three gray mahonias (*M. dictyota, M. fremontii,* and *M. nevinii*) are adaptable to gardens in Southern California and the Southwest. They will take desert heat. They complement large desert boulders, and blend well with ocotillo, yucca, and cacti. They make informal hedges (but very formidable hedges to dogs and unwelcome guests).

★**MAHONIA PINNATA.** Much like *M. aquifolium,* and has the same value. The main distinguishing characteristic is this: The bluntish basal leaflets of *M. pinnata* grow close to the branches, while the more pointed basal leaflets of *M. aquifolium* stand away from the branches on an inch or more of stem. *M. pinnata* takes up where *M. aquifolium* leaves off in the California coast ranges, extends south to Los Angeles County. Said to be as hardy as *M. aquifolium.*

★**MAHONIA PUMILA.** A dwarf alpine shrub from the Oregon Siskiyous south into the California mountains. Each leaf has 5 to 9 dull, bluish-grayish-green leaflets edged with deep, wide teeth and strongly projecting spines. Light yellow flowers clustered in an uneven ball; berries blue-glaucous. Full sun or light shade. A 12-year-old colony in full sun is 19 inches high, 5 feet across. Use on rock work and among the larger alpine rhododendrons. Hardy well below zero and adaptable to the same regions as *M. aquifolium.*

★**MAHONIA REPENS.** A creeping sub-alpine shrub widespread in our western mountains. Grows 8 inches high in the wild, usually no more than 18 inches high in lowland gardens. Leaves constructed of 3 to 7 dull green, oval leaflets with many shallow teeth. The spines are merely bristles. Use as *M. pumila* and also as a woodland ground cover. Best in half shade. As hardy as *M. aquifolium.*

MAIANTHEMUM DILATATUM. False lily-of-the-valley. A running plant with heart-shaped leaves after the fashion of its namesake, and a short rod of minute but winsome white flowers in May and June. Loves leaf mold, rotted wood, and a large space beneath trees. Height: 6 inches. N. A.

★**MAZUS PUMILIO.** A racing, invasive mat which will make you a small lawn of broad, blunted leaves and pouty-lipped flowers of lilac-violet in summer. Grow it on semi-boggy ground or as a ground cover in light woodland. Takes foot traffic well for a plant with 1½-inch leaves. Hardy down to about 5°.

MECONOPSIS. A genus of several dozen poppy-like plants which rank with the most opulently leafed, opulently flowered vegetation of our planet. Nearly all have been found on the cold, foggy meadows of the Himalayas. Most are biennial plants. In their first year from seed they form a shield-sized leaf rosette, pelted with silver or yellow. During their second year they send up yard-high stems ending in silken poppies of sky blue, violet, or pale yellow. Then they die away leaving a quarter-cup of poppy seed behind.

The species of meconopsis are little known in American gardens. Their climatic requirements can be met in very few locations. They demand high humidity combined with cool air all through the summer. The most tractable Himalayan species is *Meconopsis betonicifolia baileyi,* the blue poppy of Tibet, which some American gardeners succeed in growing under optimum conditions for large-leafed rhododendrons.

In the British Isles meconopsis as a group is easy to grow in the cool north of Scotland. Southward through the British Isles they become progressively uneasy. The success of meconopsis in the north of Scotland suggests that American gardeners in the fog-and-rain belt along the Pacific Coast might do as well with them. A garden at the edge of the rain forest of the Olympic Peninsula (where the annual rainfall is 150 inches) could prove to be ideally situated for their culture.

★**MECONOPSIS CAMBRICA.** Welsh poppy is as easy as the rest of the genus is demanding. Sow the seed in the wilder parts of the garden or in the tall perennial border, and be rewarded in early summer with a stand of poppies which seem cut out of lemon yellow *sari* silk. They'll self-sow every year from then on. Native to western Europe.

MENTHA REQUIENII. Corsican mint. A ½-inch-high creeping plant densely packed with pinhead-sized leaves. The mat stays brilliant green—like moss after a rain—the year around. In July or August the mat becomes filmed over with speck-sized violet flowers in crowded abundance. Use it between stepping stones. Corsican mint reserves its greatest attraction until you step on it and release the freshest, brightest fragrance of all the mints. Also useful as a ground cover. In the San Francisco Bay Area a plug of Corsican mint set out in spring grows a yard across by the end of summer. Farther north the plant grows at about half that rate. Likes rich moist soil, sun or light shade. Winter-kills at 20°, but self-sown seedlings carry on.

MENZIESIA. A race of bushlings akin to rhododendrons, and asking the same culture. *M. purpurea* has the brightest flowers, little bells of red with a bluish bloom on the petals. Spring flowering.

★**MERTENSIA VIRGINICA.** A stout clump of grayish spatulate leaves, 2 feet of stem, and a down-curving cluster of bright blue, tubular flowers. Virginia bluebells is one of very few mertensias which will go on living after it has been taken from its habitat. This species can be established easily in gardens in all quarters of North America. Native to moist meadows in New York southwest to South Carolina and Tennessee. Grow it in the primrose garden or with ferns in half-shady places.

MICROMERIA. Aromatic plants with the lipped flowers of the thymes. All like sunny, sandy places.

★**MICROMERIA CHAMISSONIS.** Yerba buena. See **SATUREJA DOUGLASII.**

MICROMERIA CROATICA. A neatly rounded, foot-high bush. Gives a good show of lilac flowers in midsummer. Best in a hot, dryish spot. Hardy to 0°.

MICROMERIA PIPERELLA. A 4-inch tuft of wiry stems and purple-rose flowers from Mediterranean mountains. For the collector's scree. Damaged at 10°.

MIMULUS. Known as monkey flowers for the simian mimicry of their flower faces. There are about 150 species, found mainly in western America and centering in California. Many of these are annuals; the few perennials are usually short-lived in the garden. Purple (or pink) monkey-flower, *M. lewisii,* common along streams and dripping banks in the mountains of the West, is one of the best perennial sorts for gardens. ★*Mimulus longiflorus (Diplacus longiflorus),* of the shrubby section of the genus, is one of America's loveliest wild flowers. Its apricot colored funnel-form flowers flare at the throat to 1½ inches across. They grow on a 3-foot bush found in the stony chaparral country of Southern California. *Mimulus longiflorus* grows readily from collected seed or from half-hard cuttings. Hardy to 20°.

★**MITCHELLA REPENS.** Partridge-berry. A ground-hugging creeper which grows in forests in eastern North America. Pairs of small roundish leaves decorate thin branches. The growth habit of partridge-berry recalls *Linnaea* and *Satureja douglasii.* Jasmine-like flowers, scented and long-tubed, appear in the spring. Scarlet berries follow and persist over the winter. Partridge-berry, which earns its star as a woodland ground cover, demands a cool moist atmosphere as well as a cool root run. Northern gardens only.

MITELLA. Woodland plants of the saxifrage family. Heart-shaped leaves. Clusters of tiny cup flowers from which 5 fringed petals radiate like the rays of finely crystallized snowflakes. Spring bloom. White-flowered *M. stauropetala* and greenish-flowered *M. caulescens* are the best for the garden. Divide in March. Height: 18 inches. N. A.

★**MUEHLENBECKIA AXILLARIS.** (Often listed by nurseries as *M. nana.*) Wire vine. Masses of wiry, red-brown stems, loosely strung with olive-green, fiddle-shaped leaves. Wire vine spreads both over and under the ground; it climbs bank, cliff, or tree trunk if given the chance.

Wire vine is a New Zealander often used in Mexico and California for covering rough, dry soil. It is hardy much farther north. It will kill to the ground at 10°, but it restores itself from the root. *M. axillaris* 'Nana' is more compact than the typical plant. A closely related species is *M. complexa*, a more rampant grower than *M. axillaris*. Shear the muehlenbeckias to keep them on the ground, and give them only starvation soil and menial work.

MYOSOTIS SYLVATICA. The blue, white-eyed flowers of annual forget-me-not blend perfectly among bleeding hearts, ferns, and trilliums in the open woodland. Sow fresh seed in fall; the forget-me-not will take care of its own propagation from then on. Spring blooming. Height: 8 inches. N. A.

NARCISSUS. 'King Alfred', the old, well known yellow daffodil, is a selection of *Narcissus pseudo-narcissus*, found wild over much of Europe. While 'King Alfred' daffodils are out of scale in all but the largest rock garden; they make an unforgettable picture beneath old orchard trees in a meadow.

N. poeticus, the poet's narcissus with its old-fashioned papery-white flowers with the red-edged "pheasant's eye" cups, looks best when left to return to half wildness in a meadow or sunny woodland.

Jonquil (*Narcissus jonquilla*) also settles easily in the semi-wild garden. This old favorite grows 14 to 18 inches high, has narrow leaves and heavily perfumed yellow flowers clustered on the stems. The flower form is that of the poet's narcissus—flat faced, with flower segments radiating around a short, open cup.

The miniature daffodil species are among the delights of the rock garden in spring. Some gardeners plant them in well drained soil of sandy, peaty composition. They like water in the spring, drought later on when their foliage begins to go yellow. The scree grows them well and keeps them more compact than a richer soil. Below we list several of the best miniature daffodil species.

NARCISSUS BULBOCODIUM. Hoop-petticoat daffodil. Grassy leaves 6 inches high, quaint yellow flowers. The corona (cup) of the flowers is round-flared like a hoopskirt, and the flower segments (the parts which, in the common daffodil, hang down like dog's ears) are reduced in the hoopskirt daffodil to mere slivers. For the scree and the rock pocket. Can be permanently naturalized on a grassy bank.

A number of varieties are offered in catalogues, of which *N. b.* 'Citrinus' and *N. b.* 'Conspicuus' are among the best and hardiest. *N. b. monophyllus,* a white variety from Morocco, is impermanent in the northern states, but seems a likely candidate for garden success in California, Arizona, and the southwest.

NARCISSUS CYCLAMINEUS. About 6 inches high when planted on a scree. The corona (cup) of the yellow flowers is a narrow tube and the flower segments recurve like the upraised wings of cyclamen flowers. Native to Portugal. So popular in the world bulb trade that collecting in the wild has greatly decimated its numbers. This species and the other wild daffodils can be grown and flowered from seed in 2 years.

NARCISSUS PSEUDO-NARCISSUS 'MINIMUS'. (*N. minimus.*) Grows to 3 or 4 inches high. Perfect miniature replica of a yellow trumpet daffodil. Grow it in a scree or a rock pocket.

NARCISSUS TRIANDRUS. Angel's tears is usually about 8 inches high, with slender, narrow leaf blades. The flowers are cream white in the variety most often catalogued. Pale yellow and primrose yellow forms are known. The center of this daffodil is cup-shaped, the flower segments recurved. These miniatures, native to Spain and Portugal, are growable wherever 'King Alfred' is grown.

NEPETA CATARIA. Catnip. An antique perennial, to 3 feet. Seldom sold these days, but just as distracting to cats as ever. (They love to roll and wallow on it as a dog does on a bone.) The small whitish or pale purple flowers of catnip recommend the plant to the wild garden. Start from seeds scattered where you want the plants to grow. N. A.

NEPETA HEDERACEA. Ground ivy. A dark evergreen mat of small, rounded, scallop-edged leaves, tiny blue flowers, and a rampageous habit of growth. There is also a variegated form. Ground ivy has escaped from old gardens in many areas in the United States and has become naturalized in woodsy places. Still useful as a ground cover for shady and neglected soil. N. A.

★**NEPETA MUSSINII.** An irreplaceable old-timer which makes airy, springy mounds of small grayish leaves covered in midsummer with long clusters of gray-blue flowers in summer. Much used in dry stone walls and as an edging for the perennial border. Makes a loose-textured ground cover. Best in hot sun. Drought resistant. N. A.

★**NIEREMBERGIA REPENS.** (*N. rivularis.*) White cup. Native along Rio de la Plata in South America. A rapidly ramifying mat of dark green, spoon-shaped leaves beset with white 2-inch-wide cups all through summer. A first-rate ground cover in California, but not hardy below 20°.

OENOTHERA. Evening primrose. Showy flowers during summer in dry and difficult situations. Almost all are easy to grow from seed.

OENOTHERA CAESPITOSA. Tufts of narrow, silvery, toothed leaves, and 3-inch flowers of satin white aging pink which apparently won't adapt to climates much different from those where it grows wild. See it at its best in the dune plantings at Rancho Santa Ana Botanic Garden, Claremont, California.

★**OENOTHERA MISSOURIENSIS.** A prostrate plant with fleshy, trailing stems, silvery leaves, and huge broad-faced evening primroses of clear yellow. For a rock pocket or the open ground. Fits well in the collection of desert plants. Hardy below 0°. *O. missouriensis* is a long-lived perennial. Once planted it will stay put for 20 years or more. Avoid transplanting it. Unfortunately the plant does not propagate itself in the garden by its own devices—take soft cut-

tings or sow the seed to obtain more plants. Height: 16 inches. N. A.

Oenothera oklahomensis and *Oenothera tetragona fraseri* are rather like greener-leaved, smaller-flowered *O. missouriensis* — beautiful and valuable plants, but unnecessary in gardens which have the later species. Height: 16 inches. N. A.

★**OENOTHERA PERENNIS.** (*O. pumila.*) A benign weed 6 to 9 inches high, native from Newfoundland to Georgia. It will cover cliffs or sandy banks with its green tufts and small yellow flowers.

★**OENOTHERA SPECIOSA CHILDSII.** (*O.* 'Rosea Mexicana'.) A 2-foot high, running plant with 3 or 4-inch pink (occasionally white) flowers. For a large expanse of sandy soil. Questionably hardy below 20°.

★**OENOTHERA TETRAGONA RIPARIA.** Eighteen to 24 inches high. Large yellow flowers showing red calyces. Comes up from seed year after year in the wild garden. Takes salt spray in the seaside garden.

OMPHALODES VERNA. Blue-eyed Mary, creeping forget-me-not. A low, ramping perennial with dark green, heart-shaped leaves about 4 inches long and, in the spring, tiny but intensely blue forget-me-nots in clusters. An easy ground cover beneath trees. Will take full shade. Dies down in fall. Hardy to 0°.

ONOSMA STELLULATUM and **A. TAURICUM.** Golden drops. A tuft of narrow gray leaves covered with stiff hairs. Flowers are elongate globes, nodding and soft yellow. These very similar plants of the Mediterranean and to the eastward are easily adapted to sunny gardens in the southwest United States. In the north they will winter-kill if the temperature goes much below 20°, but usually a few seedlings will show up to carry on. Height: 16 inches.

OPHIOPOGON ARABICUS. (A horticultural name; true status uncertain.) Jet-black leaves, grassy and curving, in grassy mats. A striking plant which will probably be used to broaden the palette of pattern plants, but the supply is low and the price is high just now. Found hardy at 20°.

★**OPHIOPOGON JAPONICUS.** A lily relative from Japan. Leaves are curving, grass-like blades of the darkest green. The 6-petaled flowers of violet purple, lilac, or tinted white are nodding, in short clusters. Dark blue berries follow the midsummer flowers.

In Japan, Brazil, Italy, California (where it is known as mondo grass) and in other easy winter climates, *O. japonicus* is used as a turfing plant in shady, meager soil.

The plant is more than just a substitute for grass. The rich color and the grace of its curving leaves are compatible with an amazing variety of plants and materials. Use it as a ground cover about stones, in combination with ferns and woodland shrubs, alone beneath trees, for pattern making, and to enliven bare spots alongside the house.

The form of *O. japonicus* usually sold in this country is about 6 inches tall. Dwarf forms and taller forms grow in Japan.

★**OSMUNDA CINNAMOMEA.** Cinnamon fern. Coarsely divided fronds 2 to 6 feet high; found in moist but not sopping soil in eastern North America. For a shade garden of large scale. N. A.

★**OSMUNDA REGALIS.** Royal fern. Broad, boldly-cut fronds 6 to 8 feet high which thrust from swamp soil in eastern North America. Closely similar forms grow in Asia, South America, Europe, and Africa. Grow it in a large bog garden or in deep moist woodland soil. N. A.

OXALIS ADENOPHYLLA. This remarkable plant of the Chilean Andes forms a clump of tubers which lie half-in and half-out of the soil. The gray leaves are composed of a disc of leaflets, neatly pleated along their midribs. The inch-wide, rose-tinged flowers, large on the 4-inch high plant, cup at their base and flare broadly at the upper half of their petals. Blooms in early summer. Easy to grow on the scree and elsewhere in the sunny rock garden. When tubers become crowded, divide them in March. Hardy possibly to 0°.

OXALIS ENNEAPHYLLA. From the Falkland Islands. A collector's plant which grows from tiny, pink-scaled, finger-like tubers. Leaves are pleated as those of *O. adenophylla*, but greener and smaller. Flowers are outsized on the plant—as large as those of *O. adenophylla*. Scree or pot culture. Height: 2 inches. Hardy to 0°.

★**OXALIS OREGANA.** Redwood sorrel. Creeping perennial which forms large colonies of clover-shaped leaves and 5-petaled flowers. Native to moist woodlands in western Washington and Oregon, thence southward to Monterey County in California. The plants of western Washington and Oregon south to the redwoods are white flowered. The form which grows beneath the redwoods of southern Oregon and northern California has rose pink flowers and bronze green leaves of heavier substance than the northern form, but white flowered forms appear far south. An evergreen or semi-evergreen carpet for the woodland garden. Blooms from April to September. Four to 6 inches high. Hardy to 0°.

PACHISTIMA CANBYI. From the mountains of Virginia and West Virginia. A spreading shrub usually less than a foot high, and otherwise similar to the next species.

PACHISTIMA MYRSINITES. False box. Grows on the edge of coniferous forests over much of western America. A twiggy evergreen shrub, usually under 3 feet in height. The ½-inch leaves are pointed ovals of dark glossy green. The minute greenish or purplish flowers are unnoticed by most people. Pachistimas blend well in plantings of mixed subshrubs.

★**PACHYSANDRA TERMINALIS.** A rich green ground cover for heavy shade. Leaves narrow and alternate on 6 to 12-inch stems. Small spikes of dull whitish flowers are of no garden consequence. Propagate by tearing plants apart in early spring. Set divisions out in any soil. (Grows most lushly in soft, humus-enriched soil.)

PAEONIA. The wild peonies, parents of the garden hybrids, have divided leaves which take on autumn tints of russet and wine red. Their bowl-shaped flowers are as large as those of many of their progeny, but single and simple instead of double and massive. These parent species are perfectly in character in the woodland, at the edge of the rhododendron bed, or among large stones.

Plant in rich, deep soil. Once planted, they resent disturbance and can be left alone to grow larger and more floriferous for decades, but you'll have to disturb the plants in order to increase your stock (unless you're prepared to wait a number of years for flowers from seed).

Propagate the peony species just like the hybrids by digging up the tuberous roots in the fall and cutting them apart. Leave at least 3 eyes (growing points) on each division. Divided plants grow with sulky slowness for a year or two, after which they go ahead with all their old strength.

Peonies come slowly from seed. Germination may take 2 years or more; after germination, 4 to 6 years may pass before first flowers appear.

Many of the wild peonies will take winters of 0° or less and summers of 100° or more. They require several weeks of winter chill at 35° or lower in order to flower well. Not all peony species possess garden strength and sureness, but the species described below have proved themselves easy and adaptable in a variety of climates and garden conditions.

PAEONIA ANOMALA. Two to 3 feet high. Leaves finely lobed. Four-inch summer flowers of carmine. Grows from Southern Europe over into Siberia.

PAEONIA CORALLINA. A European species with purple, whitish, or yellowish flowers in spring. Closely allied to *P. officinalis*.

PAEONIA LUTEA. From Yunnan. A shrubby species which requires years to build up 1 foot of woody stem. Yellow 3-inch flowers, nodding and half hidden among the leaves, in early summer.

PAEONIA OFFICINALIS. Found in the Alps of Italy, the dark red form of the common peony has a garden history which goes back to the Rome of Pliny. Nowadays there are innumerable garden selections and hybrids of this plant, although most modern peonies come from the Chinese *P. albiflora*.

PAEONIA SUFFRUTICOSA. (*P. moutan.*) Tree peony. After many years of growth this species makes 6 or 8 feet of gnarled trunk and branches. Clear magenta crimson or blush-white flowers vary from cup size to the size of tureens;

they bloom earlier than border peonies. Native to the remote mountainous interior of China, and cultivated in the Orient for centuries. Hundreds of selected and hybrid forms have been developed, most of which are much too gorgeous and sophisticated for the garden of wild plants.

PAEONIA TENUIFOLIA. Leaves of ferny dissection. Large, shining, crimson-magenta flowers in June. Native to the Caucasus.

PAEONIA WITTMANNIANA. An herbaceous species with leaves divided into oval leaflets, and pale yellow flowers 4 inches across. Caucasus, Asia Minor.

PAPAVER ALPINUM. The species is a miniature white or yellow spring blooming poppy from the Alps. A number of color forms exist, possibly as the result of hybridization with other species, and a packet of seed broadcast on the scree will often yield white, yellow, pink, and orange flowered plants, all about 6 to 9 inches high with a huddled tuft of dissected leaves. N. A.

PARNASSIA. Saxifragaceous plants of spongy stream-side soil in the Alps, the Himalayas, and the mountains of America. Our own *P. palustris californica* (*P. californica*) is one of the best. It grows from a creeping rootstock which can be divided if you get the plant going ahead strongly in your bog garden. Leaves are pointed ovals. Flowers are 1-inch white stars held upright on 8-inch stems. The other western American species, *P. fimbriata*, *P. intermedia*, and *P. cirrata* are similar bog plants with slightly smaller flowers. N. A.

PARONYCHIA NIVEA. Two-inch-high carpeting plant with narrow, gray, hairy leaves ⅛-inch long, in four rows along the ground-pressing stems. For weeks during the summer the mat is covered with large glistening bracts which conceal minute flowers. The bracts appear to be made of cellophane, and they rustle like cellophane if you touch them. A plant for hot sun and dryish soil, *P. nivea* will make a valuable ground cover and bulb cover for California and the Southwest, once it becomes available. Hardy to 0° or lower.

PARONYCHIA SERPYLLIFOLIA. A flat-growing mat (often less than ½ inch high) with smaller roundish leaves and smaller bracts than *P. nivea*. While the bracts are not so showy as those of other species, the olive green foliage is eye catching. Hardy to 0° or lower.

PENSTEMON. An almost exclusively American genus of more than 200 species. The only exception grows in Kamtchatka over into northern Japan. The preponderance of the species grow wild in the western United States. Penstemons are herbaceous or shrubby perennials with tubular flowers. The mouth of the tube opens into a two-lobed upper lip and a three-lobed lower lip.

Penstemons are usually short-lived in the garden, lasting 3 or 4 years, but they are easy to grow from seeds. The shrubby species can be renewed from half-hard cuttings taken during summer and rooted under glass.

Almost all species grow readily and flower copiously on fertile, well watered, well drained soil in full sun. Shrubby penstemons are excellent subjects for rock walls. Clump-forming species prefer open-ground culture.

The American Penstemon Society distributes penstemon information, penstemon seed, and penstemon enthusiasm to its members.

★**PENSTEMON ANTIRRHINOIDES.** Chaparral beard-tongue is a 3 to 8-foot shrub with small narrow leaves and yellow flowers tinged with russet. Grows on chaparral slopes in Southern California and Baja California. Best adapted to Southwest gardens. Blooms April and May.

★**PENSTEMON BARBATUS.** A 3-foot perennial well-known in European and American gardens. Basal clumps of long narrow leaves; 2 to 3-foot stems bear pink, scarlet, or carmine flowers, bearded on the lower lip. Similar, but having larger, scarlet, nearly beardless flowers is *P. torreyi (P. barbatus torreyi)*. Native to Utah and Colorado southward to Texas. Blooms in summer. N. A.

★**PENSTEMON BARRETTAE.** Low, wide clumps of blue-green leaves, oval and pointed in form, thick and leathery to the touch. Stems end in clusters of 1¼-inch rose-purple flowers. Restricted to basalt cliffs and talus slides along the Columbia River in Washington and Oregon. This comparatively long-lived penstemon is perfectly adapted by nature to wall gardens. Blooms April to June. N. A.

★**PENSTEMON CENTRANTHIFOLIUS.** Scarlet bugler. So named for its narrow tubes of scarlet which have, instead of the lips of other penstemon flowers, the merest suggestion of a rim. The perennial on which they grow is gray-green, a foot or a yard high with its main leafage gathered in a basal clump. Good company for tall gray native perennials in a dry planting. Grows wild on dry slopes and outwashes in the Coast Ranges of California. Best in Southwest gardens. Blooms April to July.

PENSTEMON CORDIFOLIUS. A 3 to 10-foot shrub with dark green heart-shaped leaves and dull scarlet flowers, split for half their length into an arching upper lip and a recurving lower lip. From chaparral slopes of the California coastal mountains. Best in Southwest gardens. Blooms in late spring.

★**PENSTEMON CORYMBOSUS.** An 18-inch shrub with dark, glossy green leaves and bright scarlet flowers from June to October. A northern California native. Hardy to 10° or lower.

★**PENSTEMON FRUTICOSUS.** Shrubby penstemon. Spreading clumps of green, oval leaves. Flowers 1½ inches long, mottled lavender and blue. Central Washington and Oregon east to Montana and Wyoming. Will thrive and flower in half shade as well as in full sun. Blooms May to July. N. A.

★**PENSTEMON GLABER.** Strap-shaped leaves, thick and bluish green, in a basal cluster. Stiff and straight flower stems, 18 to 24 inches high, carry large broad-tubed flowers of clear blue in early summer. From Montana and the Great Plains. N. A.

★**PENSTEMON HARTWEGII.** Large, long leaves in a clump. Orange-scarlet flowers on rods 3 or 4 feet high. Mexican. One of the more widely cultivated penstemons. Parent of a number of garden forms. Hardy at 0°.

★**PENSTEMON HETEROPHYLLUS.** A 10 to 18-inch perennial with long-bladed leaves and flowers as blue as lapis lazuli. (There are rose-violet forms as well.) This is a California native most often cultivated in the form *P. h. purdyi*. N. A.

PENSTEMON LINARIOIDES COLORADOENSIS. A mat of glaucous needle-like leaves and light blue flowers. An alpine plant of the Rocky Mountains. Frost-damaged in the garden at 10°. For sandy soil or scree. Full sun.

PENSTEMON MENZIESII. A creeping plant 1 to 4 inches high with a woody base. Thick, rounded, green leaves with toothed or smooth margins. Large flowers of magenta-purple, occasionally of clear rose, pink, or white in summer. From screes and crevices in the mountains of British Columbia and Washington. N. A.

★**PENSTEMON PINIFOLIUS.** An 8-inch shrub with yellowish-green leaves the size and shape of hemlock needles. Salmon-scarlet flowers. A rare and local inhabitant of rocky places in the Southwest. Likes a sunny, dry position in the garden. Hardy to about 5°.

★**PENSTEMON PROCERUS.** Basal rosette of dark green, lance-shaped leaves. Small, blue-purple flowers in whorled heads on 8-inch stems in July and August. A meadow plant found in the mountains from Alaska to Oregon, east to Wyoming and Colorado. N.A.

PENSTEMON RICHARDSONII. Cut-leafed penstemon. Grows 2 to 3 feet from a shrubby base. Lance-like leaves with toothed margins. Lilac-rose flowers average a little less than an inch in length. From dry cliffs and rock slides east of the Cascades in British Columbia, Washington, and Oregon. Blooms July and August. N. A.

★**PENSTEMON 'ROEZLII'.** This is a hybrid well known in British gardens, not the blue-flowered *P. laetus roezlii* of California. It appears to contain the blood of *P. rupicola, P. newberryi* and/ or *P. menziesii*. Brilliant crimson-magenta flowers over 5 or 6 inches of grayish-green leaves. For sunny rockwork. Will renew and extend itself from seed in gardens where it is at home. N. A.

PENSTEMON RUPICOLA. A crevice plant, 4 or 5 inches high with spreading

Penstemon menziesii

Left: *Picea abies* 'Remontii'
Right: *P. a.* 'Capitata'

Pinus densiflora 'Umbraculifera'
Right: *Artemisia absinthium*
Lower left: *Thymus nitidus*

stems of thick rounded leaves, glaucous-green and shallowly toothed. Inch-long rosy flowers clustered just over the leaves from June to August. (There is an albino in cultivation.) From cliffs in the Cascades of Washington, Oregon, and northern California. Best in a sunny wall. Grows well but flowers shyly in half shade. N. A.

★**PENSTEMON SPECIOSUS.** An upright clump of blue-gray leaves and large, bright blue flowers of heavy, waxen texture. Blooms from June to August. Found in dry plains east of the Cascade-Sierran spine. N. A., but not satisfactory in regions with wet, open winters.

PENSTEMON TOLMIEI. A more condensed, higher alpine version of *P. procerus*. Four to 6-inch stems ending in round clusters of blue-purple or blue-violet flowers in summer. Mountains of British Columbia and Washington. Delicately scented. N. A.

★**PERNETTYA MUCRONATA.** Native from the tip of South America up into Chile. An ericaceous shrub with small prickly leaves and berries of white, rose, slate, and maroon. A leggy, rangy 4 feet when mature—and in scale only in the largest rock garden. Berries cling through a mild winter, making a classic combination with the various forms of *Erica carnea*. Let the pernettya and the heather intergrow for the closest color and texture harmony. Frost-damaged at 5°.

PERNETTYA NANA. Like a 6-inch-high *P. mucronata* with rose-purple berries (sparsely produced). Placed among dwarf rhododendrons this subshrub will run about and bind the soil, insulating and benefitting the rhododendron roots. Hardy to 0°.

PHLOX. A genus of about 67 species widespread over the United States and confined almost exclusively within our borders. One species grows in Siberia, several cross into Canada and Mexico.

Relatively few phlox have been found amenable to cultivation away from their native climates. These few, however, comprise one of America's major contributions to horticulture. Our list below includes a number of species of great garden promise which are not yet widely known and not now available commercially. (*P. paniculata*, the summer phlox of borders, is too gorgeous for a place in a garden of wild plants.)

The phlox are one of those restless groups of plants, intergrading in nature, hybridizing in gardens. Every botanist who works with them has quite different ideas about their classification. Our notes follow the nomenclature and in part the horticultural evaluations put forth by Dr. Wherry in his monograph *The Genus Phlox*.

PHLOX ADSURGENS. Periwinkle phlox. A famed woodland plant from the Siskiyou region of Oregon and Northern California. Creeping stems 6 to 12 inches high with pointed oval or elliptical leaves, dark green and glazed. Flowers of clear rose pink (in the best forms) with a darker rose stripe down the middle of each petal. Periwinkle phlox will grow and flower prolifically from June to August in half-shaded gardens in the Northwest, Northeast, and the Southeast—for about 2 years. Then almost invariably it weakens and dies. But for gardens in its home territory this is one of the best rock garden plants.

★**PHLOX BIFIDA.** A bushling with long thin leaves and lavender flowers, deeply notched and star-like in effect. The plant grows in Indiana, Illinois, and thereabouts. There are forms of white and pale violet-blue which rank among the best garden plants in the genus. Takes readily to cultivation in the northern states and wherever else its near relative *P. subulata* will grow, yet at present it may be unavailable in the trade. Blooms in April.

PHLOX CAROLINA. A leafy phlox with 18-inch to 3-foot stems, and flowers of purple, pink, or (occasionally) white. Grows across the southern states in open woods and meadows. Deserves much more frequent cultivation, especially in the form *P. carolina* 'Gloriosa'. Probably hardy to 0°. Blooms May and June.

★**PHLOX DIVARICATA.** An eastern American woodland phlox which spreads through humusy soil by means of stolons, sends up foot-high stems of broad green leaves, and opens clusters of large flowers of light violet, lavender, or tinted white. In typical *P. divaricata* the petals are notched; in form *P. divaricata laphamii* the petals are full and rounded. Both are commercially available and easy in cultivation. There are also albinos in the trade. Plant in the woodland or at the edge of the shady border. N. A.

PHLOX MACULATA. A 3-foot phlox of meadows and wooded stream-banks in New York over into Iowa and down into Kentucky. Purple-pink or white flowers in summer. Similar to *P. paniculata*, from which it is readily distinguished by the narrower cylindrical flower clusters. (Flowers of *P. paniculata* are clustered in pyramidal style at the top of the stem.) In the garden, *P. maculata* prefers damp soil. N. A.

★**PHLOX NIVALIS.** A flattish clump of fully evergreen needle-like leaves. Typical wild plant has usual purple-pink spectrum of the genus; but rare individuals, found and brought into cultivation, have given the species color versatility. *P. nivalis* is similar to *P. subulata* in superficial appearance and has long been confused with it by botanists and gardeners alike. The essential difference in the landscape value of the species is this: *P. nivalis* is taller and looser-growing than *P. subulata*, and has evergreen leaves. About half the leaves of *P. subulata* wither during the winter.

Certain of the selected forms of *P. nivalis* ('Dixie Brilliant', 'Camla', 'Gladwyne', 'Scarlet Flame') are without peer among the moss phloxes. However, 'Camla' and some other of the older selections seem to have been propagated beyond their strength. They may die out after a season or two of vigor. N. A.

PHLOX PILOSA OZARKANA. A richly fragrant woodland phlox a foot or 18 inches high, with narrow green leaves and purple, pink, or near white flowers in spring. Found in Alabama, Missouri, and Arkansas. Probably hardy to 0° or lower.

PHLOX PULCHRA. This Alabaman is closely related to *P. ovata*, a plant well known to British gardeners. Both species are foot-high tuffets with clustered flowers in June and July. From a gardener's standpoint they differ in that many of the garden selections of *P. ovata* are in the raucous magenta and purple range, while *P. pulchra* can be had in pastel intergrades of lilac, lavender, pink, and white. *P. pulchra* is at present barely in the trade. Hardy to 0°.

★**PHLOX STOLONIFERA.** Makes large mats by means of overground stems which root down on leafy loam. The violet, purple or lavender flowers are carried on stems of 8 inches or so. *P. stolonifera* ranges along the Appalachian chain. *P. procumbens*, a valuable hybrid of *P. stolonifera* and *P. subulata*, is in the trade under the name *P. amoena*. Grow both *P. stolonifera* and *P. procumbens* in light shade and humus-rich soil. N. A.

Available from several nurseries.

★**PHLOX SUBULATA.** Moss pink. One of the great rock plants. A widely spreading mat, richly green and densely furry with little narrow leaves. In May the mat is solidly surfaced with flowers. Varied is the word for the flowers: The scores of named varieties now in commerce have flowers that are either round and full-petalled or narrow, notched, and starry. Colors range from rose, magenta, gray-violet, and lilac to white, pink, and subtle shades in between. Even their scent varies from sweet to pungent.

P. subulata and its varieties grow wild from Pennsylvania west to Lake Michigan and southward to North Carolina. A native of colonial America, the bright-flowered little plant was one of the first American wildflowers to catch the gardener's eye. Samples were sent to England in 1745, and prospered there. N. A.

PHLOX TRIOVULATA. From rocky hillsides in New Mexico, west Texas, and adjacent Mexico. The plant spreads about by stolons and comes up here and there between the stones in tufts of needle-leafed stems 4 to 16 inches high. The flowers are striking—large, wide-petalled, varyingly colored lilac, pink, or white. In the British Isles, a bright-pink form of this species is grown as an alpine house plant under the name *P*. 'Mesoleuca'. American gardeners in the northern states have had no success with *P. triovulata* or its forms, but the species should take to Southwest gardens like the native it is. *P. nana* and *P. mesoleuca*, two closely related species or subspecies, share the same range as *P. triovulata* and are just as promising for Southwest gardens.

PHYLA NODIFLORA. *(Lippia repens.)* Makes a tough mat of grayish leaves and small clusters of pink, lavender, purple or white verbena-like flowers from May to October. Used in California as a ground cover in hot dry soil. Will grow in the desert. Frost-damaged at 20°.

PHYLLITIS SCOLOPENDRIUM. *(Scolopendrium vulgare.)* Hart's tongue. A fern with narrow, undivided fronds about 8 inches long and of glossy yellow-green. The plant makes clumps in woods, rocks, and walls in Europe. In North America it grows with finicky rarity in Tennessee, New York, and Ontario. An easy fern for the shade garden.

There are hundreds of named horticultural forms developed mainly in the British Isles. Several of the more distinctive and outstanding are 'Undulatum', 'Capitatum', 'Cristatum', 'Crispum', and 'Ramosum'. N. A.

PHYTEUMA. Perennial relatives of campanula. Smallish, tight-clustered violet flowers of peculiar mold (they are globed at the base, then stretched out into a tube). *P. pauciflorum*, *P. hemisphaericum*, *P. scheuchzeri*, and *P. orbiculare* are strong enough to be trusted out on a rich scree in the collector's garden. N. A.

★**PICEA ABIES 'CAPITATA'.** This tree is rather more a midget than a dwarf—it is a perfectly proportioned forest tree in miniature. Color: somber green. Habit: a broad cone, with drooping branches. A 15-year-old tree is 36 inches high, 27 inches broad at its base. Use: one of the most effective dwarf trees for setting an alpine scene in a small garden.

★**PICEA ABIES 'CLANBRASILIANA'.** One of about 60 horticultural forms of Norway spruce, a spire-form forest tree of Northern Europe. For best growth, most of the *P. abies* forms prefer full sun and ample moisture. They are hardy even in New England.

P. a. 'Clanbrasiliana' grows in the form of a round, flat-topped cake, at a rate of about 2½ inches a year. The color is grass-green. This is a tough, undemanding variety, one of the oldest dwarf conifers in occidental gardens. Century-old specimens are still growing without decline.

PICEA ABIES 'COMPACTA PYRAMIDALIS'. A seedling form which grows into a slender pyramid about 80 inches high and 34 inches broad at the base in 20 years, indicating a vertical growth of 4 inches a year.

★**PICEA ABIES 'NIDIFORMIS'.** Natural-looking growth—low, almost flat, but with branches springing up independently at low angles. At 8 years it is 2 feet across, 1 foot high. Annual rate of growth: 3 inches. Appears to be a seedling.

★**PICEA ABIES 'PENDULA'.** *(P. a. 'Reflexa'.)* Many gardeners dislike this tree when it is trained upright. It appears tormented, as if it were struggling to right itself, and yet as if at the same time it

were being pulled down by its limp, dark green branches. Other gardeners find a drama in this struggle which makes the tree worth using as the dominant specimen in the small alpine garden.

The tree has a quite different value and appearance if it is allowed to follow its naturally flat habit from the first year. Planted high on the rock work, in time this tree will send its branches trailing down several yards.

PICEA ABIES 'PROCUMBENS'. A roughly mounding form with a number of leaders competing for top place. Intriguing. Medium-dark green needles on fine branches. A 35-year-old specimen is full branched and strong, 5 feet across and 2 feet high, indicating an average growth rate of about 2 inches a year.

PICEA ABIES 'REMONTII'. Grows slowly into a ragged pyramid. *P. abies* 'Pygmaea' grows more slowly into a more ragged pyramid. Light pruning will improve these varieties, but don't mention having done so to purists. They consider the raggedness of these conifers their essential characteristic.

PICEA BREWERIANA. Brewer's weeping spruce is a pyramidal tree 100 feet high in its limited range, centering about the Siskyous of southern Oregon and northern California. The needles are fine and gray-green. The horizontal branches bear 6 or 8-foot pendant branchlets which sway in the breeze like Spanish moss.

Grows about 2 inches a year for the first 10 years; no more than 6 inches a year when established. In Great Britain this tree is famous for its grace. In America it is little known and perhaps available from only one or two collectors.

★**PICEA GLAUCA 'CONICA'.** *(P. albertiana 'Conica'.)* A distinctive variety, one of the most popular. A dense cone of bright, grassy green needles which—unlike those of most spruces—are soft instead of prickly. The tree itself has a much softer appearance than most rock garden conifers.

The rate of growth is about 3 inches a year, and at about 5 feet (or about 20 years) the tree often begins to deteriorate. Under less than ideal growing conditions the deterioration may begin earlier than age 20. Ideal conditions for this tree are plentiful moisture; a friable, light and fast-draining soil; partial shade; and shelter from cold winter winds.

This little tree has been used as much in cottage gardens as in rock gardens, and often with charming effect. Its prim outline and new-green color are in keeping with white clapboard, chintz curtains, and beds of geraniums.

★**PIMELEA COARCTICA.** (The name is an untraceable mystery.) A creeping shrub related to daphne. Spreads at a rate of 6 to 9 inches a year, but never reaches up more than 3 inches. Stems are purple; leaves tiny, pointed and blue-gray-green; flowers are tiny, waxen white, innumerable along the stems, and of daphne form and fragrance. There are waxen white berries afterward, shaped and sized like short-grained rice. Grow it in sand, but only in a sunny garden—

where it will be hardy to 0°.

★**PINUS ALBICAULIS.** In its youth (up to about 80 years of age) the mountain whitebark pine is usually found as a cluster of slim, bent gray trunks. As many as seven of the sparsely branched trunks grow in a cluster which eventually fuses at the base. These fused trunks begin as separate seedlings which often sprout from a single cone buried and left by a chipmunk. Within 10 years in the open garden soil this tree will form a densely branched pyramid with a growth rate of about 4 inches a year.

This is also an excellent container plant. The pale, bending trunks and grayish-green needles show up strikingly against darker walls of natural wood or stone.

★**PINUS ARISTATA.** In the desert White Mountains of California, magnificent ruins of this tree—fortresses of driftwood with strips of living bark and limbs—have attained an age of well over 4000 years, making them the world's oldest living things.

In the rock garden, bristlecone pine has a mature appearance and a distinctive individuality from the time it is 6 inches high. The limbs are heavy, irregular, and ground-sweeping. Gray-green needles dotted with pitch and densely packed in circular, brush-like arrangement are carried for 6 years or more, even on the older inside portions of the limbs. They give the tree a thickly pelted, faintly bearish aspect, which is in good character on a rocky knoll in the garden. Growth rate: 4 inches.

★**PINUS BALFOURIANA.** Foxtail pine. Not unlike *P. aristata*. The brushlike branches are shorter than those of the bristlecone pine, and form a narrower top. California mountain native rare in cultivation. Collectors consider it an acquisition. As with many alpine trees, it is slow to give up its infancy. It may grow an inch a year for the first 10 years, then enter its adolescence and put on 4 inches a year.

★**PINUS DENSIFLORA 'UMBRACULIFERA'.** Tanyosho pine, often called umbrella pine because of the flat, spreading habit of its branches. At about 3 years this dwarf begins the same heavy production of cones for which its parent has received the name *densiflora*. At 15 years it is a 5 foot high, flat-topped, horizontally branched tree, which with a little knowledgeable pruning can be made classically Japanesque. (It is a Japanese native to begin with.)

This pine, like all dwarf pines, is grafted on a sapling root of its parent species. Pines are almost impossible to root from cuttings. The Japanese say that grafted pines live only about a century, but then perhaps only the Japanese are concerned about their gardens a hundred years hence.

★**PINUS MUGO.** Partly by inheritance and partly by the operations of the gardener's clippers, mugho pine has infinite variety. Mugho pine may be a shrub or tree from 2 to 20 feet high—with one, several or many trunks; dark green needles; and small cones produced spar-

Pinus aristata

Polemonium amoenum

Picea abies 'Reflexa'

ingly or abundantly. One sowing of seed will yield slow, flat-growing forms, and upright forms which grow a foot a year. When buying a mugho pine at a nursery, walk down a row of this tree and select an individual that seems to be taking on the right character for the job you have in mind.

In books on plant taxonomy the name *Pinus mugo* is sometimes restricted to the taller, more treelike form, while the name *Pinus mugo mughus* is used to designate the smaller, more shrublike form. But in common nursery practice both forms are sold as *Pinus mugo*. Trees sold as *P. m.* 'Pumilio' should be (but are not always) smaller and more compact than the average.

Mugho pine can be pruned to grow in any direction. An entire bank of it can be pruned to grow as a low blanket of interlocking branches. Single specimens can be heightened into 20-foot trees. As a container plant a mugho pine can be left alone to form a vigorous casual branch pattern; or with thoughtful pruning it can be sculptured into a bonsai.

Pinus mugo is hardy to below zero and once established it will get by on very little water.

PINUS STROBUS 'NANA'. A loosely rounded shrub developed from an eastern American forest tree. At 20 years it is 5 feet high, 7 feet across, with no visible bark or branch structure. Attractive if you accept it on its own terms, or it can be shaped to take on a more tree-like appearance. It has softly textured, bluish gray-green needles and small slender cones, sparsely produced. Growth rate of young trees is about 4 inches a year. After about 10 years in one position (or when the tree has had time to drive heavy roots deeply into the soil), the rate of growth picks up to 8 inches a year.

PLATYCODON. Balloon flower, and well named; the big inflated flower buds appear to strain atop their stems like archaic balloons at their moorings. They open into blue-violet or white saucers 3 inches wide. The leafy, deciduous stems of the plant grow upright from a long radish of a root. *P. grandiflorum* is 2 feet high; *P. g. mariesii* a foot. They are found mainly in Japan. Meadow plants in nature, they blend well in meadow plantings in the sunny garden. Blooms in June, July. N. A.

PODOPHYLLUM. May Apple. Tropical-appearing herbs from woodlands of the temperate zone. Umbrella-like leaves a foot across on 2-foot-high fleshy stems. Sheltered and hidden beneath these stems are nodding flower cups of white, followed by large, squashy fruits that resemble persimmons and are delicious in pies. *P. peltatum* grows in the eastern half of the United States. *P. emodi*, with handsomely splotched, green-on-green leaves, grows in the Himalayas. N. A.

POLEMONIUM. Jacob's Ladder. Perennials with ferny, divided leaves that die down in the winter. Open-faced, 5-petaled flowers in late spring. Blue is the typical flower color.

POLEMONIUM AMOENUM. Perhaps only a rose-pink color phase of *P. car-*

neum, but quite distinct for garden purposes. *P. amoenum* is easier to grow, longer-lived, and more inclined to perpetuate itself in the garden by self-sown seedlings. From Washington's Olympic Peninsula. N. A.

POLEMONIUM CAERULEUM. A plant of many European nations which undergoes considerable transformation from place to place in response to the varying geography of its range. Height: 1 to 3 feet. In gardens, a very old-fashioned, very charming plant for borders and woodlands. The deep blue, light-eyed flowers come on again and again from April to July. N. A.

POLEMONIUM CARNEUM. Tall, spare-leaved and brittle-stemmed, with large flowers tinted a blended pale pink and pale yellow—the color often referred to as "flesh." From West Coast woods. Short-lived. Hardy to 0°.

POLEMONIUM PULCHERRIMUM. This and the other alpine Jacob's Ladders usually succumb after a winter or two of alternate freezing and thawing in lowland gardens.

POLEMONIUM REPTANS. A dwarf relative of *P. caeruleum* from open woods in eastern and midwestern America. *P. r.* 'Blue Pearl' is the garden selection usually offered. N. A.

★**POLYGONATUM.** Solomon's seal. Tall woodland plants of the lily family with creeping rootstocks and arching stems which carry opposing rows of broad, pointed leaves, upturned like raised wings. Along the leafless inner arch of the stem hang urns of ivory white rimmed with jade green. This description roughly embraces *P. officinale, P. latifolium, P. multiflorum, P. commutatum,* and *P. biflorum. P. verticillatum* differs in having the leaves arranged in whorls.

Planted in a woodland which is neither too dark nor too dry the Solomon's seals will take care of themselves, widening their colonies and flowering unfailingly each spring, decade after decade. N. A.

POLYGONUM AFFINE. A dense, low mat of spoon leaves or lance leaves which in frosty climates develop attractive red-brown autumn color at the same time the small spikes of pink flowers appear. Let it trail over cool, half-shaded soil and stones. N. A.

★**POLYGONUM VACCINIFOLIUM.** A ramping, rooting-down mat of thin, yard-long branches with little elliptical leaves and, in the fall, rose pink flower spikes. First-rate on a low, sunny wall. Hardy to about 15°.

POLYPODIUM SCOULERI. Dark green with large, leathery, triangular fronds. This and the bright green *P. malahatense*, with long fronds of raggedy-edged leaflets, are easy-going, long-lived ferns for woodlands or the shady side of the house. *P. scouleri* grows on trees and rocks along the Pacific Coast from Vancouver Island to California. *P. malahatense* is a rare plant of local distribution on Vancouver Island. N. A.

★ **POLYPODIUM VULGARE.** An evergreen fern of global distribution in the temperate zone. The furry rhizomes and narrow leathery fronds of polypody follow the fissures of oak and maple trunks, of cliffs, and of boulders half-buried in the woods. Polypody transplants readily to half-shaded stonework, or to open soil in the woodland garden where it makes a refined ground cover.

Both in nature and in gardens, this is a species of many and varied forms. *P. v. columbianum* is the western American form. *P. californicum* and *P. glycyrrhiza* are closely related species. N. A.

POTENTILLA. Perennials or low shrubs of the rose family. Typically their flowers are like small yellow wild roses, and their leaves are divided into 5 leaflets (which gives them their common name, "cinquefoil"). Almost all species are easy to raise from seed. N. A.

POTENTILLA ATROSANGUINEA. Dark scarlet flowers on a rangy 2-foot plant. An easy doer which will self-sow on a rock wall, in the border, and in the woodland. Blooms June to August.

POTENTILLA CINEREA. An alpine mat, 2 to 6 inches high, of 5-divided leaves and stemless pale yellow flowers. In Pacific Coast fog-belt gardens, the mat spreads at a fast rate; in drier gardens and in colder areas, it grows well but slowly. Amazingly, for a Swiss alpine, this plant is successful in many gardens in our southwestern states. Fog-belt gardeners find *Potentilla cinerea* useful as a ground cover in sun or shade. In other areas it should probably be considered a collector's plant. Blooms April through June.

★ **POTENTILLA FRUTICOSA.** One to 4-foot shrub found in the mountains and boreal plains of North America, Europe, and Asia. Several varieties and named seedlings are in cultivation: *P. f.* 'Vilmoriniana' with cream-white flowers; 'Katherine Dykes', a rounding 3-foot bush with large yellow flowers throughout the summer; 'Sutter's Gold', with even larger flowers on a lower bush. Foot-high, spreading forms are common in Western American mountains.

Effective on stepped-back walls or on flat, open ground, in sun or light shade. Combines nicely with blue veronicas.

POTENTILLA NEPALENSIS. Rough and rangy (2 feet) with green leaves and vivid rose-crimson flowers. Said to be one parent (with *P. atrosanguinea* the other) of all the border-bred cinquefoils. Variety *P. n.* 'Willmottiae' (*P. n.* 'Miss Willmott') is a foot high or less, with flowers of clearer rose. For borders, walls, woodlands, and large rock gardens. Blooms in summer.

POTENTILLA NEVADENSIS. From the Spanish Sierra. A 4-inch-high scree plant of compact gray-green growth and yellow flowers. Winter-hardy, drought resistant. Blooms July, August.

POTENTILLA NITIDA. For the collector's scree. A half-woody mat of gray leaves and rose-pink flowers. This is one of the famous European alpines that

hikers trek to see. Most collected plants are shy flowering in lowland gardens, but the form 'Alannah' gives a good show every year. Blooms in summer.

★ **POTENTILLA RECTA.** (*P.* 'Warrensii'.) A stout basal clump of green leaves held flat like outstretched hands, and cut into 5 to 7 finger-like parts. Large yellow flowers in branching and rebranching clusters on 2 foot stems, June to September. The prolific seed may give you ten plants for one the second year, a hundred plants or more the third year. Give this one space and tall companions in meadows, in woods, and on walls.

POTENTILLA RUPESTRIS. A clump of long, feather-form leaves with the leaflets few, paired, and wide-spaced. White flowers in loose clusters on stems vary, in different geographical forms, from 6 to 18 inches. Flowers June to September. A vigorous plant, tolerant of dry soil. Seeds about, but not enough to be troublesome. Useful on walls.

POTENTILLA TORMENTILLO-FORMOSA. (*P.* 'Tonguei'.) An herbaceous plant of garden origin. About 10 inches high with clusters of apricot colored flowers. Grow it in rich soil. Divide every spring.

POTENTILLA TRIDENTATA. Grows in rocky places in several of the eastern states. Forms a network of underground stems which run about (at a controllable rate) and send up tufts of glossy dark leaves and white midsummer flowers. 3 inches.

POTENTILLA VERNA. Virtually a smaller, slower *P. cinerea*, suitable for the well watered scree and the edge of the primrose bed.

POTENTILLA VILLOSA. A Northwestern native with beautiful silvery, downy leaves and yellow flowers. Give it a rich scree and ample moisture. About 7 inches high.

PRIMULA. Primrose. The genus contains 500 to 600 species of 1 to 30-inch herbaceous plants, the majority of which are found in the Himalayas of western China and Tibet. The European and Japanese primroses are few but important. America's several species have proved nearly ungrowable in lowland gardens.

All primulas respond to the same soil composition, but since some species are bog plants and others are woodland and alpine plants, their water requirements vary. An ideal soil for primulas is an airy, friable mixture of about equal parts humus, sand, and clay. Most primroses do best in half-shaded places, where both soil and air stay cool and moist in summer. In the language of rock gardeners this optimum arrangement of soil, shade, and moisture is known as "primula conditions." The term describes as well the best garden situation for most woodland plants and the larger-leafed rhododendrons.

★ **PRIMULA AURICULA.** The wild progenitor, nearly four centuries removed,

of innumerable garden forms. The wild auricula is a rock dweller in the Alps, a tuft-maker with broad blunt leaves, smooth surfaced, smooth or saw-edged, and grayish with a powdery coating of "farina" (absent in certain varieties). Butter yellow flowers, a few in a cluster, are held well above the leaves on stiff stems. From this plant have descended:

1. The highly stylized show Auriculas, whose flowers are circled about the base, the middle, and the edge of the petals with three concentric bands, the innermost of white farina, the middle of color, and the outer of farina or of leaf green.

2. The alpine Auriculas, with large clusters of yellow or, rarely, white-eyed flowers, and usually a single ground color which fades outwardly toward the margin of the petals.

3. The garden Auriculas, which are larger, stronger plants than either the show or the alpine Auriculas, and which have red, white, brown, purple, yellow, and pastel flowers with little or no farina.

Most of the show and alpine Auriculas grow too weakly to be trusted out in the open, nor do they perfect the powdery cosmetics of their flowers in the rain and wind. But the garden Auriculas are as easy in the open and as quick to make themselves into divisible clumps as the Polyanthus. Hardy much below 0°; best adapted to cool areas.

PRIMULA BEESIANA. One of the Candelabra section of the genus; this section has tall flower stems carrying superimposed, spaced tiers of flowers. A wet-soil plant with massive thirsty leaves shaped like long tongues, and 2-foot stems carrying up to as many as 7 tiers of magenta flowers. Spring and early summer bloom. N. A.

★ **PRIMULA BULLEYANA.** Candelabra section. As hearty and long-lived in the garden as *P. japonica*. *P. bulleyana's* floral collars are reddish orange in the bud, opening into chrome yellow flowers. Hybridizes freely with other species of the Candelabra section, producing rose, apricot, salmon, buff, and orange-flowering plants. Early summer flowers. N. A.

PRIMULA BURMANICA. A Burmese plant closely akin to *P. beesiana*. Told from that plant by its larger leaves, with broader and more rounded ends gradually tapering to longer leaf stems. N. A.

PRIMULA CLUSIANA. This and *P. glaucescens*, *P. wulfeniana*, *P. hirsuta*, *P. glutinosa*, *P. minima*, and their natural hybrids are small relatives of *P. auricula*, all plants of high rocky places in the Alps where they make clumps of hard leathery little leaves and outsized flowers of lilac and magenta rose. These plants are easy enough to grow in rich, half-shaded scree, but their flowers are rarely produced. N. A.

PRIMULA DENTICULATA. From Himalayan meadows spongy with snow water. Growable in moist shade gardens in the Pacific Northwest and in the Northeast. The plant spends the fall and winter as a cluster of huge buds. In early spring the buds open into rosettes of long floppy leaves like those of a fat dandelion, but with uncut edges. Deep winey-

Primula sieboldii

Primula burmanica

Primula elatior

lavender flowers are arranged in dense round clusters atop 18-inch stems.

PRIMULA FRONDOSA. For the collector's garden. A 4-inch tuft of bicolored leaves, dark green above, powdered white below. The flowers (held 6 inches high) are clustered, notch-petaled, and pink, with a darker eye. This plant of the Balkan mountains is a pleasant surprise in the garden. Despite its small size, it thrives and even seeds itself in any garden soil that is partly shaded and moist yet well drained. This species can adapt itself to drier garden atmospheres than most other primulas. *P. farinosa* is closely related, but smaller and far less good-natured. April bloom. N. A.

PRIMULA INVOLUCRATA. Low clumps of dark green leaves. Tall slender stems bear sparsely flowered clusters of white. *P. yargongensis* is a similar, rose-flowered species. Both are easy in moist shade and both bloom in May. Divide in March, April. N. A.

★ **PRIMULA JAPONICA.** A tall candelabra primrose from wet places in the Alps of Japan. The wild plant is purple. After a century of selection in European and American gardens we have white, rose, lilac, salmon, carmine, striped and bi-colored varieties. None tops 'Miller's Crimson', the old crimson, maroon-eyed variety. *P. japonica* grows most lushly in a large bog—but not in standing water. The plant will grow readily in upland soil if given abundant water. Adaptable to west coast and east coast states. Blooms in summer.

PRIMULA JULIAE. Discovered in 1901 in the Caucasus Mountains of Asia Minor, the species itself is known only to collectors, but its hybrids are widely grown. It quickly produced a wide range of garden hybrids with *P. elatior* and *P. vulgaris*.

Bright magenta ★*P.* 'Wanda' was one of the first of these Juliana primroses and is still one of the most popular.

Wild *P. juliae* is a dwarf dense plant about 2 inches high. It makes spreading masses of dark little ear-like leaves and small, nearly stemless magenta flowers. N. A.

PRIMULA MARGINATA. A relative of *P. auricula* from cliff crevices in the Alps. The narrow, saw-edged leaves have on their surface a silvery powder which thickens into a definite margin along the teeth. The flowers of all the cultivated forms are light blue, lavender, or white. An easily grown species of first importance to collectors. N. A.

★ **PRIMULA OBCONICA.** From warm, low elevations in Western China, Burma, and Tibet. Will not survive more than a few degrees of frost, but is much used in California as a bedding annual (actually it is a short-lived perennial). The rest of the country knows *P. obconica* as a florist's plant worthy of a place beside African violets on a well-lighted windowsill. The large and lovely flowers open continuously for months. Leaves of this plant can cause a rash on some allergy-prone people.

★ **PRIMULA POLYANTHA.** This is America's universal garden primrose, a clump of elongate and netted dark green leaves and a clutch of flowers on 9-inch stems. There is no end of colors—white, yellow, scarlet, purple, and pastels by the legion. The English call them "Polyanthus", reserving the name "primrose" for the various forms of *P. vulgaris*. The Polyanthus is either a form of *Primula vulgaris*, or a hybrid of this and two other primulas, *P. veris* and *P. elatior*.

Popular interest in the development of the Polyanthus began in England about 1700 and intensified during the 18th century to something like the frenzy of the tulipomania in Holland the century before.

The early taste in Polyanthus ran to freak forms such as hose-in-hose (duplex flowers, one inside the other), and Jack-in-the-green (flowers resting in a ruff of little leaves at the top of normal stems). Most of these freaks were lost to cultivation when the intense popular interest in Polyanthus subsided in the 19th century.

The modern Polyanthus, with its larger flowers and great color range, is a product mainly of the 20th century. It will grow in most of the 50 states, will survive winter temperatures far below zero, and requires at least a cool winter's rest. The desert summer is too much for it.

PRIMULA ROSEA. Ideal for soil saturated with fresh running water. There it expands oblong, glossy, reddish leaves in the earliest spring. Stout 8-inch flower stems arise with the leaves and part at the top into clusters of bright rosy-pink flowers.

This primrose will also adapt to drier-than-bog conditions. If Juliana primroses grow to special lusciousness in your garden, you can probably grow this one under the same conditions. N. A.

★ **PRIMULA SIEBOLDII.** In April the large, soft, crinkly leaves and the flowers stretch simultaneously from mats of winter-dormant buds. Each of the 8 to 12-inch rod-like flower stems holds a cluster of flat-faced upright flowers which are like phlox in their form, carriage, and color range (rose, pink, white).

This native of Japan was cultivated there for two centuries and selected into uncounted garden forms. Some have flowers with rounded petals, other forms have petals intricately pinked. One of the half dozen most easily grown Primula species, it asks only a rich, cool soil in part shade. Combine it with woodland plants. Divide it in March every third spring. Hardy in the west and east coast states; a successful plant in New York gardens. Blooms in May.

PRIMULA VERIS. The cowslip ranges over most of Europe and much of Central Asia. It has long been grown in the gardens of wildflower enthusiasts but it has never created any general stir. The yellow flowers of the cowslip have smallish petals and puffed-up, baglike calyxes. Yet these unlavish flowers have horticultural significance for the fact that they are held clustered on 6 to 8-inch stems.

The clustered habit and rod-like stems of polyanthus are thought by some researchers to have been inherited from the cowslip, and the fullness of petal and variety of color are believed to have come from *P. vulgaris*. Where the cowslip and the primrose grow wild together on the same grassy banks, they produce an intermediate plant which has been called *P. elatior,* the oxlip. The true *P. elatior* is a larger plant than the cowslip and has flowers of a more decided yellow.

★ **PRIMULA VULGARIS** *(P. acaulis.)* The primrose. This is the "prime rose" of springtime in the British Isles and in Europe. It is the original title holder of the name—now contracted to "primrose"—by which we call the whole genus. The primrose makes clumps of dark green leaves and bears short-stemmed single flowers of light "primrose-yellow," with a saffron-yellow eye. The Polyanthus primroses of modern gardens were developed from this wild plant (perhaps in hybrid combination with *P. veris* and *P. elatior*). The wild primrose imparts a soft yellowness like April sun to woodland gardens.

PULMONARIA. Clumps of low, ample leaves and short stems of tubular flowers. Pulmonarias grow in oak woods in England and on the Continent. There are several species described below, all useful in the woodland garden—and one is splendid.

★ **PULMONARIA ANGUSTIFOLIA.** Dark green leaves, long and narrowish. Blue flowers of dark, yet glowing, purity on 6 to 12-inch stems in April. A drift of this easily grown plant, flowering together with soft yellow *Primula vulgaris,* is one of the great rewards of woodland gardening. Divide in the fall after the leaves die down.

PULMONARIA OFFICINALIS. Spotted dog. Evergreen clumps of heart-shaped leaves liberally splashed with pale dots and blotches, and bristly with transparent hairs. Flowers of mottled muscat red and violet on 8 to 12-inch stems. April flowering. N. A.

PULMONARIA SACCHARATA. A larger edition of *P. officinalis;* grows to 18 inches. Reddish-violet or whitish flowers. Both this and *P. officinalis* are easy and permanent in shady places. N. A.

PYROLA. Stoloniferous forest plants. With their leathery, glossy leaves, they look as if they would transplant with ease. Actually they are so difficult to cultivate that almost no one has succeeded.

RAMONDA MYCONI. *(R. pyrenaica.)* An alpine relative of the African violet. Hardy to sub-zero temperatures. Makes a wide rosette of broad blunt leaves pressed flat on the ground. The surface of the leaves is ridged and furrowed like a relief map. Each leaf lives 5 or 6 years; the rosette may live to be 20, widening to dinner-plate size. The flattened and beaked, lilac-violet flowers are similar to African violets. Blooms in May.

Ramonda is a collector's plant which can be grown flat in soft, humus-rich primrose soil, but it prefers a wall in cool mossy shade. Drainage must be swift; the great flat rosette is subject to decay. Adaptable to the northeastern states and to the Pacific coast from California to Alaska.

RANUNCULUS. Buttercup. Fillers of pastures, but there are also alpine buttercups.

★ **RANUNCULUS CORTUSAEFOLIUS.** Grows 3 feet high in wet soil. Round, cut-edged leaves and light yellow flowers are both of tropical bigness. From the Island of Teneriffe in the Canaries. Won't take much frost. Summer flowers.

RANUNCULUS MONTANUS. From the Alps. A refined slow-growing clump of small rounded cut and lobed leaves and large single buttercups that open in March. Leaves and flowers together are no more than 6 inches high. A tough plant, permanent in the garden with the least care. Grow it among primroses. N. A.

RANUNCULUS REPENS. A creeping, invasive buttercup that makes a dark, shining green (although somewhat floppy) ground cover for neglected places in the garden. *R. repens* 'Pleniflorus', with fully double, button-like flowers of waxen yellow, is planted more often than the species. N. A.

RAOULIA. Carpet makers from New Zealand—packed masses of minute rosettes which cover the ground as tightly as a scab of lichen. The raoulias are composite plants (relatives of the daisy family) whose flower heads are like minute daisy centers without the daisy rays. They need hot sun, sandy soil, and water every few days during the summer. San Francisco grows them well.

RAOULIA AUSTRALIS. An unplant-like silver-gray carpet, sprinkled in April with light yellow button flowers. A wonderful collector's plant, fruitful of garden conversation. Visitors sometimes mistake it for a piece of cloth. Frost-damaged at 20°-25°.

RAOULIA LUTESCENS. A yellowish-green mat. Pinhead-size button flowers solidly surface the mat in late April and early May, turning it bright yellow. Slow growing. Frost-damaged at 20°-25°.

★ **RAOULIA TENUICAULIS.** Olive green with glints of silver. Minute, pale yellow flowers bead the mat in March. They exude nectar and an opiate sweetness detectable a good many feet down the air stream. Makes a long-lived ground cover. Growth is rapid (up to 2 feet across in a year), but the mat is persistent and should need dividing and replanting no oftener than every 5 years. Use as you would thyme, or in pattern planting. Frost-damaged at 15°. Kills back ominously at 0°, but restores itself.

RHODODENDRON. English translations follow the Latin names of some of the rhododendrons discussed below, usually those names which hold clues about the plant's culture or identification. Rhododendrons vary widely, even within a given species. If you possibly can, get named forms. One hallmark of an outstanding rhododendron is the symbol "F.C.C." appearing after the species name. This symbol means that the plant you are getting has been propagated from a plant which has received a First Class Certificate from the Royal Horticultural Society. For a discussion of the garden requirements of rhododendron, see page 32. The azaleas are rhododendrons, botanically speaking, and are so treated here.

RHODODENDRON. Native species. Except for the untamable *R. albiflorum* of western mountains, our native rhododendrons transplant easily from the wild. Both collected and nursery-grown shrubs of a number of the species are on the market.

Use the evergreen species such as the eastern ★*R. catawbiense* and ★*R. carolinianum* and the western ★*R. macrophyllum* as background foliage in the woodland garden. Use such tall deciduous rhododendrons as ★*R. calendulaceum* (the flame azalea) and ★*R. occidentale* (the white or pink yellow-splotched western azalea) for brilliant May color in sunny borders or woodland glades. They don't flower well in shade. Shell-pink ★*R. vaseyi* has a restrained elegance that suits it for the company of primulas, ferns, and the other soft leaves and flowers of cool half-shaded places. *R. canadense* is a low stoloniferous shrub which can go in the foreground. It grows 15 inches high, 15 inches wide at 10 years. This species' magenta-rose, lilac, or (rarely) white flowers—with a corolla split into butterfly-like wings—sit in sprightly fashion on bare branches.

★ **RHODODENDRON AUGUSTINII.** Upright and open (3 to 5 feet high, 30 inches wide in 10 years). Leaves are narrow, as long as 3 inches, with an attenuate point. They have a downy covering which reminds the fingers of felt. The best of this species' named seedlings are clear blue-violet. The wild plant runs to beet purples. ★'Blue Diamond' and ★'Blue Tit' are semi-dwarf *R. augustinii* hybrids of rich amethystine hues. April, May.

★ **RHODODENDRON CAMPYLOGYNUM.** Variable. 'Patricia', a selected seedling, grows 19 inches high and 30 inches across in 10 years, has bright rose flowers and blunt-tipped, 3-inch leaves. Seed will produce flowers of pale rose-purple to black-purple in May.

★ **RHODODENDRON CANTABILE.** (Worthy of song.) A fine leafed, twiggy bush 3 feet high. Scarce in cultivation and not readily obtainable. Selected forms have startlingly clear and deep blue flowers.

RHODODENDRON CHRYSEUM. (Golden yellow.) A shrublet of twiggy growth and rough form (about 16 by 16 inches in 15 years). Blunt leaves ⅜ inch long, dull green beneath a furry coating of pale yellow. When bruised the leaves are sweetly aromatic with a scent between leather and sage. Dense clusters of tiny lemon yellow flowers with their thready inner parts noticeably exserted.

Best in sun with plenty of moisture. Damaged at 15°. May bloom.

★**RHODODENDRON CILIATUM.** (Fringed.) Branches few, irregular, and stocky (13 inches high, 24 inches across in 10 years). Hairy 3-inch leaves, rough and abrasive to the touch. The big (2-inch) pale rose-pink flowers come in such numbers that they can weaken the plant. Some gardeners thin the flower buds. ★'Racil' and ★'Cilpinense' are valuable *R. ciliatum* hybrids, but no handsomer than their parent. March, April.

RHODODENDRON DIDYMUM. A somber shrublet, stout and slow in growth (14 inches high, 16 inches across in 10 years). The small black-crimson flowers tucked beneath the leaves do nothing to liven the plant until the low sun strikes through them. Then they glow ruby-red like stained glass. To get the full effect of this glass fire, plant *R. didymum* where both the rising and the setting sun will reach it. Shade during the midday. Flowers in June and July.

★**RHODODENDRON FASTIGIATUM.** The name *fastigiatum* implies a "narrow and columnar" habit, but most forms in cultivation are flattish. (The F. C. C. form is 8 inches high, 18 inches wide in 10 years and has amethyst flowers.) The blue-green leaves are like the wing cases of some neat little beetle—rounded on the end, rolled down along the edges, seamed down the middle. *R. impeditum* is so closely related to *R. fastigiatum* that one authoritative grower asks whether they are distinct. Either name will buy you something special.

RHODODENDRON FERRUGIN-EUM. The alpine-rose of Switzerland. A low, stout shrub (16 inches high and 24 inches across in 10 years). Leathery leaves are narrow, 2 inches long, and deep green. Small flowers, but selected forms are of a bright and cheerful cherry rose. Blooms in June. Takes full sun well.

RHODODENDRON FORRESTII REPENS. In Yunnan and Tibet, where it is a creeping, stem-rooting dweller of dripping moss-covered rocks, this ivy-like growth erupts in its season with chubby, glowing crimson bells, and becomes one of the incomparable marvels of the world of flowers.

Nothing of the sort happens in the garden. With us *R. f. repens* is a reluctant grower (a wizened 6 inches high, 14 inches across in 10 years) which struggles to bring forth a flower or two a year. Quite out of reason, hybrids of this species are sound, easily grown garden plants. ★'Carmen' is low and dwarf with dark red flowers. ★'Little Joe' has bright scarlet flowers on nearly prostrate branches. ★'Elizabeth' is taller, with blood red flowers (eventually it is 5 feet, but it can be kept at half that height by pruning). April blooming.

★**RHODODENDRON GLAUCOPHYL-LUM.** (With bluish-gray leaf.) In some forms this is a gnomish growth (8 inches high, 10 inches across in 10 years) of thick, stubby branches and hard little egg-shaped leaves that are a dark polished green on their upper side, bluish-white beneath. Nodding bell flowers of magenta or clearer rose pink. Light shade. May flowering.

★**RHODODENDRON GLOMERULA-TUM.** (Having dense clusters.) A rounded shrub (28 inches high, 25 inches wide in 15 years). Gray-green leaves less than an inch long, petiole and all. Mauve-purple flowers. Full sun.

RHODODENDRON HANCEANUM NANUM. A tidy, clipped-looking shrub (12 inches high, 18 inches wide in 10 years). Tufts of 1½-inch leaves are leathery and brownish green—like old Morocco book-binding. Flowers are pale yellow (rarely white) in a stalked truss. Needs shade. Spring flowers.

★**RHODODENDRON HIPPOPHAE-OIDES.** Upright and somewhat leggy (3 feet high, 17 inches wide in 10 years). Leaves grayish, olive green, 1¼ inches long, elliptical. Inch-wide flowers of lilac, lavender-rose (or in selected forms, light violet) open abundantly in May, and smatteringly through the growing season. Full sun or light shade in coastal climates. Survives sub-zero temperatures. Successful at the Brooklyn Botanic Garden.

RHODODENDRON KEISKEI. Usually a dense low shrub (2 feet high, 3 feet across in 20 years). Abundant cream or lemon yellow flowers in April. Shade it from the midday sun and water it well.

RHODODENDRON KELETICUM. (Charming.) A Tibetan closely related to *R. radicans,* but a couple of inches taller with some exposure of bare twig.

RHODODENDRON LEPIDOTUM ELAEAGNOIDES. An elfin shrub for a guarded spot (10 by 10 inches in 10 years). Bright yellow or dull plum flowers, inch-wide and solitary, above the pointed leaves in June. Native to various elevations from 10,000 to 16,000 feet in Sikkum, Burma, and Yunnan. Its garden hardiness depends on the degree of cold to which it is natively accustomed. Usually survives a drop to 10° or lower.

RHODODENDRON LEUCASPIS. (White shield—a reference to the flat form of the 2-inch-wide white flowers.) A low bush (10 inches high, 17 inches across at 10 years). Hairy, oval, olive-green leaves 1¾ inches long. Flowers appear in February if frost hasn't killed the buds. Give it shelter and half shade. Bud damage occurs at 25°; damage to branches at about 18°.

★**RHODODENDRON LUTESCENS.** (Yellowish.) A sparse, upright shrub (37 inches high and 22 inches wide in 10 years). Leaves olive-drab, narrow, pointed, 2½ inches long, and evergreen if temperature doesn't drop much below 20°. Open-faced flowers about 1½ inches across. Typically this species is pale yellow; richer yellow selections are available. Use it toward the back of a shrub grouping. Let lower rhododendrons branch through its sparse stems. February to April bloom.

★**RHODODENDRON MICROLEU-CUM.** A thin, twiggy little bush (14 by 14 inches in 10 years). Narrow ½-inch-long leaves and small paper-white flowers. Needs part shade.

★**RHODODENDRON MUCRONA-TUM.** (*Azalea ledifolia.*) Half-evergreen with soft, hairy, grayish leaves and white flowers with a hothouse look. But the plant is hardy to zero. Grows to 2 by 2 feet in 10 years. Blooms in May.

★**RHODODENDRON MUCRONULA-TUM.** (Sharp pointed.) An upright shrub (7 feet high in 30 years). Narrow pointed leaves drop in the northern winter, persist in the south. Bright warm magenta flowers in February. Combine with *Erica carnea* and *Pernettya mucronata.* Native to the north of China, Korea, and Japan. Thoroughly hardy on our west coast and even in New England, but frost blights the opening flowers.

★**RHODODENDRON OBTUSUM.** (Blunt.) A shrub of mountain flanks in Japan. Parent of the well-known Kurume azaleas, which probably are superior selections of (and hybrids within) the species developed in Kurume, Japan, over a long period.

In this country we now have scores of varieties colored pink, salmon, scarlet, crimson, or white, and bearing the delicately poetic names the Japanese give their garden flowers. The commonest of these is 'Hinodegiri' which has fading red crêpe-paper flowers and is one of the least attractive. In form the Kurume azaleas are low and dense—with a compact, almost sheared appearance. The evergreen or semi-evergreen leaves are small, dark, and blunt. Hardy to about —10°. Used as single specimens in front of taller rhododendrons the Kurumes give standout color. In mass plantings—for which purpose they are especially adaptable—the Kurumes are a major reason for rock gardening. They bloom in early spring in cold regions; in mild winter areas some bloom in fall and winter.

★**RHODODENDRON OBTUSUM KAEMPFERI.** The Kaempferi azaleas average 4 feet in mature height. Growth habit is loose, showing much bare branch. Colors are of the salmon-orange-terra cotta range. The dull green leaves take on autumn tints as colorful as the flowers, and then they more or less fall away in semi-evergreen manner. Hardy even in New England.

★**RHODODENDRON OREOTREPHES.** (Mountain dweller.) Upright to 7 feet at maturity, but selected forms are more compact (18 inches high, 24 inches across in 10 years). The broad, 1½-inch leaves are bright blue-green when they are new, darker at maturity. The flowers are a mauve or mauve-pink as delicate and evanescent as the tints of certain rare pearls. Said to be tender in New York and New England, but safe on the West Coast. They bloom in April or May.

★**RHODODENDRON PEMAKOENSE.** (From Pemako, Tibet.) A low, dense shrub, twice as wide as high. (23 inches across, 11 inches high in 15 years). Dark, glossy green leaves, 1 inch long, blunt-tipped and narrowly oval. Covers itself with large mauve-pink flowers (which pass too quickly) in March. One of the very few rhododendrons which spreads by stolons (underground suckers). Encourage this habit by top-dressing with peat moss or leaf mold. Prefers half shade or, in coastal climates, full sun and extra water.

RHODODENDRON POUKHA-NENSE. *(R. yedoense poukhanense.)* An evergreen azalea of 3-foot dimension. A bit bare and stick-like about the older portions. Deciduous in cold areas. A common plant on grassy mountain slopes and thin pine woods in South Korea. Wild forms have cold lilac-purple flowers. Even the commonly available variety 'Yodogawa' lacks warmth in its double lilac flowers. March or April bloom.

RHODODENDRON RACEMOSUM. Varies from 1 to 6 feet at maturity (about 20 years). Taller forms make inferior garden shrubs, thin and awkward, with maverick branches that shoot up willow-fast from the body of the shrub. (Sometimes these runaway branches grow as much as 2 feet a year.)

The popularity of this species stems more from its early introduction, availability, and demonstrated hardiness than from its landscape value. But the flowers (April and May) are worth having. They are bright pink in the best forms, and borne both in terminal clusters and in clusters along the branch growth made the previous year.

Low growing forms and compact forms of middling height are available from several American nurseries. If you happen to get a leggy form, prune it.

RHODODENDRON RADICANS. (Rooting stems.) An ankle-high shrublet from stony moorlands at 14,000 to 15,000 feet near Lhasa in Tibet. Garden growth rate: 5 inches high, 15 inches wide at 15 years. Leaves narrow, densely packed, ⅝ inch long, dark green with a gloss. Purple flowers are huge (for the plant) and produced in leaf-hiding abundance in late May. Best in full sun in coastal climates. Topdress with peat moss to encourage stem roots. Rooted branches can be detached and nursed into new plants. Cuttings root with extreme ease.

RHODODENDRON RUPICOLA. (From stony places.) A twiggy mass of small narrow leaves which turn an alarming dead, leaden color in winter. Reddish-purple flowers of open funnel form in April and May. Sun.

★**RHODODENDRON RUSSATUM.** (Reddened.) A small shrub of roughly oval form, the larger end upward. Growth rate: 23 inches high, 17 inches wide in 10 years. Inch-long, oval leaves of strong medicinal smell (but only when rolled between the fingers). The flowers are dark plum purple. New growth has reddish purple bark. Best in full sun.

★**RHODODENDRON SCHLIPPEN-BACHII.** Baron von Schlippenbach's name encumbers this magnificent woodland azalea from Korea and Manchuria. Big soft pink flowers and big whorled leaves open together in April. Give it half shade, wind shelter, and much water. Growth rate: 3 by 3 feet in 15 years.

★**RHODODENDRON SCINTILLANS.** (Sparkling.) A 3-footer with an erect, open branch pattern. Lavender blue or (in the F. C. C. form) royal blue. It flowers in April.

RHODODENDRON SERPYLLIFOLI-UM. (Thyme-leaved.) Wild-thyme azalea from central and southern Japan has perhaps the smallest leaves of any rhododendron—¼ inch long in some forms. The little rosy lavender or white azaleas open along thin, twiggy branches. Sometimes frost damaged at 20°. May flowers.

RHODODENDRON TRICHOSTO-MUM LEDOIDES. (Like ledum.) An upright, vase-shaped shrub (18 by 18 inches in 10 years). The leggy branches and little narrow leaves are no garden ornament. However, the pink to white flowers are delightful—individually tiny, but clustered in ball-shaped heads, with the fragrance and the tubular form of daphne flowers. Need sun and extra moisture.

★**RHODODENDRON WILLIAMSI-ANUM.** Heart-shaped leaves—bronze when new, afterward green—on a flatened, dome-shaped shrub. Some forms are prostrate and grow only an inch a year; others grow rounded and four times faster. Unfortunately, most forms which are making the rounds of American nurseries are virtually non-flowering.

Free-flowering forms in the stock of British Columbia nurserymen will become available here sooner or later. One of these selections grows 12 inches high, 24 inches across in 15 years, and has shell pink flowers of bell form, flared to a breadth of 2¾ inches. This is one of the first plants in the garden to show signs of distress when the soil and atmosphere dry out. Give it abundant water and afternoon shade.

There are some excellent hybrids, more easily grown than wild *R. williamsianum*. 'Bow Bells', a vigorous semi-dwarf with leaves and flowers much like those of the wild form, makes a rounded shrub at a growth rate of about 4 inches a year. 'Moonstone', a compact 1 to 3-foot shrub, has cream flower cups flecked with red. 'Humming Bird' is closer to its parent than either 'Bow Bells' or 'Moonstone'. Water it well.

ROMANZOFFIA SITCHENSIS. Grows beside trickling ice water on shady mountain cliffs in the Northwest. This 6- to 10-inch perennial has a bulbous base, scalloped kidney-shaped leaves, and starry white flowers standing separately on thread-fine divided stems. Other romanzoffias of similar fragile effect are *R. unalaschkensis, R. suksdorfii*, and a tiny dweller on sea cliffs along our Pacific coast, 1- to 3-inch

R. tracyi. All require careful cultivation in primula soil and shade. N. A.

ROSA. The miniature roses, intriguing as they are, have little or no place in the rock garden. But in the rockery— why not? Four-inch-high *Rosa chinensis minima* (*R. roulettii*) with tiny double pink roses is a mystery discovered by Correvon in a windowbox garden in a Swiss alpine village. He could find no one in the alpine village who remembered its origin. N. A., but cover the plants in hard freeze areas.

ROSCOEA CAUTLEOIDES and **R. HUMEANA.** These come up late in the spring from deeply buried roots of tuberous and translucent fleshiness. They form lush, bladed leaves, like those of corn, on 12 or 16 inches of stalk. The midsummer flowers are orchid-like, with both hooded and drooping petals. The flowers of *R. humeana* are purple, those of *R. cautleoides* soft yellow. Plant the roots of *Roscoea* 6 inches deep in primula soil.

RUBUS ARCTICUS. A fine-stemmed, 3- to 6-inch raspberry from the Arctic tundra. In the sunny woodland garden or beneath alpine rhododendrons, the plant ramps about freely and harmlessly by means of stolons. Little wild rose flowers open above the lobed leaves all summer. Raspberries—composed of only about 3 to 7 beads—make rare dots over the colony throughout the flowering season. Taste one and you'll wish this tangy sweetness came in bushels. The raspberry leaves take on orangy autumn tints before they drop. This plant comes close to earning a star as a ground cover in woodsy situations. N. A.

RUBUS FOCKEANUS. Makes a flat mat of distinctive maple-form foliage. Leaves are 1½ inches across, dark evergreen, polished, eroded along the edges of their roundish maple lobes, deeply channeled over their surface with a network of sunken veins. A small start grows 3 or 4 feet across in one year on a moist sunny bank. The blackberry flowers are small, white, and picayunish. This plant may be worth a star. Hardiness proved down to 5°.

SANGUINARIA CANADENSIS. Bloodroot spreads broad, cove-edged leaves and white anemone-like flowers, 6 or 8 inches high, over acres of woods and meadowlands in eastern America. Leaves and flowers expand in the first warmth of spring from thick, brittle roots, which drip a blood-colored juice when you break them. A single joint of bloodroot can expand into a yard-wide colony within 5 years in the moist, soft soil of the woodland garden. *S. canadensis* 'Multiplex' is a slow growing form with fully double flowers like small peonies. N. A.

SANTOLINA CHAMAECYPARIS-SUS. A silvery gray shrub 18 to 24 inches high with soft, small, finely divided leaves. *S. virens* (*S. viridis*) has green foliage.

Santolina flowers are unlovely discs —the yellow centers of daisy flowers. The entire plant has a strong sage-like smell. Santolina enjoys heat, even desert heat. Plant it on sunny rockwork. Massed, it makes a rough ground cover or a hedge. If the plants become overgrown, shear them in the spring. The clippings will root easily in shade and sand. N. A.

★**SAPONARIA OCYMOIDES.** An indestructible wall plant and a handy plant for the rock garden in general. Something like a woodland phlox with baskets of procumbent stems (covered with scratchy hairs like the stems of chickweed to which saponaria is actually related), small, dark green, oval phlox leaves, and bright rose phlox-petalled flowers in loose bunches. Flowers from May to July. A foot high and, after a few years, 5 feet across. N. A.

SATUREJA. Savory. Small shrubby herbs with tough wiry stems and narrow grayish leaves. The savories are dry land members of the mint family. Nine to 12-inch-high *S. montana*, with rosy-lilac summer flowers, is offered from time to time by dealers in small plants. The savories are neat, quiet plants which take care of themselves in the herb garden and on sunny rockwork. They may winter-kill at 5°, but seedlings usually show up.

★**SATUREJA DOUGLASII.** (*Micromeria chamissonis.*) Yerba buena, a trailing plant in light woodlands from British Columbia to Los Angeles. The stems show paired oval leaves which release a delightful fragrance when rubbed or crushed. Paired oval leaves distributed along prostrate, rooting stems. Small lavender flowers. A valuable evergreen cover for garden areas under casual cultivation.

SAXIFRAGA. The saxifrages are low, rosette-forming plants with star or cup flowers on 3-inch to 3-foot stems. Most species in cultivation are alpine or woodland plants of first importance to the collector's rock garden. Several species have the toughness and beauty to qualify as landscape plants. The several hundred species in the genus *Saxifraga* have been divided into sections. The species within each section have mutual features —and thus mutual garden dispositions. Section: *Euaizoonia.* True rock plants from high alpine clefts. Leaves typically in pressed-down rosettes of leathery grayish green. Along the leaf edges is an ornamental row of white dots formed of lime drawn out of the soil and deposited by evaporation. Lime also grays the leaf blades and gives these plants their common name—encrusted saxifrages. Flowers are starry and white (usually) in simple, narrow clusters or in great branching plumes. Grow in light, fast draining loam or on a scree. Give them afternoon shade. Except in fog-belt gardens they will scorch in the full sun. Early summer bloom.

Section: *Kabschia.* Pincushion-sized alpine plants with large, white, yellow, lilac, or purple flowers on about 4 inches of stem. The species hybridize freely and the hybrids outstep the species in flower size and color range. In Great Britain and on the Continent early in this century, these tiny plants were the

improbable source of a nursery bonanza. The Kabschias were intensely hybridized, glowingly named, and briskly sold. Hundreds of hybrids were brought out before World War II. Lately, Kabschia-fancying is declining, but at least one North American nurseryman keeps a stock of many of the famous old varieties.

Kabschia saxifrages require a balanced exposure to sun and shade. They will dry up and die in the full sun; they also die of too much shade. The ideal exposure is the moving sun and shadow pattern provided by a lath covering.

Most collectors grow Kabschias in pots of scree compost. Their small size suits them well to pot gardening. Old plants of different Kabschia varieties make domed cushions about 3 to 10 inches across. They're so small, in fact, that one of their great dangers is being overgrown by moss. Use tweezers to remove moss from between the saxifrage rosettes. They bloom in spring.

Kabschias are soundly hardy (down to 0° or lower) and adaptable to open ground cultivation in the shady lee of a large stone or between raised stepping stones. But here more than in pots they are bothered by moss, liverwort, snails and slugs (which, with imperial Roman gourmandism eat the flowers but not the leaves). Place poison bait and use the tweezers once a month.

Kabschia saxifrages are the perfect plants for the sort of gardening we discuss on pages 31 to 40.

Section: *Dactyloides,* the mossy saxifrages. These make sprawling cushions of moss-green, moss-fine foliage. They grow easily in almost any well drained soil in part shade. The much-planted *Saxifraga decipiens* hybrids belong to this section. They bloom in early summer.

Section: *Diptera.* The name pertains to the group's uneven flowers, with 3 small petals and 2 large petals, which are like the fragile wings of a May-fly. *Saxifraga sarmentosa* is the best-known member. For a shady window or a shady garden. Summer bloom.

Section: *Miscopetalum* contains two woodlanders, *S. rotundifolia* and *S. taygetea.* Section: *Nephrophyllum* has one important member, the meadow saxifrage, *S. granulata.* Section: *Trachyphyllum* contains *S. bronchialis austromontana* from stone slides in western mountains. Cultural notes for these sections are given in the biographies of their members.

Saxifrages do best in our west and east coast climates from Alaska to Northern California and from New England to North Carolina. They will grow, but usually won't flower, farther south.

★**SAXIFRAGA AIZOON.** A globe-circling alpine and boreal plant of many forms. This is the type of saxifrage with lime-beaded leaves. *S. aizoon baldensis* is the smallest form—and one of the smallest alpine plants. The frost-edged rosettes are about ⅓ inch across. A large plant of *S. a. baldensis* is 4 inches across, ⅓ inch high. Pale yellow flowers of small effect held up on 3 or 4 inch stems. *S. aizoon* 'Lutea' has small, pale green rosettes which wear little lime. Primrose

yellow flowers of good value on a foot of stem. *S. aizoon major* has limy and grayish rosettes 2 inches across. Red-speckled flowers on sparsely branched 18-inch stems. *S. aizoon* 'Rosea' is a silvery clump with pale rosy pink flowers.

SAXIFRAGA APICULATA. (*S. sancta X S. marginata.*) The oldest hybrid kabschia. Compressed rosettes of glossy, yellow-green, spearhead leaves. In February and March, loose clusters of full-petaled, primrose-yellow flowers. Old descriptions classify this plant as a vigorous carpeter. Nowadays *S. apiculata* is a slow growing clump. Perhaps it has been propagated past its early strength.

SAXIFRAGA BURSERIANA. A February and March flowering Kabschia of reasonably easy garden temper. Pin-cushions of stiff grayish needles and inch-wide white flowers of full ruffled petal, on 3 or 4 inches of glossy reddish stem.

SAXIFRAGA COCHLEARIS. Mounds of hollow-centered clumps of little hard leaves in round rosettes; white flowers on 9 inch red-brown stems. Section: Euaizoonia.

★**SAXIFRAGA COTYLEDON.** A noble plant with great flattened rosettes (up to 7 inches across) of narrow, lime-edged leaves, and flocks of white flowers in yard-high panicles. Section: Euaizoonia.

SAXIFRAGA ELIZABETHIAE. A superior hybrid Kabschia with large, soft yellow flowers, full and round in the petal.

SAXIFRAGA MACNABIANA. Small-ish hybrids between the encrusted species.

SAXIFRAGA MARGINATA. Classified with the Kabschias, but more resembles the encrusted saxifrages. The small rosettes of strap-shaped leaves have a nearly continuous bank of lime beads along their edges. Full, white flowers on short stems.

★**SAXIFRAGA MOSCHATA.** Covers a group of carpet-making white to rose mossies with narrowly cleft leaves. The plant which earns the star is in the American trade as *S. moschata* 'Alba'. Starry-petaled white flowers open from April until June over ferny-fine mats 30 inches across. Section: Dactyloides.

SAXIFRAGA POLODIAE. A hybrid Kabschia with large primrose-yellow flowers over a firm dome of tiny yellow-green rosettes dusted with lime.

SAXIFRAGA ROSACEA. (*S. decipiens.*) Mossy saxifrages of innumerable variety. They have little paw-like leaves made up of bright green fleshy lobes. The big, bland, flat flowers on 8- or 9-inch stems run to wine reds (which fade in the sun). There are pink varieties which resemble the red in their faded condition, and there are whites and creams as well. Sometimes you can look at all these and welcome their bland brightness, coming as it does in March when you are eager for flowers. Then again, you can look and see the hybrid mossies coarse and blatant in flower form and color. Many people take the brighter view. *Saxifraga rosacea* hybrids are among the most-planted rockery plants in the country. Section: Dactyloides.

SAXIFRAGA ROTUNDIFOLIA. Seeks damp rocks and moist woodlands. Kidney-shaped leaves narrow into long stalks. Rose-dotted white flowers grow in an intricate 2-foot-tall cluster.

SAXIFRAGA SANCTA. A green-needled, carpeting Kabschia which will grow a foot across if you take close care of it. The loosely clustered yellow flowers are small and a little disappointing. *Saxifraga haagii* is a hybrid with the small flowers of *S. sancta.*

★**SAXIFRAGA SARMENTOSA.** A woodlander which laces old stone walls at Nikko and over much of Japan. In America we know it as "strawberry geranium," a house plant in cold-winter climates, a shade-loving ground cover in mild winter areas. Hairy round leaves white-variegated along the veins. Reddish whips extend from the leaf rosettes, search out a fresh spot of ground, and bear a new rosette at their tip. Sprays of unequal-petaled white flowers come from spring until fall. *Saxifraga sarmentosa* is hardy down to 0° or a little lower. Use it as a restrained ground cover in mossy shade. Section: Diptera.

SAXIFRAGA TAYGETEA. Resembles *S. rotundifolia* reduced by two-thirds—the round scalloped leaves packed in a 2-inch rosette. The stem and star flower ensemble rises to 8 inches.

★**SAXIFRAGA UMBROSA.** London Pride. After *S. sarmentosa* this is the most easily grown saxifrage. Rosettes of narrow, spatula-shaped leaves, pea-green and glossy, stained violet underneath. Pink or white star flowers in open spaced, graceful arrangement on foot-high clusters.

Form ★*S. umbrosa* 'Serratifolia' has saw-edged leaves. Both the typical and the saw-edged form make limited ground covers in shade. Elliot's variety of *S. umbrosa* 'Primuloides' is a miniature requiring and deserving the choicest primula conditions. Flat rosettes, 1½ inches across, of scallop-edged, spoon-shaped leaves. Pink flowers on 4-inch stems. Section: Robertsonia.

SCOLOPENDRIUM VULGARE. See **PHYLLITIS.**

SEDUM. A world-wide genus of succulent plants found nearly everywhere rocks are found, on sea cliffs and mountain tops, in deserts and woodlands. All the species need perfect drainage; most prefer full sun. Several species long have had prime importance as wall, rock, and ground plants in Europe and America. Indifferent about soil composition and tolerant of bad treatment, sedums have come to be regarded as garden drudges—useful but unstimulating. Take a fresh look at them. There is

nothing in the entire range of dwarf plants more brilliant in flower than *Sedum spectabile* and *S. spurium* 'Dragon's Blood'; nothing more subtle in leaf than the shell and sea tints of *S. sieboldii* and *S. dasyphyllum glanduliferum.* There are few if any dwarf plants of surer, longer garden life. Hardy and adaptable over most of the United States.

★**SEDUM ACRE.** Gold moss, wall pepper. A 2-inch-high carpet of waxen, yellow-green leaves less than ⅛ inch long, in tightly packed, twiggy masses. Yellow star flowers on short stems. Brilliant in flower and brightly evergreen the year around. Use gold moss as a ground cover, as a wall plant, or between stepping stones, but keep it well away from plantings of high alpines. Gold moss spreads itself by detachment. When you weed around gold moss or when a bird scratches at it, branches pull away and leaves roll off like little marbles. Every severed branch and every vagrant leaf will root and grow into a new plant in short order. *S. acre* 'Minus' is only ½-inch high and has little of the invasive abilities of the larger form; but 'Minus' grows too slowly to have much landscape value. ★*S. a. sexangulare* is an enlarged version of the species. Summer bloom.

★**SEDUM ALBUM.** Dark dusty-green leaves, tiny and cylindrical, in ever-spreading mats. The June and July flowers are white stars of thread-stemmed daintiness. Makes a first-rate evergreen ground cover.

★**SEDUM AMECAMECANUM.** A Mexican native with a name like an incantation. Much used in our Southwest for covering sunny soil and for pattern plantings. Makes 6-inch-high mats of sausage-plump yellow-green leaves and yellow star flowers. Not hardy in the north. Evergreen. Flowers in May.

SEDUM ANACAMPSEROS. Sprawls over rocks with bare, fat and fleshy, brownish stems at the ends of which are gray-green, plate-form leaves, tightly shingled like the armor of a pangolin. Purplish pink July flowers. Evergreen.

SEDUM 'CRISTA-GALLI'. A cockscomb variety of *S. rupestre,* monstrously ugly yet somehow attractive, with that quality the French call "the beauty of the devil." This plant is usually one of the first to sell out at plant sales.

★**SEDUM DASYPHYLLUM GLANDU-LIFERUM.** Tiny glaucous blue-gray clump-maker with roundish leaves like barleycorns. Pink stars of misty pallor on wispy stems. Leaves and flowers together are about 3 or 4 inches high. To propagate one plant into a large patch, pull it apart into a hundred or so pieces and leaves. Scatter these over well-softened soil and keep them watered. Evergreen. June blooming.

★**SEDUM KAMTSCHATICUM.** Makes mats of green leaves and masses of yellow June flowers, both like *S. spurium.* There is a rose-and-yellow splashed leaf form unusually attractive for a variegated plant. Deciduous.

Saxifraga cotyledon

Saxifraga sarmentosa

Sedum spathulifolium

★**SEDUM PRUINATUM.** Makes a carpet of soft bluish-gray-green needles in cylindrical masses on twigs which are capable of branching and rebranching immortally like sargassum. Hard yellow stars spray out on radial stemlets atop a straight 6-inch stem. Closely related to *S. rupestre* which it resembles in size, form, flower, and ease of cultivation. Differs from *S. rupestre* only in the brighter bluishness of its needles. Evergreen.

★**SEDUM PULCHELLUM.** A trailing plant from cool woodsy places in the southeast United States. Green needle leaves arranged cylindrically like those of *S. pruinatum.* The rosy purple flowers have the structure of *S. pruinatum.* They open from summer until late fall. Best in a shady spot. Evergreen, with winter tints of russet and purple.

★**SEDUM RUPESTRE.** The well-known, yellow-starred, gray-green needled wall drapery. Needles take on winter tints of violet-purple. Endures drought.

SEDUM SARMENTOSUM. Narrowish green leaves on ramping, rooting stems. Yellow flowers. A sprig of this can make a yard-wide patch in a single year in a cool woodsy spot. Deciduous.

★**SEDUM SEXANGULARE.** See **SEDUM ACRE.**

SEDUM SIEBOLDII. A clump of 6 or 8 inch stems which grow radially over the soil. Rounded leaves, in threes along the stems, are blue-green with a rim of pink—a chinaware or seashell look. Bright pink flowers in spreading clusters give a good August and September show. Deciduous.

★**SEDUM SPATHULIFOLIUM.** A widely distributed western American plant which makes spreading clumps of spatula-form leaves in pressed-down rosettes. The 6- or 7-inch flower stems divide at the top into spread fingers of brilliant yellow summer flowers. Typical leaf color is glaucous gray-green. Plants of this color cover miles of cliff on the coast of Oregon. A finer form with denser, smaller rosettes commemorates the Oregon coast in its name 'Cape Blanco'. Green-leafed forms grow near San Francisco and northward on shady cliffs within coniferous forests. Leaves of *S. spathulifolium* 'Purpureum' turn violet red in fall and keep this color until late spring. Rain lacquers the winter leaves to near blood redness.

Use *S. spathulifolium* in sun or half shade as a ground cover, in containers, and in rock pockets. The plant likes moisture and good drainage.

★**SEDUM SPECTABILE.** A cluster of upright 18-inch stems along which large, rounded, blue-gray leaves are attached bracket-like at right angles. From about late August to early November the stems are roofed over with flattish masses of pale pink stars, atumble with bees, mimicking bee-flies, and skipper butterflies. Does well in sun or shade, in rock pockets or as a border edging. Combine it with blue veronica. There are several named color forms. 'Brilliant' has rich amaranth-red flowers. Deciduous.

★**SEDUM SPURIUM.** Flat mats of wedge-shaped leaves tipped with one rounded tooth and six pointed ones. Leaves are purplish-green with a gloss. In flower this sedum is one of the most rewarding dwarf plants in cultivation. The season starts in July and continues two months. Great branching masses of heavy-scented, pale rose stars dome the plant over and bring the bees in droves. *S. spurium* 'Dragon's Blood' is a purple-red flowered form with the light-reflecting aniline brilliance of certain ice plants. Grows in sun or shade. Does well on shady rocks and even in starvation soil beneath conifers. Partly evergreen.

★**SEDUM 'STAR RED'.** Appears to be a form or hybrid of *S. album,* with reddish-brown leaves throughout the year and rosy stars in early summer. Useful for pattern plantings.

SEDUM TELEPHIUM. Orpine. An anciently cultivated plant once used as an herb simple for the treatment of wounds. Orpine makes foot-high stands of dark green oblong leaves. Late summer flower clusters of variously purplish flowers. Use as *S. spectabile.* Deciduous.

SEMPERVIVUM. Hen-and-chicks, houseleek. The sempervivums are succulent plants whose place in botany is beside *Sedum* in the Crassulaceae family. The species commonly in cultivation come from the mountains of Europe. Horticulturally, *Sempervivum* is a much-confused group. There are probably close to a hundred species, which have given rise to several hundred hybrids. The whole collection, species and hybrids, is generally mixed-up and misnamed.

Sempervivums grow as great, ever-widening colonies of rosettes which rest upon the ground. The leaves of the rosettes are usually broad like arrowheads and tipped with a harmless spine. Fleshy roots enter the ground directly from the base of the rosette without any intervening stem. The colony increases by forming offsets close to the mother rosettes (hence the name, hen-and-chicks). One rosette can increase into hundreds in several summers, forming tightly packed masses a yard across.

The beauty of sempervivums—and the excuse for all the minutely varied hybrids—is in their endlessly combined leaf colors. There are jade greens, soapstone greens, powdered blue-greens, mauves, carmine-violets, red-purples, and on and on. The colors (especially the reds) brighten in the late winter and early spring. In summer and fall they become duller.

The flowers of most sempervivums lack brilliance, but their production is interesting. In early summer a scattering of the colony's older rosettes loosen their inner leaves and heave up a stout stalk. The stalk rises 4 inches to a foot and splays at its tip into a cluster of waterish-lemon or raspberry ice star-flowers. The rosette dies from this effort.

Sempervivums are famous for their ability to get along in the garden with very little help. They can thrive in dry subsoil on a rockery wall. But they can also die if the air and the soil become too dry. These plants make their best growth in fertile loam with ample water. Top the soil with scree or sand to insure aeration beneath the rosettes. Some sempervivum specialists prefer growing their plants in half shade (they like the larger, more open-leafed rosettes that form in shade, and they say that the leaf colors are brighter). Most sempervivums are hardy to —20° or lower.

★**SEMPERVIVUM HYBRIDS.** A random selection of the many kinds with flattened, shield-like rosettes, 4 inches across.: 'H. Celon' with glossy, bronze-green leaves; silvery gray-green 'Silverine'; 'Engles 13-2' with pale green leaves tinted violet-purple and hazed over with down; jade-green 'Charolensis'; 'Ward's No. 2' with light green leaves tipped with grayed violet-purple.

★**SEMPERVIVUM ARACHNOIDEUM.** Ball-shaped rosettes ¼- to ¾-inch in diameter. White webbing stretches from leaf tip to leaf tip, giving the rosette a cobwebbed appearance. Sparse flowers, but of brighter rose than those of most sempervivums. A cliff dweller in nature, *S. arachnoideum* is at home on garden walls and outcroppings where its rosettes trace the joints and fissures of the stone. *S. arachnoideum* 'Stansfieldii', possibly a hybrid, has larger cobwebby rosettes (1¾ inches in diameter) which turn bright carmine-bronze in winter.

SEMPERVIVUM ARACHNOIDEUM 'DOELLIANUM'. (*S. a.* 'Glabrescens', *S. moggridgei*.) Flattened, light green rosettes, 1¼ inches to 2 inches across. Leaf tips are tufted with white hair.

SEMPERVIVUM CALCAREUM. See *S. tectorum.*

SEMPERVIVUM HEUFFELII REGINAE-AMALIAE. Queen Amelia's namesake grows in the Grecian mountains. It makes a sturdy plant in gardens, but is so slow growing that only collectors will have need of it. Rosettes are 2 to 3 inches across, light green on the inner half of the leaves, bronze-purple on the outer half. Yellowish stars with 6 petals.

★**SEMPERVIVUM 'HISPIDULUM'.** Possibly also *S. montanum.* Has domed, light grayish-green rosettes 1 to 2 inches across, made up of many small leaves. Reddish flowers. Valuable for its quick increase.

★**SEMPERVIVUM SCHLEHANII BLANDUM.** A vigorous sort, quick to widen its colony of flattened 2 to 3-inch rosettes of luminous, light bluish-green. Pale rose flowers.

SEMPERVIVUM SOBOLIFERUM. Makes rounded, green rosettes. The young offsets are nearly perfect balls which become detached by any small agency (an angleworm could do it) and then roll away on their own to start new colonies.

★**SEMPERVIVUM TECTORUM.** The houseleek received its name from the old European custom of planting the rosettes on roofs covered with earth for insulation. The rosettes soon ramped into a solid cover and kept the soil from washing away.

Houseleek is the common garden sempervivum. It has flattened rosettes 3 to 4 inches across. The pale green leaves are tipped with purple-bronze. Forms 'Atroviolaceum', 'Atropurpureum', etc., turn rich red-purple in the late winter and spring. All *S. tectorum* forms have reddish starry flowers with 12 petals. *S. tectorum* is one of the toughest, most prolific sempervivums. Form *S. t. calcareum* has light green 2-inch rosettes. The leaf tips have touches of bronze and purple, giving the rosette a spotted appearance. Rather slow growing.

★**SENECIO GREYII.** A New Zealand shrub. Open growth to 3 to 4 feet high and 6 feet across. Branches and undersides of the 2-inch-long, egg-shaped leaves are thickly coated with a pale gray felt. The felt covering brims up over the edge of the leaves, then thins inwardly, revealing something of the dark green that underlies the gray. Combine *S. greyii* with other tall grays in dry plantings. Contrast it with mugho pine. Cut the branches freely for arrangements. They last weeks in water.

In cool-summer climates this good foliage plant may be excused for its sparse production of little yellow daisies. In warm summer climates its profusion of flowers in 5-inch-wide clusters is one of its glories. Frost damaged at 15°. Kills to the ground at 5°, but springs back to full size in a year or two. Best in hot sun. Endures half shade.

SHORTIA GALACIFOLIA. From the mountains of North Carolina. Adapts easily to primula conditions in east and west coast gardens. One of America's most desirable wild flowers. Shortia has the glossy, round, leathery leaves of pyrola or galax, and incomparable flowers with 5 flared white petals, waved along the edges. Spring and early summer bloom.

North Carolina nurserymen sell collected shortia, but the plant is too rare and local to encourage the wholesale collecting of it for mass planting. For that reason the star of landscape worthiness plus beauty is withheld from this species, which otherwise would deserve it. Seed sown and cared for like rhododendron seed will produce 4-inch clumps and a few flowers in four years.

Pink-flowered *S. uniflora* is a similar species from Japan.

SILENE. Kruckeberg hybrids. Arthur Kruckeberg, botanist and gardener, has gathered most of the hundreds of silenes (a monumental task) and is engaged in producing a range of important new hybrid rock plants. One of these, *S. baldwinii* x *S. wherryi*, blends 2 eastern plants into a mat of spatulate leaves and stemless rose flowers, deeply fringed and 1¼ inches across. Needs moist, well drained soil, half shade. N. A.

SILENE ACAULIS. A bright green moss-like mat which grows around the northern world, on the rock ribs of mountains just below the eternal snows and in Arctic pastures. Nearly stemless, bright rose, 5-petaled flowers crowd the mat in earliest spring. *S. acaulis* 'Pedunculata' is a strong-growing, large-flowered form. For the collector's scree. Northern N. A.

SILENE ALPESTRIS. A favorite alpine plant. Stoloniferous tufts of small narrow leaves, dark-evergreen and shining. Flower stems — slim, bare and openly branching — rise 8 to 14 inches from the tufts during spring. Flowers are small and remarkable — made of pure white star-shaped petals, notched and lobed into a lacework as uselessly lovely as a carved ivory fan. There is a double form which, surprisingly, compounds rather than cancels the daintiness of the single. Light shade or sun, moisture, drainage. For the collector's garden. N. A.

SILENE SCHAFTA. A 6- to 16-inch upright, green, leafy tuft, bent down from mid to late summer with bright rosy flowers. Needs sun, moisture, drainage. N. A.

SISYRINCHIUM BELLUM. Blue-eyed grass. An iris relative with 8 inches of grassy-bladed leaves and upturned, eye-like flowers of dark violet. Native to moist sunny meadows in western America. Establishes easily in moist garden soil and seeds itself into colonies. N. A.

★**SISYRINCHIUM CALIFORNICUM.** Golden-eyed grass grows in wet soil and in sphagnum bogs on the coast of California and Oregon. Flat-bladed grayish leaves; rich yellow flowers all summer. Height: 8 to 12 inches. Valuable in a large sunny bog, where it will seed itself into a solid turf. Adapts to upland soils, even to the point of becoming a pest in choice plantings. Hardy to 15°; seedlings will renew the planting if temperature drops below the kill point.

SOLDANELLA. A primulaceous genus, but quite unlike primrose in appearance. The soldanellas are high alpine plants with matted clumps of small, roundish, dark-leathery leaves and fringed violet bell flowers which pierce up through the crust of melting snow during the mountain spring. There are several species differing mainly in size. *S. montana*, 6 to 14 inches high, is the largest and generally the only species strong enough for open ground cultivation. This plant is a notable success in many west and east coast shade gardens, in the same climate zones where primulas thrive. Flowers in March. Divides easily in June.

SOLIDAGO. Goldenrod. Dwarf goldenrods such as 8- to 12-inch *S. cutleri* (*S. brachystachys*), and *S. algida*; 12- to 18-inch *S.* 'Pulcherrima' and *S. pallida*, have a place on the rock wall and in the alpine meadow planting. In flower these alpine dwarfs are no more or less than miniatures of the tall roadside goldenrods. They seed about freely, but stay in a clump instead of sending out invasive stolons. Tall goldenrods like *S. caesia* and *S. speciosa* are the perfect complement to cool violet Michaelmas daisies in the late summer wild garden. N. A.

Soldanella montana

Sempervivum in variety

Silene acaulis

★**SPIRAEA BULLATA.** (*S. crispifolia.*) A compact 2- to 4-foot shrub with small, deep green, crinkled leaves in clusters along upright branches. Flat clusters of bright magenta-rose flowers dome the branchlets in July and August. Plant singly or in masses. Can be held at 18 inches by pruning. Needs sun. N. A.

SPIRAEA PALMATA. See **FILIPENDULA.**

STATICE LATIFOLIA. See **LIMONIUM.**

TAXUS BACCATA 'REPANDENS'. The English yew, *T. baccata,* is a dark and somber tree whose flexible wood, whittled into bows, helped the English archers shape the course of history. It has red, berry-like fruits. *T. baccata* is highly tolerant of shade and will succeed in a mostly shady garden. There are a number of dwarfs with dark or golden needles. *T. b.* 'Repandens', as somber as the species, makes a rough, spreading bush at a rate of about 8 inches a year. It can be considered mature at a height of 4 feet and a spread of 15 feet or more. *T. b.* 'Pygmaea' is a condensed mound.

TAXUS CUSPIDATA 'NANA'. Dwarf forms of the Japanese yew are of a fresher, lighter green than forms of the English yew. *T. c.* 'Nana' is rather equivalent to *T. b.* 'Repandens' in the rate and habit of its low, spreading growth. *T. c.* 'Minima' grows about 18 inches high and 8 feet across at a rate of 6 inches a year.

★**THALICTRUM AQUILEGIFOLIUM.** A 3-foot perennial in most nursery catalogues. There are also forms as low as 1 foot. Yard-high *T. aquilegifolium* makes a noble border, woodland, and wild garden plant with lacy leaves of bleeding heart, columbine, or maidenhair fern. Above the lacework in May and June burst billowing masses of many-stamened rose-purple to white flowers. N. A.

★**THALICTRUM DIPTEROCARPUM.** Grows 2 to 5 feet high. Each pale green leaf is divided into 3 groups of 3 leaflets each. Flowers are an inch wide with lilac colored petals and a fluff of cream colored stamens. They are individually larger than the flowers of *T. aquilegifolium* and of most other thalictrums, and are arranged in looser sprays. N. A.

Thalictrums are long-lived plants, asking no more than growing space and a moderate supply of moisture. To increase your stock, you can divide the clumps in March. They may self-sow.

THUJA OCCIDENTALIS 'GLOBOSA' and **T. O. 'FASTIGIATA'.** These two dwarfs of the American arborvitae are grand old-timers. Globe arborvitae (*T. o.* 'Globosa') is now quite old-fashioned and fussy looking, but it is still much planted. For nearly a century this globe, which grows only to 4 feet, has been planted in rockeries and along foundations and walks, like rows of buttons. Columnar arborvitae (*T. o.* 'Fastigiata') is still invaluable. Its richly green columns aligned against walls or at the property edge make the narrowest of hedges or screens. Closely planted, columnar arborvitae will form a solid wall of green 25 to 30 feet high and no more than 3 or 4 feet through. By clipping, this tree can be held to a width of 18 inches. The upward growth is 6 inches or more a year. Few other trees and shrubs can give this height and solid greenness in such narrow space.

More than 60 forms of American arborvitae were listed in nursery catalogues in the 1920's and 30's. Beside 'Globosa' and 'Fastigiata' a few others are worth remembering. *T. o.* 'Little Gem' is a globose bush, more compact and globular than the original *T. o.* 'Globosa'. *T. o.* 'Ericoides' is a juvenile form with feathery, heather-like foliage on a compact pyramidal bush to 4 feet in height. *T. o.* 'Ellwangeriana Aurea' and *T. o.* 'Ellwangeriana Rheingold' are bright, clean yellow the year around.

Thuja occidentalis forms appreciate heavy watering, but they don't demand it.

THUJA ORIENTALIS. The Chinese arborvitae has been as prolific of juvenile forms (they are tenderish and wind-subject) and seedling forms as the American arborvitae. *Thuja orientalis* dwarfs are highly entertaining from one season to the next for their chameleon-like ability to change colors. *T. o.* 'Rosedalis Compacta' became enormously popular after its introduction in the early 1920's. It is a juvenile with fine branches and foliage compressed into an egg-shaped shrub which grows 3 or 4 inches a year. It puts on a color extravaganza in 3 acts: In the spring it is brilliant gold; through summer it is sea-green; during winter it is plum-purple with a gray bloom.

T. o. 'Hillieri' is an egg-shaped adult form, soft yellow in summer, pea-green in winter. *T. o.* 'Minima Glauca' is a little globe of juvenile foliage, glaucous green in summer, yellow brown in winter. Grows about 1½ inches a year.

THYMUS. Evergreen shrubs which grow as mats 1 to 3 inches high or as wiry-stemmed footlings, and which have a pervasive and refreshing herb scent about their pinhead-sized leaves. They have clusters of small, two-lipped flowers, rose-purple or white, characteristic in the mint family (Labiatae) along with rosemary, garden sage, and marjoram.

The thymes come mainly from Mediterranean countries, where they are born to sun-heated stones. In American gardens thymes make valuable ground covers in hot, droughty soil—even in pure sand. They must have fast drainage, both of air and soil moisture. *T. serpyllum,* the hardiest and most adaptable species, can even be used as a woodland ground cover in half shade.

THYMUS CIMICINUS. A ½- to 1-inch high mat of minute, dark green leaves. Fast-growing (to 16 inches across in one year), but shows little tendency to die out in the center of the mat as do many fast-growing ground covers. Hardy to 0°.

★**THYMUS HERBA-BARONA.** Once used in royal kitchens to flavor baron of beef. This thyme is a 3- to 6-inch mound of springy branches. The scent of the leaves is brisk, head-clearing, and distinct from all other thymes. Corsican, but found hardy down to 0°.

★**THYMUS LANICAULIS.** A shrub with trailing branches in open, airy arrangement. The soft gray leaves and white flower spikes are larger than those of most other thymes. Frost-damaged at 20°. Not readily obtainable.

★**THYMUS LANUGINOSUS.** (*Thymus serpyllum lanuginosus.*) Grows 1 or 2 inches high, makes foot-wide mats in one summer from plugs set out in the spring. Rounded, gray-green leaves, frosted with down and soft to the touch. Practically flowerless. Occasionally the mat will carry a sprinkling of lavender flowers. This fast-growing sort tends to mound up and die out in patches. Pull out the brown areas if they occur and stir the soil. The mat will soon heal itself. Frost-damaged at 10°. Many nurseries carry this thyme.

THYMUS NITIDUS. An upright shrub to 16 inches high and 20 inches across. The leaves are narrow, dull gray-green, and powerfully aromatic. Showy spikes of lilac flowers. *T. nitidus* is a *T. vulgaris* relative from Etna, the Sicilian volcano. A bush of *T. nitidus* is old at 15 years, with a heavy, woody base and sparse limbs — like an old, gnarled lavender. Has been found hardy at —5°. Rare.

★**THYMUS SERPYLLUM.** The wild form of creeping thyme from stony places in Europe makes dark-leaved mats with lavender rose flowers. In America this old, unimproved form has escaped from gardens and established itself on road cuts and waste areas. There are brighter garden forms of creeping thyme. Here are a few of the more outstanding:

T. s. 'Albus'. Abundant white flowers on close-growing medium-green mats. Moderate growth rate (a plug grows 12 inches across in a season). Many nurseries have this. N. A.

T. s. 'Argenteus' (*T. citriodorus* 'Argenteus'.) Silver variegated leaves and lavender-rose flowers on a foot-high bush of upright, slender, billowy branches. Damaged at 10°.

Thymus serpyllum 'Aureus' (*T. citriodorus* 'Aureus') has yellow variegated leaves on a shrub very like *T. serpyllum* 'Argenteus'. Damaged at 10°.

T. s. 'Clear Gold' has bright chartreuse leaves on mats 3 to 4 inches high. The few lavender flowers do the plant no credit. Hardy to 0°.

Thymus serpyllum 'Coccineus'. Bright rose-purple flowers massed over 1- to 2-inch-high dark green mats. Moderate growth rate. *T. s.* 'Coccineus Splendens' has even brighter flowers. Hardy to about —10°. Readily obtainable.

T. s. 'Vulgaris' (*T. citriodorus.*) Lemon Thyme. Lemon-scented leaves on a mounding 3- to 6-inch shrub. Herb specialists stock this thyme. N. A.

★**THYMUS VULGARIS.** An upright shrub, 9 to 12 inches high in its best growth. Later it legs up to 16 inches. The dark grayish-green leaves are either narrow or egg-shaped. Lavender-purple flowers. The leaves of this species provide the thyme of commerce. You will find the shrub easy to grow in a sunny position. Renew it from half hard cuttings every 2 or 3 years. Comes easily from seed and may self-sow. Plants are obtainable from herb specialists.

★**TIARELLA CORDIFOLIA.** Foam flower. A foot-high member of the saxifrage family from moist, luxuriant woods in eastern America. Handsome heuchera-like, toothed, heart-shaped leaves, green in the summer, bronze tinted during winter. Star flowers filled with a thread-fluff of stamens and assembled in steeple-like racemes. Two varieties are in the trade: white-flowered 'Albiflora' and salmon-pink 'Collina'. Bailey lists in his *Standard Cyclopedia of Horticulture* several other varieties, perhaps no longer available, but worth finding (if they still exist) and preserving from extinction. They are: purple flowered 'Purpurea'; 'Purpurea Major', with salmon-rose or wine-red flowers; 'Purpurea Major Compacta', a more compact grower with bronzy chamois-colored flowers; and 'Purpurea Marmorata', with attractive bronze foliage passing to blackish green and marbled with purple, plus very numerous maroon flowers.

A drift of *T. cordifolia* can be one of spring's high points in the moist shade garden. Flower steeples last from late April until well into June.

Western American *T. unifoliata* and *T. trifoliata* have small white flowers in filmy clusters. Divide tiarellas in fall every 2 to 4 years. N. A.

TRILLIUM. Wake-robin. Woodland plants of the lily family. Trilliums grow from a deeply buried rhizome. Their pointed buds push out of the ground in early spring. A broad collar of three horizontal leaves expands at the top of a fleshy stalk. Just upon the juncture of the three leaves or just above it on a bit of stem, three sepals part and release petals of white (in the best loved species) or of maroon, rose, or lemon yellow.

Grow trilliums under primula conditions. Plant rhizomes of the larger species with their tops 5 or 6 inches below ground. Plant *T. rivale* and *T. nivale* 2½ inches deep. To increase your plants dig the rhizomes up in early March, cut them apart, and replant them before the roots attached to the rhizome dry out. Don't divide more often than once every 3 or 4 years. Trilliums are slow growing plants which may never need dividing for their health's sake. Some gardeners have 25-year-old clumps of *T. grandiflorum* and *T. ovatum*. These old plants carry about 100 flowers, and apparently have not yet reached their full production.

Seed sown as soon as it is ripe (it must be fresh) will yield the first few small flowers 3 or 4 years after germination. Most trilliums sold by American nurseries are collected in the wild. A few nurseries sell nursery grown and divided stock. If you want to collect your own you may as well dig them while they are in full flower (with permission of the landowner or government agency in charge). You'll need a large shovel, wet newspaper, and a box large enough to lay the plants in flat.

Dig away the surface soil from the trillium. Plunge the shovel blade up to the hilt in a circle around the plant and then pry the plant upward slowly and carefully so that you don't break the brittle stalk. Roll the roots, rhizomes, and stalks in the wet papers; lay the plants in the box and get them home before they wilt. If you can't plant them until the next day, or if despite your care they begin to wilt, unwrap the trilliums and stand them overnight in a bucket of water. Of course trilliums are much easier to transplant in the fall when they have died down, but then you may never find one in woods which were alive with them in April.

TRILLIUM CERNUUM. Twelve to 20 inches. White flowers turn downward on their stems and hide beneath the ample leaves. This eastern species makes a vigorous garden plant but you have to stoop to see the flowers.

TRILLIUM CHLOROPETALUM. Un-scented maroon, greenish-yellow, or white flowers. Grows on wooded slopes in our west coast states. All the forms are easy in deep moist soil and shade. The leaves have attractive dark marbling.

TRILLIUM ERECTUM. Twelve to 16 inches. "Stinking Benjamin" to the country children who romp its woods in eastern America. Maroon flowers that are inoffensive unless you get right down and sniff them. There is a white form. An easily grown species.

★**TRILLUM GRANDIFLORUM.** Twelve to 20 inches. The leaves come up bronze green and retain a slight metallic tint all summer. Flowers are large (up to 3 inches across), of full and slightly ruffled petal, and pure white; they age to a pale rose. This eastern American woodlander grows readily in shady gardens.

TRILLIUM NIVALE. Four to 5 inches. A collector's plant with small, dark-blotched leaves. The inch-wide white flowers are in perfect scale. An eastern woodlander closely allied to the western *T. rivale*.

★**TRILLIUM OVATUM.** From western American woods, this is the fraternal twin of *T. grandiflorum* and just as easy and beautiful as the eastern species. The foliage of *T. ovatum* is clear green. The petals average narrower than those of *T. grandiflorum* and the sepals of *T. ovatum* are longer than those of the eastern white trillium. They usually almost equal the petals.

TRILLIUM PETIOLATUM. Three round leaves on long leaf stems rise directly out of the ground, resembling old-fashioned palmetto fans. A small maroon flower sits in the juncture of these leaves. This curious plant is neither willing nor worthwhile in the average garden.

TRILLIUM RIVALE. A dwarf plant (usually about 4 inches high) from wooded mountain shoulders in southwest Oregon and adjacent California. Small leaves of dark shining green, often with darker marbling; white, purple-spotted flowers with broad, blunt petals. Provide scree conditions and half shade for this exquisitely proportioned collector's plant.

TRILLIUM SESSILE. Twelve to 20 inches. Large, broad leaves, usually marbled with dark splotches and spots. Long, urn-shaped wine purple or greenish flowers sit stemless on the collar of leaves. They have the scent of ripe grapes. *T. sessile* is widespread in the eastern states. *T. sessile luteum,* also eastern, has pale yellow, lemon-scented flowers. This form is smaller and less vigorous than the others.

TRILLIUM STYLOSUM. Twelve to 18 inches. A slender-stemmed plant with narrow leaves and wavy-petalled, clear rose-colored flowers. Native to North Carolina southward to Florida. Not an easy species to establish in northern gardens.

TRILLIUM UNDULATUM. Eight to 12 inches. White flowers marked red, with narrowish, wavy-margined petals. Woods of eastern America. Not an easy species to grow.

TSUGA CANADENSIS 'NANA'. An inverted bowl with horizontal branches, down-curving at their tips. Growth rate about 2 inches a year. A 15-year-old specimen is 30 inches across, 22 inches high. Needles are yellowish in hot sun, greener in partial shade. Said to be a wild seedling.

★**TSUGA CANADENSIS 'PENDULA'.** (*T. c.* 'Sargentii'.) Fine grayish needles in flat arrangement; weeping branches of gracefulness unsurpassed among rock garden conifers. Grows about 5 inches a year. An 8-year-old specimen is 24 inches across, 15 inches high. The first few olive-sized, olive-shaped cones usually appear on trees this size.

Tolerant of half shade, it is most graceful trailing over shady stones. A wild seedling

★**TSUGA MERTENSIANA.** Over a broad range of western American mountain slopes, where the snow lies in deep, shifting drifts, mountain hemlock grows in a yielding manner. The limber trunk often lies flat on the ground for several yards, and the branches grow down-swooping like the roof of a chalet.

Much of this graceful, languid manner of growth is retained in lowland gardens. The typical tree grows 6 inches a year when established—an open pyramid of blue-gray suitable for large rock gardens or shady banks.

Dwarf seedlings of prostrate, rounded, or pyramidal form are discovered rather frequently in the mountains. But they are scarcely known in the trade, due partly to the difficulty of propagating them. One of the most distinctive of these is *T. m.* 'Elisabeth' (flat growing, 30 inches across in 12 years).

TULIPA. Tulip. Most tulip species grow wild in dry Mediterranean and Near Eastern countries. The species tulip bulbs sold in America come mainly from nurseries in the Netherlands. The bulbs are coddled to peak flowering conditions (sometimes under a glass roof) and marketed with the expectation that they will flower well the first and perhaps the second year and then decline. Gardeners in many areas in the United States should buy them with the same expectation. Wild tulips almost never establish in gardens where winters are moist and open (the Pacific slope north of Monterey.) However, many of the species grow, flower, and seed into colonies as readily as native plants east of the Washington and Oregon Cascades and the California coast ranges. They can be expected to do the same in the Southwest and in the Great Plains.

Several of the more striking wild tulips are *T. linifolia,* with long narrow leaves and satiny-scarlet, star-petaled tulips close to the ground; *T. kaufmanniana,* with huge, almost stemless water lily-like yellow flowers; dwarf, moon-pale *T. batalinii;* tall *T. clusiana* with pearl-white purplish-eyed cups. These and the many other tulip species look most in place among desert stones.

★**UVULARIA GRANDIFLORA.** A lily relative springing perennially in the woodland garden from its tough base and wickerwork of coarse roots. Twelve to 18-inch stems of bright oblong leaves and soft yellow pendant bells in May. Grows in eastern woods from Canada and the Great Lakes south to Georgia and Iowa. *U. perfoliata* has smaller, paler flowers than *U. grandiflora.* N. A.

VANCOUVERIA. Three forest ground covers close to *Epimedium.* Blunt-tipped leaflets clustered by threes; tiny, suspended flowers formed somewhat like descending parachutists. All three grow on our Pacific slope.

VANCOUVERIA CHRYSANTHA. A Siskiyou plant with dull grayish-green leaves in foot-high, slowly spreading clumps. Soft yellow flowers. Does not like a wet, freeze-and-thaw winter. Best adapted to western California and southwestern Oregon. Blooms in June.

★**VANCOUVERIA HEXANDRA.** Deciduous leaves which keep a tender green, new-leaf look all summer. Cream-tinted white flowers on a foot of stem. Spreads rapidly in woodland duff, slowly in full sun. N. A. Blooms May to July.

VANCOUVERIA PLANIPETALA. (*V. parviflora.*) From western Oregon and California. Dark, shining evergreen leaves in loose 3- to 6-inch-high mats. Slow spreading. Frost damaged at 15°. White flowers in May and June.

★**VERONICA FILIFORMIS.** Spreads its mat at the wonderful or detestable rate (depending on where you've planted it) of 4 feet a year in moist, sunny soil. The evergreen leaves which dress the thin, interminable shoots are a quarter inch across, pale green verging on yellowness, and shaped like blunted hearts. In April and May the mat opens light blue flowers no larger than the leaves, but in numbers sufficient to haze the plant over with its own pale sky. From spring until late the shoots go forward, keeping tidily close to the bare ground, but jumping up and infiltrating every low plant in their path.

V. filiformis behaves as a monstrous weed when released among small plants or near lawns, where it invades the grass. But used correctly it can be one of the most valuable mat forming plants. Use it in place of a small lawn or as a path plant. The mat will take a fair amount of foot traffic. Use it as a covering for harsh stones. Let it come up against only the largest, toughest rock plants such as mugho pine, *Cotoneaster dammeri,* and *Juniperus squamata meyeri.* N. A.

VERONICA GENTIANOIDES. Has the glossy, tufted leaf rosettes of gentian. There are 6-inch and 2-foot forms, but 1 foot is the usual height of the spikes of pale blue summer flowers. Native to the Russian state of Georgia, where it grows in sunny alpine meadows squashy with spring water. Adaptable to shade and dryish soils of all characters. N. A.

VERONICA INCANA. A prostrate clump of oblong or narrow willow-like leaves, silvery gray with a dense pile of microscopic hair. Clusters of intense blue summer flowers on 12 to 18 inch stems. Full sun. N. A.

★**VERONICA LATIFOLIA.** (*V. teucrium.*) Grows upright to 20 inches, a clump of stiff shoots set with dark green, roundish or narrowish, toothed leaves. Spiky clusters of dark blue, rose, or white flowers in June.

★**VERONICA PECTINATA.** Makes flat, evergreen mats of felted, ½-inch gray-green leaves edged with deeply rounded and uneven teeth. There is a bright show of May and June flowers, deep blue with a white eye, loosely arranged in short clusters. Variety 'Rosea' is the same plant with rose flowers. In a sunny, sandy position *V. pectinata* is as valuable for its long-lived mats as for its flowers. Spreads 2 to 3 feet a year. Will not climb or invade taller plants.

★**VERONICA PROSTRATA.** (*V. rupestris.*) This has the leaves and flowers of *V. latifolia,* but a flattened habit of growth. Only the tips of the branches turn upward—to a foot or less. Narrowly oblong, smooth, or serrate-edged leaves and rigid racemes of purplish flowers through the summer; plants die down to the ground in the fall. N. A.

★**VERONICA REPENS.** Makes perhaps the flattest mats of any of the rock plants (⅛- to ¼-inch high). Tiny overlapping leaves — egg-shaped, glossy, and evergreen — dress the creeping stems with a dense shingly coat. Milky blue or rose flowers in slender clusters sit flat on the foliage in May. A small start planted out in the spring in moist soil, sun or shade, may grow a yard across by fall. The mat never climbs, and roots so shallowly that it is harmless to other plants. For paths (where it takes moderate foot traffic), mixed ground cover planting, or bulb cover. Evergreen and hardy to at least 10° below zero.

VERONICA SATUREIOIDES. A small mat of yellow-green shoots which lie along the ground, then turn up 1½ inches at their tips, holding evergreen tufts of oblong, pea-green, glossy leaves. Short, blunt spikes of dark violet flowers expand from the leaf tufts in the spring. Divide the mat every 2 years, or when it begins to weaken at its center. Replant only the stronger outer portions. N. A.

VIOLA. Violet. Small, clump-forming plants whose flowers are celebrated in song and poetry as the shy sprites of the woods and the agents of romance. Violet leaves have many shapes, but violet flowers always show 5 petals in ruffed, irregular arrangement, vaguely like mild faces.

The flowers of *V. odorata,* the sweet violet, fill a considerable volume of March air with a heady perfume which inspires swains to buy violet corsages, gardeners to get out their rakes and trowels, and children to regret the violets' lack of palatability. There is no catalyst in human experience quite like the scent of violets.

Violets settle best in half-shady places where the soil is a well drained loam, dark with humus. When happy, they seed about and make large colonies. To prevent uncontrollable invasions, don't plant violets nearer than 15 feet to primulas and small woodland plants. This precaution applies to all the starred violet species in the following biographies. The best garden violets are also benign weeds.

★**VIOLA ADUNCA.** A meadow plant which ranges across Canada and through our Pacific states. The leaves and flowers are small; the flowers dark violet in color. A rapid colonizer on a well watered, sunny bank.

★**VIOLA HEDERACEA.** (*Erpetion reniforme.*) Kidney-shaped leaves along creeping, rooting stems. The flower petals have an interior zone of light blue, rounded outwardly with white. This Australian plant makes an all-summer flowering ground cover in California and the Gulf states. Winter-kills at about 20° to 30°.

★**VIOLA LABRADORICA.** Makes large, woodland-filling colonies of heart leaves, dark green with an overcast of metallic violet-purple. Violet flowers during spring and summer. Fully evergreen through a mild winter.

★**VIOLA ODORATA.** Sweet violet. The star goes to the wild form, a self-sufficient woodland plant with small, intoxicatingly fragrant violets. The heart-shaped leaves of sweet violet are a deep woodland green. They stay fresh through a warm winter, disappear partly or completely if the weather drops below 20°. The dark violet-blue flowers rise in February and March together with the new leaves.

In one old garden there was a 60-year old sweet violet planting beneath fir trees. The violets seeded about in the needle duff, filling the woodland floor with a nearly uniform lawn of sweet violets in March (when walking there was as soporific as the poppy field before the city of Oz) and heart-shaped leaves the rest of the year. House and garden were razed recently.

Variety 'Sulfurea' (rare in American gardens) has dull yellow flowers. The flowers of variety 'Rosina' are an unusual and attractive shade of light rose pink. The florists' doubles have little place in woodland gardening.

VIOLA PALMATA. At its best, has such clear-water purity in its large blue-violet flowers that you half expect it to evaporate overnight. This can happen if you forget to put out slug bait, but otherwise *V. palmata* is a strong, hardy garden plant. In this species the broad heart-shaped leaves are deeply and irregularly slashed into lobes and teeth. Native to New England west to the Great Lakes and south to Florida. Adaptable to gardens in all wooded regions of North America, except for the palmetto fringe. Blooms in April and May.

VIOLA PAPILIONACEA. Pointed heart leaves and dark violet (rarely white) flowers. Widespread woodlander of the northeastern states. Sound garden constitution. N. A.

VIOLA PEDATA. Bird-foot violet. Leaves cleft into 3 to 5 strips; flowers as large as 1¼ inches across. There are two color forms, the first with the 2 upper petals dark, velvety violet and the lower three petals light lilac; the second (or the more common) with the uniformly lilac flowers. April to June bloom.

In nature, this famous eastern American wildflower keeps to sandy soil and rock places exposed to the sun and the brunt of the weather. For some reason *V. pedata* seldom settles down in gardens, even those close to its native places.

VIOLA PEDUNCULATA. Leaves heart-shaped, with scalloped edges. Orange-yellow flowers, an inch wide and full petalled, the upper pair brown on the back. Grows on grassy hillsides in western California, where it dies down in the heat of the summer to a deeply buried cocoon-shaped root. Not hardy in the North.

★**VIOLA PRICEANA.** The Confederate violet from Kentucky is a close relative of *V. papilionacea*. Confederate violet is one of America's showiest wild flowers and a nearly indestructible garden plant. Inch-wide flowers, white with dilute blue centers and broad-faced like small pansies, adorn the plants for several weeks in April and May. Hardy north and south. Seeds itself quickly into large colonies. N. A.

★**VIOLA RUPESTRIS.** (*V. arenaria*.) Probably the most recklessly invading and colonizing of all violets. Only tall tough ferns and woodland plants can keep a place in its vicinity. A violet of small heart-shaped leaves and lavender-lilac flowers, but form 'Rosea' with dull rose flowers is probably better known in gardens.

★**VIOLA SEPTENTRIONALIS.** A New England and Newfoundland species with blunt-tipped heart leaves, inch-wide violet-purple flowers, and a strong will to live and multiply in the garden. There are albinos in cultivation. N. A.

VIOLA TRICOLOR. The wild parent of the garden pansy. The parti-colored flowers are distracting when planted among other wild flowers.

★**WOODWARDIA FIMBRIATA.** (*W. chamissoi*.) Giant chain fern. Vast palm fronds up to 10 feet long, the pinnate divisions boldly proportioned. Grows in moist shade on the Pacific side of California, Oregon, and Washington. Use this fern for architectonic effect in woodlands and against structures. Plants from the southern end of its range are sometimes winter-killed at about 20° to 25°. Plants collected in northern woods are hardy to 10° or below in a sheltered position.

★**WOODWARDIA VIRGINICA** is an eastern American woodlander with 12- to 18-inch fronds for fern beds and north walls in all forested sections of the country.

★**ZAUSCHNERIA CALIFORNICA.** California fuchsia, hummingbird fuchsia. A bright scarlet California native which spreads underground by means of somewhat woody stems, and above ground by woody, arching branches. The aboveground portion starts growth in the late spring (from the ground if the winter has been cold), lengthens into 9-inch to 3-foot-high arching or trailing stems, lined with gray-green, slightly toothed, lance-shaped leaves.

The salmon-scarlet flowers open about the ends of the stems in August, September, and October. They are trumpet-shaped, 1½ to 2 inches long on outstanding plants. Four petals spread wide at the mouth of the trumpet; pistil and stamens shoot forth. This is a flower which brings hummingbirds zooming and shimmering to probe for the nectar deep inside.

The other zauschnerias described below have similar flowers.

Although *Z. californica* grows on the coast of California, it is hardy to 10° or lower in sunny northern gardens. In warm California winters the branches live over from year to year, build into a shrubby tangle. Prune overgrown zauschnerias right to the ground in the spring. The zauschnerias like to trail over sunny rock walls and banks. Once established, they seldom need watering.

★**ZAUSCHNERIA CANA** (*Z. microphylla*.) Makes 3-foot high stems, lined with short, thin twigs and dressed with short gray needles. The scarlet trumpets flare from the top foot of the stems in September. Spreads into a 6-foot-wide colony in about 10 years. Hardy to below 0°. N. A.

ZAUSCHNERIA LATIFOLIA. The broad-leafed California fuchsia is best known in its silvery and prostrate variety 'Etteri' from low elevations. This variety suffers frost damage in the low 20's. The species is hardy to below 0° in the Siskiyou mountains of Oregon, south and east into California and Nevada high country. The alpine species has green leaves and creeping stems which die down completely to the ground in the fall.

Woodwardia fimbriata

Senecio greyii

Viola priceana

Index of Common Names

Aaron's beard—*Hypericum calycinum*
Alpine fir—*Abies lasiocarpa*
Alum root—*Heuchera americana*
American arborvitae—*Thuja occidentalis*
Angel's tears—*Narcissus triandrus*
Autumn crocus—*Colchicum*
Azalea—*Rhododendron*

Baby's-breath—*Gypsophila*
Baby's-tears—*Helxine*
Balloon flower—*Platycodon*
Balsam fir, dwarf—*Abies balsamea* 'Nana'
Basket of gold—*Alyssum saxatile*
Bellflower—*Campanula*
Berry bladderfern—*Cystopteris bulbifera*
Bird's-foot trefoil—*Lotus corniculatus*
Bitter root—*Lewisia rediviva*
Bleeding heart—*Dicentra spectabilis*
Bloodroot—*Sanguinaria*
Bluebell of Scotland—*Campanula rotundifolia*
Blue fescue—*Festuca ovina* 'Glauca'
Blue marguerite—*Felicia*
Blue poppy—*Meconopsis*
Blue-eyed Mary—*Omphalodes verna*
Bluets—*Houstonia*
Bog-rosemary—*Andromeda polifolia*
Broom—*Cytisus, Genista*
Bugle-weed—*Ajuga*
Bunchberry—*Cornus canadensis*
Buttercup—*Ranunculus*

Campo pea—*Lathyrus splendens*
Candytuft, evergreen—*Iberis sempervirens*
Cardinal flower—*Lobelia cardinalis*
Carpet bugle—*Ajuga reptans*
Catnip—*Nepeta cataria*
Cats' paws—*Antennaria*
Chain fern, giant—*Woodwardia fimbriata*
Chinese arborvitae—*Thuja orientalis*
Christmas rose—*Helleborus niger*
Cinnamon fern—*Osmunda cinnamomea*
Columbine—*Aquilegia*
Coral bells—*Heuchera sanguinea*
Corsican mint—*Mentha requienii*
Cowslip—*Primula veris*
Creeping thyme—*Thymus serpyllum*

Daffodil—*Narcissus*
Daphne, February—*Daphne mezereum*
Deodar cedar, Weeping—*Cedrus deodara* 'Pendula'
Dog's-tooth violet—*Erythronium*
Dogwood, creeping—*Cornus canadensis*

Edelweiss—*Leontopodium*
Ellwood false cypress—*Chamaecyparis lawsoniana* 'Ellwoodii'
English daisy—*Bellis perennis*
English yew—*Taxus baccata*
Evening primrose—*Oenothera*

Fairy bells—*Disporum*
False box—*Pachistima myrsinites*
Fawn lily—*Erythronium*
Fig, creeping—*Ficus pumila*
Fireweed—*Epilobium*
Five-finger fern—*Adiantum pedatum*
Flax—*Linum*
Foam flower—*Tiarella cordifolia*
Forget-me-not—*Myosotis*
Fuchsia, California—*Zauschneria*
Fumitory—*Corydalis*

Globe tulip—*Calochortus*
Gloxinia, hardy—*Incarvillea delavayi*
Gold moss—*Sedum acre*
Golden drops—*Onosma*
Golden-eyed grass—*Sisyrinchium californicum*
Goldenrod—*Solidago*
Golf ball cypress—*Chamaecyparis obtusa* 'Caespitosa'
Ground ivy—*Nepeta hederacea*
Guinea hen flower—*Fritillaria meleagris*

Harebell—*Campanula rotundifolia*
Hart's tongue fern—*Phyllitis*
Hay-scented fern—*Dennstaedtia punctilobula*
Heath, Cornish—*Erica vagans*
Heather—*Erica*
Heather, Scotch—*Calluna vulgaris*
Hellebore—*Helleborus*
Hellebore, Corsican—*Helleborus corsicus*
Hemlock, mountain—*Tsuga mertensiana*
Hens and chicks—*Sempervivum*
Hinoki cypress—*Chamaecyparis obtusa*
Hoop-petticoat daffodil—*Narcissus bulbocodium*
Houseleek—*Sempervivum*

Indian paintbrush—*Castilleia*
Irish heath—*Daboecia cantabrica*
Irish moss—*Arenaria verna caespitosa*
Ivy—*Hedera*

Jacob's ladder—*Polemonium*
Japanese yew—*Taxus cuspidata*
Jonquil—*Narcissus jonquilla*
Juniper, shore—*Juniperus conferta*

Kenilworth ivy—*Cymbalaria muralis*
Kinnikinnick—*Arctostaphylos uva-ursi*

Lady fern—*Athyrium filix-femina*
Ladies' slipper—*Cypripedium*
Lavender—*Lavandula*
Lenten rose—*Helleborus orientalis*
Leopard's-bane—*Doronicum*
Lily turf—*Ophiopogon*
Lily-of-the-valley, False—*Maianthemum dilatatum*
Lippia—*Phyla nodiflora*
London pride—*Saxifraga umbrosa*

Maidenhair fern—*Adiantum pedatum*
Maidenhair spleenwort—*Asplenium trichomanes*
Maiden's wreath—*Francoa ramosa*
Manzanita—*Arctostaphylos*
Maplewort—*Aceranthus diphyllus*
Mariposa tulip—*Calochortus*
May apple—*Podophyllum*
Mock-strawberry—*Duchesnea indica*
Mondo grass—*Ophiopogon*
Monkey flower—*Mimulus*
Morning glory, shrub—*Convolvulus*
Moss pink—*Phlox subulata*

New Zealand bur—*Acaena microphylla*
Noble fir—*Abies procera*

Oregon grape—*Mahonia aquifolium*
Oregon grape, Low-growing—*Mahonia nervosa*

Partridge-berry—*Mitchella*
Pasque flower—*Anemone pulsatilla*

Peach leaf bluebell—*Campanula persicifolia*
Periwinkle phlox—*Phlox adsurgens*
Persian candytuft—*Aethionema*
Pine, bristlecone—*Pinus aristata*
Pine, foxtail—*Pinus balfouriana*
Pine, mugho—*Pinus mugo*
Pine, umbrella—*Pinus densiflora* 'Tanyosho'
Pine, whitebark—*Pinus albicaulis*
Pink—*Dianthus*
Polyanthus—*Primula polyantha*
Prickly-thrift—*Acantholimon*
Primrose—*Primula*
Prophet flower—*Arnebia echioides*

Rockrose—*Cistus*
Rock-cress—*Arabis*
Rock-jasmine—*Androsace*
Rose of Sharon—*Hypericum calycinum*
Royal fern—*Osmunda regalis*

Sagebrush—*Artemisia tridentata*
St. John's wort—*Hypericum*
Salal—*Gaultheria shallon*
Sand lily—*Leucocrinum montanum*
Sand myrtle—*Leiophyllum buxifolium*
Sawara cypress—*Chamaecyparis pisifera*
Sea lavender—*Limonium*
Sea pink—*Armeria*
Shooting star—*Dodecatheon*
Silvery yarrow—*Achillea argentea*
Snowdrops—*Galanthus*
Snow-in-summer—*Cerastium tomentosum*
Solomon's seal—*Polygonatum*
Southernwood—*Artemisia abrotanum*
Spotted dog—*Pulmonaria officinalis*
Spruce, dwarf—*Picea abies* forms
Spruce, dwarf Alberta—*Picea glauca* 'Conica'
Statice—*Limonium*
Strawberry—*Fragaria*
Strawberry geranium—*Saxifraga sarmentosa*
Sun rose—*Helianthemum*
Sweet amber—*Hypericum androsaemum*
Sweet woodruff—*Asperula odorata*

Tarragon—*Artemisia dracunculus*
Tennis ball cypress—*Chamaecyparis obtusa* 'Tetragona Minima'
Threadleaf false cypress—*Chamaecyparis pisifera* 'Filifera'
Thrift—*Armeria*
Thyme—*Thymus*
Trailing arbutus—*Epigaea*
Twinflower—*Linnaea borealis*

Veronica, shrubby—*Hebe*
Violet—*Viola*

Wake-robin—*Trillium*
Walking fern—*Camptosorus rhizophyllus*
Wall pepper—*Sedum acre*
Wall-cress—*Arabis*
Wand flower—*Galax aphylla*
Welsh poppy—*Meconopsis cambrica*
White cup—*Nierembergia repens*
Wintergreen—*Gaultheria procumbens*
Wire vine—*Muehlenbeckia*
Wood sorrel—*Oxalis oregana*
Wonder of Stafa—*Aster frikartii*
Wormwood—*Artemisia absinthium*

Yarrow, silvery—*Achillea argentea*
Yerba buena—*Satureja douglasii*